Mark Johnson personifies the past as he welcomes us once again into his parent's letters of courtship. It's **A FASCINATING READ THROUGHOUT** as Mark examines the innermost feelings and desires of two people trying to make sense of their ever-changing world through the lenses of their Christian faith. One leaves the book feeling as if they personally know Walter and Margaret and hoping that their future turns out bright in an increasingly troubling time. – Will Griffin, Staff Writer for *Fuller House,* Netflix

Having read and enjoyed Mark Johnson's first book containing the love letters written by his parents during their long-distance courtship, I was thrilled to read this second work as well. … This book is a reminder of what **HEART-TO-HEART COMMUNICATION** should be. … Mark's commentary and questions for discussion add to the value for study groups and book clubs also. – Cheryl Johnston, Managing Editor, Focus Magazine, Focusplantcity.com

Mark Johnson has written yet another interesting book/study guide … The letters serve as a launching pad for his unique exploration of the tensions some scientists have with religion, and some Christians have with evolutionary science … His explanations and conclusions are submitted in a kind and loving way, leaving the reader with a sense there might actually be **A PLACE FOR AGREEABLE DISAGREEMENT**. – Paula Johnson, wife and partner of a Colorado Farmer, mother, grandmother, author of children's book series, *We Serve Too*! ™, and most importantly, a follower of the risen Jesus

Dr. Mark Johnson searches his parents' letters to find the way into their love, their faith, and their values. Along the way, he ponders his own life choices and the deepest motivations for all human behavior. What emerges is **A THEOLOGY OF LOVE**. How are people to best discover and embrace their future? How do hardship and denial, even self-denial, strengthen intimacy over time? … I found myself repeatedly drawn to the longing and the intimacy of this slower … painstakingly crafted, form of communication. – Rev. Dr. J. Mark Stanley, Trinity Presbyterian Church

Mark Johnson's second book featuring his parents' letters is a testament to Christian faith and love! It shows true devotion between a man and his future wife within the context of their social, economic and personal challenges. Many of its pages are devoted to explaining the true meaning of biblical passages and I found this **MOST ENLIGHTENING**! I recommend this fine book without reservation! – David Sullivan, CEO at Coulter Boyd Simulations, LLC and producer of *Christmas with Winston*.

What **A SPIRITUAL LEGACY**! The courtship letters of Walter and Margaret absolutely breathe their devotion to Christ and to each other. In all honesty, I struggled through the discussion concerning our four fundamental sources of truth … Other than that, the letters and brief reflections are faith-building. – Larry A. Greene, M.Div., Senior Pastor, River Cities Community Church.

PAST, PRESENT, FUTURE! That is Mark Johnson! My family back in Michigan taught me: "Keep your eyes on the past and do your best to improve the strain." Discover and grow with these words of faith/works. – The Rev. Dr. Lyle E. Harper, retired Pastor and District Superintendent of the Baltimore Washington conference of the United Methodist Church and Leader of the InterFaith Conference of Metropolitan Washington

Questioning God … [is] an insightful autobiographical non-fictional exploration of Mark's own search for answers. His parents' … strong faith in the God depicted in the Bible … apparently strengthened their faith. My interest … lies … in Mark's discussion … regarding how "The letters my parents exchanged during their year-long courtship prior to World War II provide **A FEEL FOR THE RATE OF CHANGE** over the past century". – Dan Kincaid, Principal at Distributed Power Consulting and Energy Advisor, Waste Reduction Partners

Mark Johnson cogently analyzes the letters exchanged between his parents during their courtship during the Great Depression and the years just before WW II in an era when private telephone conversations were uncommon and, of course, long before email and text messaging dominated our lives. At a minimum, financial concerns greatly delayed their engagement and he describes in vivid detail how their religious faith gave them **THE COURAGE TO ENDURE**. … He then puts this issue in greater perspective in the face of modern science and society. A fascinating read! – Robert Safford, MD, PhD, Emeritus Professor of Medicine, Mayo Clinic

Mark Johnson's own search and pilgrimage began with reading his parents' personal love letters. In reflecting on their beliefs and actions for his own understanding of faith in God's promises and providence, he formulates **STRIKING DISCOVERIES** … The reader becomes immersed in a personal way that gives good reason to gain the underlying and penetrating meaning as events unfold. This will draw any thoughtful person into such beguiling reactions. – M. Div. P. Gerald Leaf, retired Pastor and Vice-President Lutheran School of Theology at Chicago Foundation

This book is **AN ENGAGING THREE-WAY CONVERSATION**. Mark provides a unique perspective on his parents' faith. His search for spiritual understanding, recollections, historical timelines, and questions for discussion invite you to revisit the past and explore questions of faith … I highly recommend it. – David Carlson, retired Pastor in the Evangelical Lutheran Church of America.

Every Christian feels the two separate life styles of being a holy Christian on Sundays to going back to their normal lives once the week begins. It is important to be a good Christian but it is often difficult … The book is a great resource to **FIND ONE'S OWN DIRECTION** … in a world with so many issues. The author illustrates through his parents an example of what it means to live as a holy Christian by practicing their faith in their daily life. – Rev. Do In Kim, Hebron Korean Church

Questioning God's Will

Philosophical Reflections on Pivotal Concerns in My Parents' Letters

Mark Johnson

Published by EA Books, Inc.

EAbooksonline.com

ISBN: 978-1-945976-05-06

CONTENTS

INTRODUCTION

Walter met Margaret at an autumn church outing when she visited her sister in Greeley, Colorado. Shortly afterward, Margaret returned to Washburn, North Dakota, to direct choral groups and teach high school English. Aside from two brief visits, their premarital exchanges took place entirely through letters.

The springtime of their courtship is covered in the first book of their letters, *Encountering God: Reflections on the Courtship Letters of My Religious Parents*. There were a few initial rough edges, but mutual visions of a heavenly father bringing them together, caring for them, and responding to their thoughts and prayers quickly evolved. Meanwhile, world affairs were deteriorating economically and militarily. Clouds gathered as war threatened, Walter was refused a needed loan, and

Margaret wondered why the stock market had to "fluctuate so much."

Their worries materialize in the wintertime of their courtship. Walter wonders about God's will, and Margaret wonders about Walter's. It's an intimate and detailed look into the inner thoughts of two educated young adults as they encounter vexing issues while seeking to know God and each other better.

As a grateful son and retired scientist, I contextualize and reflect on some of the consequences of their thoughts and choices and give my take on three issues arising in the letters on which many have contended and pivoted: the complementary nature of our fundamental sources of truth, the oncoming world order, and the extraordinary events surrounding the open tomb.

A word is in order concerning this transcription of the letters. Conversation is the most natural way of sharing our thoughts. We unthinkingly color the literal meaning of what we are saying with appropriate pauses and inflections. We may mispronounce our words, but we don't misspell them. To aid reading and to make the letters more conversational, they have been transcribed into mechanical type. The punctuation has been edited to better correspond to the pauses and inflections of natural speech, and the spelling has been corrected — except when Walter and Margaret intentionally speed things up by writing, for example, "thot" for "thought." Postscripts, which occasionally wind around the edges of their letters, have been appended after their signatures. A few photos of the letters have been added to help the reader gauge what is lost in this transcription.

ONE QUESTION DWELLS ON MY MIND

In Colorado, Walter read the *Greeley Tribune*. There he learned on February 7 that the English and French were countering German and Italian support for Franco's fascist takeover of Spain and had sent warships to blockade the Balearic Islands between Spain and Italy. On February 9 he learned that Roosevelt wanted billions for economic relief. In North Dakota, Margaret read the *Washburn Leader*. On February 11, she learned that Franco had declared himself dictator of Spain.

February 5 [Postmarked February 7, 3:00 p.m.]

Dear Walter,

"And God gave Solomon wisdom and understanding exceeding much, and largeness of heart, even as the sand that is on the seashore." I Kings 4:29

God surely answered Solomon's prayer. This section is so very interesting. It was so sad to read of Absalom's sin against David, his father. It was marvelous the way David treated King Saul, the anointed. God took care of him. Well, He will do the same toward us. He can hear us at all times. It is strange that Martin Luther could spend four or five hours in prayer when he was so very busy. Was that statement in the book Prayer *by Hallesby? I really would enjoy reading that book. I believe I could have time to read it. Those other books which you mentioned I also would like to read. I believe such reading gives added strength. …*

We got our checks this morning. I don't believe that I have told you what my salary is. I get one hundred dollars a month. I put thirty dollars in [a] *savings account. I don't have a checking account. Formerly I have sent quite a lot home, but they don't want me to do so now as they want me to save for my own use later if I can possibly put some aside. I plan to send at least twenty dollars to pay for church dues and house rent. I don't know if the folks will accept the money for* *house rent. In that case I plan to have them use it for the Clarissa Church building fund. Ebba, Mother, and I pledged $100 to be paid within three years, and I want to pay at least forty dollars before May. …*

Walter, I am glad that you are a farmer. Farmers can do so much for humanity. My father's and mother's folks were farmers, and here none of their children have lived on the farm, so I think that maybe I am the one that should. Really, I don't care much for living in town. It will be fun to see things grow. Just think if we were living in the time of pioneering; it would be entirely different. Stock might be cheap now, but think how hard it is for other businessmen to make a living. There are very few callings of today that are as honest and honorable as farming. The teaching field is certainly not safe and secure. Some teachers receive only warrants, which are difficult to get cashed and when cashed must get it at less than full value. …

Today you were to move to your home. I bet you are tired tonight. I hope that you will soon be able to send me another plan of the house. I hope we can get a piano as soon as possible. You know you want to learn to play, and I want to be your teacher. I have enough music books to keep you busy. I want to play too. When your sister Mabel comes, you know we will want to hear her play. Evodia and she can play duets together. Won't it be fun, though? …

May God bless and keep you in the grace and peace which is found in His Son. I am glad that you talk and walk in Christ. I know when He comes the second time, He will draw you up to Him wherever you may be, out in the field irrigating or in town, or in the house or up in the mountains. May He take me, too, altho I am not as near to Him as my heart longs to be. May He forgive me. …

May God help you in your work and in your new environment.

Margaret

February 5 [Postmarked February 7, 4:30 p.m.]

My Dear Margaret:

"The heavens declare the glory of God: And the firmament showeth his handiwork." Psalm 19:1

It has always seemed very strange to me that anyone could walk upon this wonderful earth and not recognize this truth but, rather, deny God and His creation. I have known times, when, in order to justify my own convictions, I have tried to recognize the theory of evolution, but it just will not work. Only one, with an unlimited resource of power, could create this world and the surroundings and then keep the whole thing in order, year after year. Indeed, the heavens do declare the glory of God. …

Walter and Margaret were in high school when the Scopes trial of 1925 dramatically voiced conservative and fundamentalist objections to teaching evolution in school. Margaret may have taken a special interest in that trial. She had spent her first ten years in a Swedish community in Tennessee Ridge where her parents helped start a Lutheran church before they moved to Lindsborg, Kansas.

No, I have not read Babbitt *by* [Sinclair] *Lewis, at least not all of it. I have read* Main Street *quite thoroughly and also scanned through* Arrowsmith *quite well. I do not care much for his writings, especially his viewpoints. They are not the viewpoints of a Christian; in fact, he is a rank atheist. It is said — in fact, I read it in a daily newspaper some years ago — that he strode into the middle of one of the streets, in St. Louis, Mo., and defied God to strike him dead. Of course, God did not answer such a request, and Lewis said that it was proof that there was no God. I do not believe his works are nearly as popular as they were a few years ago. We should thank God that many of the writings of our most popular modern authors point to a much better moral outlook, for instance:*

Magnificent Obsession

Green Light *by Lloyd C. Douglas*

A Lantern in Her Hand

A White Bird Flying *by Bess Streeter Aldrich*

How to Win Friends and Influence People *by Dale Carnegie*

Walter read *Main Street* "quite thoroughly" even though he strongly disagreed with the author's view of God. Why would he read it? I read it to find out.

This 1920 novel portrays the struggle of Carol Milford, a liberal-minded woman. She grew up in a big city. After finishing college, she met and married Will Kennicott, a medical doctor living in a small midwestern town. Although Carol was not the girl of Walter's dreams, he might easily have pictured an independent and spiritually minded woman coming to live with him on the farm.

As the book progresses, Carol's free spirit slowly withers. Her thoughtful considerations are discounted by Will Kennicott. He tries to accommodate her interests, but he owns the house and dispenses her allowance. Her cultural drive conflicts with the then-current small-town midwestern traditions in which women dutifully catered to men, who played the leading roles in the community. In trying to elevate the cultural interests of the town, she became a target of its gossip.

Although in one sense the views of Walter and of Sinclair Lewis are poles apart, Walter did not want to end up like Will Kennicott, with a wife whose spirit has been suffocated. He is off to a good start when, in his November 11 letter, he writes, "your letters contain messages of thot, wisdom, and rich knowledge" and, in his January 26 letter, that he feels it would be a "privilege to be [her] husband."

During their married life, Dad treated Mom with respect. He was courteous to her in all matters. They shared the major budgetary decisions. He never termed household or child-rearing duties "women's work." He helped gather us around the piano to sing. He enthusiastically sang along, sometimes with a monotone approximation when unfamiliar with the melody. He encouraged and helped her in elevating the cultural interests in our church and farming communities. His reward? A high-spirited woman who always returned his love and admiration.

I am quite sleepy tonight. I cross my I's and forget to cross my t's, and my margins look even worse than usual if that be possible. I just got partly cleaned up and moved up this afternoon. Tonight I am spending my first night up in our house. Irene and Bernice helped me this afternoon. Mr. Heard moved Friday, so that leaves the old bachelor in full possession. Now I shall be able to take some measurements and send you a detailed plan of the house, but I will not be able to do so at this time. …

The cattle price does not look good, and it is hard for me to pray for God's will to be done and not my own desires. Though there are so many things that I want to get and need money for, I shall try to leave it all in the hands of Him who knows what is best. I am asking Him to help me in this. …

In his earlier October 7 letter, Walter was thankful for his "fortunate purchase" of "25 head of very good cattle." During the fall, the cattle were fattened on leavings and weeds still in the fields. Now they are being bedded down with straw and fed hay and grain. Spring is rapidly approaching, and come spring, Walter must sell his cattle before preparing the seedbeds for his sugar beets, barley, and alfalfa.

Tho several hundred miles separate us, sometimes I feel very near to you, Margaret. I feel that Jesus has one arm around you and one around me. When I see some seeking pleasure in the world and talk to some of them and hear their viewpoints, I am so happy that I have found Jesus, who is a friend so precious. And then I also thank God, for you and other friends who pray that I may always be found in Him.

I seldom dream, so I have not dreamt about you, but I often think about you and the days when you will be with me in our own home.

May God make me the kind of husband I should be, kind, loving, and considerate. Margaret, if it were so that we might see each other, we could discuss and talk about many things. Here is one question that dwells on my mind a great deal. That is the one of money. If we trust entirely upon God, who has been so gracious unto us, we may never have much money, altho I am sure He will provide plenty for us. Now I am not sure that we can bring ourselves to the point where we will leave all in the hands of God. It is something that very few people living today can do, even if they feel they want to. Now I do not say this just because I have not a great deal of money now, or because I am lazy, for I do not believe God will provide for those who are unwilling to work. "If any will not work, neither let him eat." 2 Thes. 3:10. *Were money to be my goal in life and my great desire, I know that by pursuing the right course I could amass a fortune, but that does not seem right to me. Does it to you? Now I want to provide for you, to make you comfortable and happy, but I am going to take God at His word, and He has said, "But seek ye first his kingdom and his righteousness; and all these things shall be added unto you."*

Walter's last sentence restates the verse, Matthew 6:33, found in Margaret's October 30 letter. His choice is preceded by a prophetic statement: "If we trust entirely upon God … we may never have much money, altho I am sure He will provide plenty for us." Sounds good, but the bend he senses in the river isn't going away. We hear the faint roar of the rapids ahead when he writes, "one question that dwells on my mind … money."

The old fire is getting pretty warm now, so I shall take a bath and then go to bed in order to be able to get up and get ready for S. S. [Sunday school] *& church. I will not seal this letter, as there may be something interesting to* [write] *concerning the events of tomorrow.*

Monday Morning: 9 a.m. [Continuation of February 5 letter]

Good morning, Margaret

How are you this morning, and is Helen strong enough to go to school this morning?

I plan to wash the woodwork and scrub the floor in the kitchen today. I plan to use only the two south rooms, the kitchen, bedroom, pantry, and clothes closet. We did not finish cleaning the kitchen Sat., so I will do that today. But I want to get this letter off to the dearest girl in all the world, to me. Instead of just writing, "good morning," I should like to have taken you in my arms and kissed you good morning. But you know that, and you are safe in the arms of Jesus.

As I was looking for suitable songs for S. S. last Thurs. eve., I came upon this song and copied a verse to send to you. I forgot to copy the no. of the song, but I am sure you know it. I like it very much.

Watch and pray, my soul,
Flesh and blood control;
When the world in tempting story,
Tells of pleasure, wealth and glory,
Watch, my soul, and pray. …

This kitchen has green, calsomined walls and gray woodwork. [Kalsomine is an inexpensive paint that gave rise to the saying, "Too proud to whitewash, too poor to paint."] *The woodwork in this house is pretty good but needs redecorating, as does the whole house. Aside from cleaning it well and perhaps painting the kitchen floor, to make it easier to scrub and clean, I will not do anything to any of it until you come. If I sell my cattle pretty well and get a fair crop, I know we will have enough to furnish this little house pretty well. Mr. Brown will furnish the material, paint, and varnish & paper, but I may have to do the work. It is a good farm, and I would gladly do that. …*

Wed nite I am going to the midweek service and to the rifle shoot afterwards. I plan to finish with the rifle club this year and drop it after it is over sometime in March. You could not go with me, and there are so many things which we can go to and do together. Since I cannot do as most men do, call on their girls and take them with them, at least once a week I will have to do my courting after we are married. I begin to see the plan God has laid out for us — "At least I think I do." I always felt it should be no different after marriage than before, so now I am glad that it is arranged as it is. Then, since we have seen so little of each other, it will be even easier to plan things together. For one thing there will be no debating about going to church on Sunday morning. We'll always plan for that. Then there will be hiking trips to the mts. and hikes up there. I can think of many things to do, and though I have seen you so little, yet I know pretty well your likes and dislikes concerning many things, and I can only thank God that they are as they are. I am so glad that you like little mts., little and big flowers, birds and animals, and all nature. Some afternoons when the work is a little slack, and there are such times, we can take a short drive into the lower mts. and have a little beefsteak fry. Perhaps Rueben & Evodia will find time to go with us also.

It is such fun to write to you, darling, but I must sign off and attack this woodwork. One thing which helps is an abundance of warm soft water. It's going to be a snap to wash that beautiful hair for you. I'll get a chair of the right height, put you on it, and bend you over the sink and go to it. But now, you'll have to imagine you're getting just a little spanking and a kiss, because I am leaving you, in the keeping of our blessed Redeemer and his merciful father.

Yours in Christ,

Walter

One can easily appreciate that the theory of evolution might not explain the "wonderful earth" that Walter sees. But Walter felt that the theory's failure to do so to his satisfaction implied that God must have been involved. I see this as a God-yes reasoning fallacy. There is no problem with Walter's inferring or believing God brought about his world. A person is free to infer and believe whatever he or she wishes. However, the fact that science could not explain the existence of Walter's physical world does not imply the existence of God. Nor does a current inadequacy of a scientific explanation of one's world exclude the future emergence of a scientifically satisfying explanation.

In my early exposure in college to the theory of evolution, I found the evidence for the theory quite compelling. At the same time, God and biblical truth were simply a part of my life. The need to reconcile my "scientific" understandings of the creation of the world with the biblical accounts of creation in Genesis naturally emerged. One day I asked Dad what he thought of the theory of evolution. His characteristically succinct reply satisfied my young need: "The problem arises when our God is too small. Should God have wanted to create the world through evolution, he certainly could have."

The difference between this answer and the viewpoint expressed in the opening of this letter puzzled me — until I ran across Mother's college text *English Prose of the Nineteenth Century* edited by Hardin Craig and J. M. Thomas. It lay among a number of her books she left behind at her death.

The selections in the anthology were grouped by author. Mom had penciled in her reading assignments on the table of contents. There were groups of selections from the works of Charles Lamb, Thomas De Quincey, Walter Landor, Thomas Carlyle, William Thackeray, and John Newman. Her May assignments were from Matthew Arnold's works. The last one, "Literature and Science," was marked May 15. While reading this article, I kept thinking, "so that's where Dad got his arguments for why one should get a liberal college education before focusing on a more specialized interest."

But what really caught my attention was a group of selections following Arnold's, two of which were unobtrusively marked in ink. They were by Thomas Huxley, sometimes called

Darwin's bulldog. One was his autobiography; the other was "A Liberal Education; And Where to Find It." In between was another of Huxley's articles, "On a Piece of Chalk."

The title took me back to the times Dad invariably pointed out the chalk cliffs in southern Wyoming on our occasional trips to the dry lands in northeastern Colorado. The article by this eminently gifted writer showed how the chemical, biological, and geological arguments for the existence of the chalk cliffs had been written in stone long before the story of the days leading up to the creation of man had been inscribed on parchment. The arguments were simple and straightforward, the type Dad loved. I believe that Dad, after carefully digesting the central force of Huxley's arguments for the theory of evolution, had a new appreciation for the origin of the cliffs he liked to point out. If so, he would have had to thoughtfully reconcile those arguments with his own understanding of God. That reconciliation might be the one I heard when I later asked him what he thought of evolution.

MATTHEW ARNOLD (1822–1888)

THOMAS HENRY HUXLEY (1825–1895)

WALTER HORATIO PATER (1839–1894)

February 8 [Postmarked February 10, 8:30 a.m.]

Dear Margaret:

"But if we walk in the light, as he is in the light, we have fellowship one with another, and the blood of Jesus his son cleanseth us from all sin." I John 1:7

The last twelve words in this verse were the theme of Dr. Maier's sermon last Sunday. It was a very good address and gave me a new and greater value and respect for that great gift; as one reads it over and over again, and meditates upon it, he cannot help but thank God, for making it possible for all men to be free from all sin.

This was the first time I had heard Dr. Maier on the Lutheran Hour. I had at one time planned to get myself a small cheap radio set, but I lack the necessary funds, and anyway, I want you to help pick one out. …

I may wait to have my picture taken until I am better off, financially. I think everything will work out for the best, but at the present time, I have to be pretty careful of my money. Perhaps there is a divine purpose in this. I hope I learn the lesson, to always spend carefully.

The cattle market has been much stronger today, and that is encouraging. I think the potato market is showing some strength also. …

Did I answer, last time, your wish concerning the yellow or white gold ring? I shall certainly remember that. I long for the time when I may send it, and Oh! How I do wish I could come and put it on that little finger.

I certainly have a hard time getting much reading done. That is, in my estimation, one of the great drawbacks on the farm. It is necessary to spend the daylight hours at your work and then the evening [hours] *are all that you have left. With some necessary reading to do, such as S. S. study and preparation and my daily Bible reading with some correspondence, I find it hard to do much reading on the side.*

It is soon time to go milk. I milk Brown's cow. Then I will get all the milk I need when I move or, rather, start batching. For I sleep over here now, but I go home to eat.

I have time to say thank you, for the letter. There is one thing I seldom mention, as you so often do. That is my own unworthiness. I am truly thankful that I have found Jesus and know him. But Oh! How I long to be much closer to him. I would even like to lay my head upon that strong bosom. Margaret, I am not at all worthy of his wonderful mercy and goodness. And I am not perfect in any way. I pray much that I might be worthy of you and be the kind of husband I should be.

I am so thankful we can each of us turn to God for strength, else we would have nothing.

It was in a conversation with my sister, Anna, about some ties between the Song of Solomon in the Bible and these letters that I realized how deftly Walter expressed his deep desire for Margaret. One can only wonder how the thought of "that strong bosom" arose.

Now again I say that I love you, not for what you could be or might be but just for what you are. Not counting myself worthy of your love but ever thanking our Gracious God for making that love possible. How glad I am that someday we will, "God willing," take these problems to God together.

Now I go to milk and then home to supper.

Yours in Christ,

Walter

Although Walter's feeling that there may be a "divine purpose" in his discouraging financial circumstance is not a God-yes reasoning fallacy, notions of purpose and intention are terms rigorous science has ceased to use in its explanations. Two simple anecdotes will illustrate the need for both the mechanistic-based explanations of science and the intention-based explanations of ordinary life.

First anecdote: An instructor opened a technical writing workshop in our pharmaceutical research division with a rhetorical question: When you throw a rock into the air, why does it fall to the ground? When nobody spoke up, I volunteered, "Because it wants to get closer to the earth." My answer suited his goal of pointing out that scientific explanations address *how* something happens, not *why*.

My proffered explanation actually agrees the behavior of all of the rocks I have thrown into the air, but *why* are they drawn to the earth? Science would agree that they are drawn to the earth — but by gravitation, not by intention. Given the initial velocity and direction of the rock, science can predict its path. Moreover, the predictive equations can be generalized to the point of predicting the path of rockets. However, we would not have such terms as *purpose* and *intention* if they did not bestow significant capabilities as well.

Second anecdote: You're driving down a road. You notice a little café for the first time and decide you and your friend might enjoy meeting there for lunch. You call your friend and set up the time and location of your luncheon date.

Whether or not the two of you meet at the designated location is an objective test of your ability to predict a critical event in your future. The next day arrives. Should your friend not show and your prediction thereby fail, you would want to know the reason why and maybe even modify your method of coordinating and predicting similar future luncheon dates.

Unlike landing a rocket on the moon, we have been taking such coordinations for granted ever since the human mind began to recognize the power of speech. Yet setting up and predicting these commonplace coordinations lie forever beyond the realistic dreams of science. There are no measurements, no brain scans, and no probing questionnaires that could have been collected prior to your phone conversation that would have enabled science to predict the occurrence of your luncheon date — nor will there ever be.

Suppose science could know the states of all of the neurons in your brain, and the states of all the molecules that make up *each* of those neurons, and all of the electronic states of all of the atoms that make up *each* of the molecules of each of those neurons. Even so, science could never complete the needed predictive calculations before the event occurred — not when the simulation of the interaction between just two molecules is so computationally time-consuming that current simulations on our most powerful computers are restricted to molecules with only a handful of non-hydrogen atoms!

The time may come when you could converse with a robot that will agree and be able to meet you for lunch and may even know your daily routines. But until you share your particular plans with that robot, it cannot know them. It would be stuck in the same simple, computationally insurmountable predictive problem faced by science even it if could know all the factual details of your brain.

As a scientist, I don't despair. Neuroscience is unveiling aspects of the structure, functioning, and organization of the human brain that underlie a variety of mental experiences and behavioral patterns that our intuitions can only vaguely discern. I'm only suggesting that the rapidly evolving terminology of science will not replace the core aspects of our language that have been honed to convey the evolving intentions of the human heart.

February 12 [Postmarked February 12, 3:00 p.m.]

Dear Walter,

"And Jabez called on the God of Israel, saying, Oh that thou wouldst bless me indeed, and enlarge my border, and that Thy hand might be with me, and that Thou wouldst keep me from evil, that it be not to my sorrow! And God granted him that which he requested." I Chron. 4:10

This is such a wonderful verse that seems like a fountain in a dry land. It seems much of Chronicles is just [a] *listing of names. I am using Mother's Bible, which contains the diacritical markings for all the names. I enjoy pronouncing them, altho it really doesn't mean much to me. I am sure that just the above verse has helped me enough so that I am glad that I am reading the book.*

I found out that I can send a bank draft much cheaper than a money order. I am sending thirty dollars home. There are some things that I need from the cities, so that takes some of the money. A portion goes for house rent, building fund (church), and church dues. ...

I told Miss Foster concerning that thot you had of Sinclair Lewis's defying God. She said she knew it and also could see this same viewpoint in his works. In English IV one of the boys reported on the life story of Vachel Lindsay. Did you know he committed suicide? From his childhood he had always suffered financially, and it finally caused his killing himself. I don't believe writers have a very easy life. …

We have had quite cold weather. This morning we had weather that was somewhat like a blizzard. I was up to school checking some Eng. I workbooks for about half an hour. It was very cold up on the hill. When I came downtown at noon, the thermometer registered five above. One day this week we had no train service. It has been predicted that next Monday we will again experience the same loss of mail. I decided to send this letter this afternoon. …

Walter, there is another boy, Raymund Goehring, whom I wish you would pray for. Last year he was a real problem. He would not study and didn't care if he failed his subjects. He is studying now, and I believe his grades for this six weeks' period will average a B. He has a good bass voice; I would like to have him in my glee club. I believe if we pray about it, that when I approach him he will join the group. Byron is doing fine singing. …

I would enjoy surprising you tonight by knocking at the kitchen door and bring[ing] *my crocheting with me to spend the evening. I am afraid the ride back by plane would be too swift, cold, and costly, though. I can imagine what fun we would have together. You would show me all over the house, wouldn't you? …*

Helen is melting snow for our hair. I wouldn't mind having you wash my hair, too. I hope to save fifty cents; therefore, I am washing it and fixing it myself. I hope it gets thoroughly dry before six o'clock.

It seems strange to hear of the snow's melting and completely off the ground. Soon, I presume, you will be plowing. What seed do you plant first? You don't plant potatoes for a long time, do you? ...

Now I will have to hurry to get this letter off in time. May God be with you while we are absent from one another and even be with us when we are together.

Yours in Christ,

Margaret

Feb. 14 [Postmarked February 14, 4:30 p.m.]

Dear Margaret:

"And he went out, and followed; and he knew not that it was true which was done by the angel, but thought he saw a vision." Acts: 12:9

In our S. S. class we studied the 12th chap. of Acts yesterday. The book of Acts is very interesting. But I was much impressed by the fact that even Peter had a hard time casting himself entirely upon God and his boundless grace. I can almost imagine that Peter pinched himself to make sure that he was awake, alive and on the outside of prison. How much like Peter we are after all: Sometimes hardly daring to ask God for some things because we can hardly believe that even He can give them to us. ...

Although Dad especially liked reading the writings of the Apostle Paul, he seemed to identify more with Peter. Once when I was a young teenager, Dad was asked to lead the church service on a Sunday when the minister was absent. How proud I felt when he stepped into the pulpit. Speaking as one talking to someone on the street, Dad pointed out that doubt and fear were things Peter, too, had experienced before becoming a wholehearted follower of Jesus.

Here are some of the questions which arise in class. Do miracles happen today? Is prayer answered in dreams and visions? Why do we end our prayers by saying "In Jesus's name and for His sake? What was the purpose of Christ's coming upon the earth? Why did He have to die to save us from our sins?

Now you may not have time to try answering these questions. I merely mention some of the questions arising in the minds of these boys. If you do have some time, please give the 3rd question some thot. It is a difficult question to answer. Perhaps you can give me a better view and wording of it. …

I am becoming accustomed to the bachelor life by now. Of course I only sleep here. Some tell me I will not like it. Of course they do not know that I am going to have such a fine little helper. (Do you mind that "little"?) My heart is not as big as it should be, and I know that you completely fill it. So from that I come to the conclusion that you are a little girl. …

It was said that 100 miles south of here near Colo. Springs there were millions of young grasshoppers coming out. Of course not many will admit it, but I know that it is God helping the farmers. For we will have a cold spell after that, and it will kill what otherwise might have been the worst grasshopper epidemic in history. It had been predicted by some very prominent entomologists. There comes to my mind an old saying, maybe from the Bible, but I am not sure of it right now, but it says, "If God is for us, who can be against us?" It certainly seems to me, as far as the farmer is concerned, that God is for us.

I traded my shotgun for $20 worth of merchandise at the hardware store in Eaton. … I still have my rifle. I do not use even it very much anymore. …

That changed. As early as I can remember, Dad had a .22 target rifle with a high-powered scope, a slide-action .22, his childhood single-shot .410, and a 10-gauge lever-action shotgun. He later bought a slide-action 20-gauge shotgun and a 12-gauge double barrel for my two older brothers. My sisters, when interested, were trained in shooting tin cans with the .22 and clay pigeons with the .410.

Duck hunting with Dad was a treat — laying out decoys before sunrise along the edge of a river or lake and then hiding back in the brush with him as he called to ducks off in the distance, "QUAAAACK, QUACK, QUAck, Quack, quack, quack, quack, quack." When he caught the attention of some approaching ducks, the calling changed to contented chuckles, "Tuk-kah-tuk-kah, Tuk-kah-tuk-kah, Tuk-kah-tuk-kah-tuh-kah. …" As the circling ducks came within range, the whispered excitement, "Here they come!" was palpable. Those were moments I'll never forget.

I also won't forget an even more memorable moment that happened many years later. A friend was showing me where I might take my son duck hunting. I carried a 16-gauge Browning automatic and brought along a box of shells I had reloaded for hunting doves and quail in North Carolina with my father-in-law.

We eased his canoe into a clear Michigan stream meandering through the cattails. About a half hour later, we surprised a pair of wood ducks as we floated around a curve. I shot the drake and would have shot the hen had the reload ejected. While trying to free the casing, I kept my eyes on the hen. More than once I had seen a duck circle back over the very spot where some of the flock had just been shot. Sure enough, she turned and headed back toward us. After failing to pry the casing loose, I decided to enjoy the moment.

Here she came, just above the treetops, close enough for me to see her probing eyes and feel her throbbing heart as she risked her life in search of her silenced mate.

I understand the lure and camaraderie of duck hunting, but I will never again kill a duck just for the sport of it.

This is the month of birthdays and also St. Valentine's Day. I sent a little valentine box to you. I am sorry it could not be more. …

I still have my cattle and potatoes. The cattle are certainly doing well. Now if the price will pick up 25 cents each week for a while, I shall come out very well. I may sell some potatoes soon. I need a little money. I have expected a check from the govt. for the soil conservation program I carried out this summer.

Mr. Brown, my landlord, has certainly been on a long spree, about 2 months. He is trying to quit now, but it is very hard because when the effect of the alcohol leaves him, his nerves are all shot to pieces. If he does not quit pretty soon it will kill him. Yesterday, right after dinner, Mable wanted to come up and see our house. While we were walking around looking at the cattle, Mr. Brown asked me to come in. I did, and he was shaking like a leaf and wanted me to stay with him as his wife and daughter were away to dinner. I took Mable home and then came back. He was some better later in the evening and this morning. Margaret, Mr. Brown is a rank atheist and has lived a hard life, so it is hard to talk with him. Will you pray and ask God to call him? Ask Him to help me in order that I might show him [Mr. Brown] *the way. He is very stubborn; otherwise, I think he secretly acknowledges a supreme being, but in order to justify his own actions, he will not admit it.*

Now I must close. I cleaned up in the house some this morning, and I am going to walk home because I have a horse, which has crossed the fence. I will take a bridle along and ride him back after dinner. …

Now may God make His face shine upon you and keep [you] *always, in Christ.*

Walter

Of the four questions Walter, my dad, puts to Margaret early in this letter, I am more interested in the first: Do miracles happen today? Dad seemed to think there were more miracles in biblical times than today because of our pervasive lack of faith. But Dad had faith. I dramatically experienced that faith the summer that Mary, his oldest child, was preparing to go to college.

Dad and I were standing a half mile north of the house on the bank of the head ditch of our bean field. We had finished directing the irrigation water down roughly thirty bean rows and were surveying our work. Irrigation tubes were laid out along the ditch, each funneling an allocated stream of water down the furrows separating the rows. The water sparkled and glistened through the green leaves under the bright Colorado sun.

Dad began talking about a bean crop yielding possibly forty-plus bushels to the acre. The bumper crop would yield enough to send Mary to Bethany, the private Lutheran college Mom had attended. I liked the thought. We didn't have much in the way of material possessions. What we had was seldom new. Yet it was understood that Dad's oldest child was going to the college of her choice. Dad had missed the opportunity of a college education; his oldest daughter would not.

A week later, a churning thunderhead darkened the sky. White curtains of hail reaching all the way to the ground were headed our way. We rushed inside to pray. Shortly after, the hail began pounding on the roof. We prayed harder; it hailed harder. After the storm passed and the prayers ended, the outcome was clear. There wasn't going to be much of a bean crop. The flowers and leaves were stripped from the plants in the lower part of the bean field next to the house.

But a hailstorm can be spotty. It can cut out a quarter-mile strip or widen into a two-mile swath. Dad and I climbed in the pickup and drove to the top of the bean field to see the extent of the damage. We got out and walked to the bank of the head ditch where we had stood the week before — totally wiped out, only naked stems.

Dad did not cry, curse, or even complain. Like so many farmers, he had taken out bank loans to cover the costs of raising the crop. Those had to be repaid. They were not mentioned. Instead, he turned from this financial loss to a more insistent concern somewhere along the spiritual path he had chosen to take as he pointed out the importance of Mary's college education and what it was worth.

All that remains of my experience of this conversation is his refrain, "Somehow God will provide," and my young stomach tightening around a silent promise, *We'll see.*

A few years later, Mary was completing her degree after transferring to a nursing school, and my two older brothers and I were studying at Colorado State University. A comment of my botany professor particularly intrigued me when he related why he had only two children. He wanted to assure that he would have the needed funds to send them to college — and they were attending in-state colleges. As I thought of our family with limited financial resources and eight children, something within me chuckled, *Where there's a will, there's a way.*

More years passed. My three younger sisters graduated from private colleges — Lois from Saint Olaf, Ruth from Bethany, and Anna from Kalamazoo College. I still did not have Dad's understanding and Mother's eye for seeing God's hand in this. I saw Dad taking a winter job at the sugar beet factory. I saw Mom going back to college to renew her teaching certificate and then taking a job teaching grade-school children. I saw each of us working to pay our college costs. I saw loans, scholarships, and for two of us, fellowships being granted. On receiving my doctorate, I had no problem in saying, "I earned my way through college."

A few years later, the blinders finally lifted from my mind's eye. I saw that my going to college was premised on there being an affordable college; that my getting loans, scholarships, and fellowships was premised on there being granting agencies; and that my finding good-paying, part-time jobs was premised on there being jobs. I had taken such things for granted, much like food, clothing, health, sunlight, clean water, and fresh air.

Although my college degree required an effort on my part, the opportunity rested on a social structure for which I can only be grateful. These thoughts slowly directed my mental focus to the source that gave rise to, and on which ultimately rested, the necessary social structure of mutual trust and environmental concern. Dad was referring to that source when he said, "Somehow, God will provide." And my willingness to work my way through college? Another gift opened up for me through the prayers and encouragement of my parents.

February 14 [Postmarked February 16, 3:00 p.m.]

My dear Walter,

"I know also, my God, that Thou triest the heart, and hast pleasure in uprightness." I Chronicles 29:17

This evening it is Valentine's Day. I wanted to write a few words to my valentine because he has already promised to be mine. ...

Tuesday evening ...

This evening I received a box of candy from you. It tastes very good. I wish you could share it with me. You should have taken out some pieces for yourself. This evening when I passed the candy to Helen, she asked if I had received it from a former student. I, of course, told her who it was from. She got the idea because last Saturday, Vivian Rising, a student of the Minnesota University who was a pupil of mine at Clarissa, sent me a heart-shaped box of chocolates, and another girl sent me a letter and a valentine. You know it just makes me so happy when my former pupils remember me. You, however, can guess which candy I enjoy the most. Thank you very much. ...

Mrs. Swanson's daughter, Laura, ... asked me to sing an appropriate missionary hymn or solo. I just couldn't seem to find anyone suitable except "The Ninety and Nine," which went way up to g and stayed on that tone for quite a few measures. I didn't want to sing it because that would sound strained and put on for me to sing for church, altho for someone who could have sung it easily it would have been very impressive. About an hour and a half before the program, I got two Methodist hymnals from Allagene Jefferis, and then I prayed again especially for a suitable song, and I found "Sowing the Seed." When I came to church, here the words of the devotionals were concerning the sower who went forth to sow. Laura's entire talk was about the text. I was so thankful that God was so gracious to answer my prayer. All that Laura had told me concerning her talk was that it was on missions. May I always seek divine guidance in singing. …

I am glad that the cattle market has been somewhat stronger. That is a term that I have never used in that connection before. I presume it is a correct usage because you used it. I am glad that you feel encouraged about the prices. Money isn't everything. I am sure that you could amass quite a fortune, as you said, if that were your goal of life. It isn't worth it. Sometimes the thought of just heaping up gold like Silas Marner did just makes me feel sick. I am glad that you see the folly of money not rightly and justly earned, saved, and spent. Your efforts are needed in more important fields. Should God wish you to have a substantial income, He will supply it. I do pray that I might be [a] *thrifty helper to you, but if I get too extravagant or too stingy, you just tell me how to change and to improve.*

Walter, I appreciate that you wrote that you love me for what I am, but again I am afraid you don't know me well enough. May God do much refining of my personality these few months that will pass so that your statement can be applied to me. My mother and brothers and sisters love me, but that is natural. I thank you for the expressions of love to me in your letters as well as in the valentine which you sent. May I be of joy to you from the very first time we met as long as God wishes. May I never cause you to stumble, and if I do, may God quickly pick you up and punish me.

With sincere Christian love,

Margaret

Wednesday morning.

Dear Walter, I found such a wonderful strengthening verse this morning that I want you to enjoy and receive nourishment from it with me. It is [2 Chronicles 16:9]*: "For the eyes of Jehovah run to and fro throughout the whole earth, to show himself strong in the behalf of them whose heart is perfect toward Him." …*

Weren't you afraid to stay with Mr. Brown? I plan to remember him in my prayers. Walter, I am thankful that you do not drink, and I am more thankful that God will always help to refrain you from tasting it. We should do more to prohibit the use of alcoholic liquors. …

To think that you sold your shotgun. I hope you won't miss it too much. I am sure that the articles you bought will help you.

Now may God bless you and give you all that He wishes to do. I am glad that you are able to do your work well. I shall try to answer those S. S. questions next time. I wish that you were here so that we could talk together.

Margaret

Feb. 16 [Postmarked February 17, 4:30 p.m.]

Dear Margaret:

"But as for me and my house, we will serve Jehovah." Josh. 24:14

I came upon this verse this evening, as I was finishing the book of Joshua. I have seen it on plaques in various homes many times. It had always been my desire and prayer to be able to sincerely say this of my home, were it ever God's will that I have a home of my own. When I stop sometimes and think upon the fact that I have been privileged to meet you and that you love me enough to be willing to help me create and share such a home with you, I know that the age of miracles and answer to prayers is not at all past.

I am certainly thankful that God so directed my path that I might meet you. I do believe that two people should be physically attracted to each other and that mating is important, but I also believe that most important of all is that both parties be Christians and in Christ, our redeemer and Saviour. Then He will help them in all their other problems. Do you not think so? I am so glad that words can hardly express my joy that you like the mts. (little & big), the plains, flowers and plants, traveling, children, the church, music, and even washing dishes. You know, it is very important that we like to work. It is God's command and His will. I am glad that you like to wash dishes, crochet, knit, sew, and other housework. I am also glad that you want children.

Do you know that I believe motherhood to be the greatest career a woman can enter upon, else why did God fit them for that, first of all? I also believe that the father should share the responsibility of parenthood and not just the privilege. It is a wonderful privilege and great art to be a true & good parent. Don't you think so? I know that too many men take the task of childbearing and motherhood too lightly. For that reason I will continue to ask God to be with me as well as you and to make me kind and considerate and thoughtful.

Perhaps I should explain here why I have written or, rather, used the expression "our home," which you wondered about. If it is wrong, I will hope for forgiveness, but I am so afraid that I will do as many men do. [They] *say: "I own this." "This is mine." "I am going to do this or that," forgetting that they have a partner who has very likely worked as hard as they have to achieve these things; yea, even their daily plans should be discussed and planned and prayed about together. Margaret, will you plan to do this with me and help me with it? I want to say "We and our" and not "I and mine."*

Margaret, I am praying for Raymund Goehring, … and all the other requests which you sent and for you always, in order that you may be used to lead many to God.

I have a sort of system. I start around here, with my near and dear ones, then to Cheyenne around and back to Denver. Then I go out into

Kansas, include all our synod and other true ministers of the gospels, then into Minnesota, to those who are near and dear to you and then last of all to you. I guess I do this so I may concentrate better, "My last stop so I do not have to remember any more," while I am praying for you. …

My little lady, I guess it is just as well you cannot come tonight and visit and crochet. Not because I would not like it, but because I am afraid I would never let you leave. …

I would certainly like to see those pillowcases, which you are working upon. Oh! Oh! I was just up to put some coal on the fire, and as I looked into that cold bedroom, a suggestion came to me. You had better learn quilting also because we get some mighty cold weather here too. …

The first crop which I plant is barley and alfalfa, then corn and beans, then cabbage and potatoes. Barley & alfalfa, 1st of April, corn & beans, 15th of June. I am busy all the time, with cattle feeding, hay & straw hauling, potato sorting, and soon fieldwork. But I feel very well. …

I am sending you the promised plan for the house. Together with the pictures, you may get an idea of the plan.

I still have the cattle. They are doing fine, and the price is some better. I have not much cash, but I expect a soil conservation check from the govt within a few days. That will help a great deal.

I have not taken a picture yet, for lack of money. But if that check amounts to anything I will do so immediately after.

Now may God's grace and peace be yours always.

Yours in Christ,

Walter

February 20 [Postmarked February 22, 3:00 p.m.]

Dear Walter,

"Yea, forty years didst Thou sustain them in the wilderness, and they lacked nothing; their clothes waxed not old, and their feet swelled not." Nehemiah 9:21 …

It was a miracle how God protected, saved, and preserved the Israelites while they journeyed in the wilderness. …

Thanks for sending the plan of our home. I haven't studied it very carefully as yet, but I hope to during this week. So you don't think you'd let me leave if I would come to spend an evening with you? I like the verse which you quoted, "but as for me and my house we will serve Jehovah." My father used to quote that very often. Walter, I am so glad that you want a Christian home. May it ever be our aim to have such a home, and may He accomplish it. …

I am glad for the cold spell that you have had. Probably the grasshoppers are frozen to death. We have had quite cold weather also. One morning while I was walking up the hill with Ruth Mitleider, a freshman girl, she told me that I had a frozen spot on my nose. She told me to just hold snow on the spot. I did so, and in a short time the whiteness had disappeared. That morning the thermometer registered 26° below. When you froze your face, maybe there was no snow handy. …

Walter, today in English II class we discussed Milton's sonnet "On His Blindness." He was but forty-four years of age when his sight was taken from him. I believe he was a sincere Christian. I wish there were more like him. He is ranked next to Shakespeare as a poet. What couldn't many of the poets do for spreading the gospel if they but had the true Light.

This evening just before supper I again hiked down to the river. A portion of the river is open so that one can see and hear the ripples of the water; the other part is a solid piece of ice. The reason that the water flows is that the power plant uses the water and lets hot water flow into the river all the time. …

Walter, I have never sewed a quilt in all my life. I began one when I was about ten years old, but I never finished it. …

Soon I hope to receive a large picture of you for my dresser. It doesn't have to be large, but I hope it is clear and natural. … The time, if God wills, will come when we can have our pictures taken together.

Now may God bless you as He has blessed those who trusted Him in the Old Testament, and may you lead others to Him.

Yours in Christian love,

Margaret

I enjoy reading the clippings you send. I haven't finished reading Dale Carnegie's book yet. I plan to finish it by next Wednesday of next wk.

I heard the "Wedding March" from the opera Lohengrin *by Wagner. It rather thrilled me. Thus far we haven't made many plans for the great event, but we'll need to start in pretty soon, don't you think, my big man?*

The following figure illustrates the difficulty in editing and transcribing the letters into a mechanical and easily readable typeface.

6

Walter, I have never sewed a quilt in all my life. I began one when I was about ten years old but I never finished it. I still have the remains of it so maybe this summer I can finish it. I know this much that it takes much time and energy to quilt one so I believe I had better not attempt making one until I am through with school. This coming Saturday I plan to finish my pillow cases and put them in my trunk. It is fun to sew for our home. I can just imagine that when you pass the furniture stores you would like to be able to buy all that we will need. Won't it be fun to buy and arrange the furniture?

Soon I hope to receive a large picture of you for my dresser. It doesn't have to be large but I hope it is clear and natural. I haven't taken a picture for a long time it seems at least two years ago. The time, if God wills, will come when we can have our pictures taken together.

Now may God bless you as He has blessed those who trusted Him in the Old Testament and may you lead others to Him.

Yours in Christian love,
Margaret

I heard the wedding March from the Opera Lohengrin by Wagner. It [illegible] thrilled [illegible] [illegible]

I enjoy reading the clippings you send. I haven't finished reading Dale Carnegie's book yet. I plan to finish it by next Wednesday [illegible].

Margaret's response to Walter's comments on the grasshopper infestation is surprising. She mentions God's involvement in so many aspects of her life. In her January 11 letter in *Encountering God,* she notes God's promise to help farmers. Walter captures the seeming essence of that promise when he writes, "as far as the farmer is concerned ... God is for us" and then notes how God is going to send a cold spell that will kill the grasshoppers jumping about. Margaret recognized that the recent cold spell probably killed the grasshoppers, yet she forgets to thank God even though she recognized God's hand in it? I doubt it. More likely, she didn't see God's hand in it because she already had a rationally satisfying mechanism by which it came about.

Nothing wrong with that. Individuals are free to explain things to themselves however they wish. The fortunate ones find understandings that bring joy and meaning to their worlds. However, having a satisfying material mechanism by which something comes about does not logically rule out God's involvement. How strange it would be if God could not act through material means. What would it even mean for God to act if not so much as an atom or wave of materiality was involved?

When I shared with Mom some of my "scientific" understandings, she would sometimes say, "If you lose faith in God because you went to college, then I wish you had never gone." One might well ask, How is it that college, an institution dedicated to discovering truth and a better understanding of our world, could possibly cause one to lose faith in any of the fundamental sources of truth? The next chapter, easily skipped by those wanting to get on with the letters, explains why that need not be the case once the grounding of religious truth is clearly distinguished from that of scientific, artistic, and philosophical truth.

A Glimpse Back

Ferreting out what is key to your joy can be a rewarding task. Successful searches often begin with a question. Here are some self-exploratory questions tied to the foregoing letters of Walter and Margaret. There are no "right" answers. There are only your answers, for you are the world's authority on how you see things — and on what you look for and what you find in how others see things.

February 5. Margaret notes that she is glad Walter is a farmer because "Farmers can do so much for humanity." In what helpful ways do you look upon your vocation? What are some ways a spirit of serving can add meaning to your work?

February 5. Walter writes of a "wonderful earth" kept in order "year after year." In what way is his view of the world similar or dissimilar to your view?

With the cattle prices still down, Walter found it "hard ... to pray for God's will to be done and not [his] own desires." What understandings help when you are being denied something you earnestly desire?

"Tho several hundred miles separate" Walter and Margaret, he shares a figurative understanding by which he "sometimes feels very near" her. What understandings bring you a feeling of closeness when you can't be near a loved one?

February 8. Walter says he loves Margaret not for what she could be but just for what she is. What joys might that understanding bring Walter? Bring Margaret?

February 12. How do you see the many ways Walter, Margaret, and Raymund Goehring might benefit by her thoughts about getting Raymund to join the glee club?

February 14. Many people in Colorado noticed "millions of young grasshoppers." Some entomologists saw a coming epidemic. Walter saw "God helping out the farmers." In what ways do you feel spiritual interpretations of natural events add joy and meaning to his life? To your life?

February 14. Margaret gives a spiritual interpretation of how it came about that her selected song fit the text of Laura's talk.

In what ways might that particular interpretation have added something special to the joy surrounding her performance?

Many books have been written on ways of amassing a fortune, yet Margaret draws Walter's attention to *Silas Marner,* written in 1861 by George Eliot (the pen name for Mary Anne Evans). What spirit of life and source of truth guided her choice?

February 16. Walter covers many things he likes about Margaret and what he thinks is important in a marriage. Which of those things do you feel will prove most rewarding to him, and which do you feel most appealed to Margaret?

When talking about their anticipated home, Walter wants to say, "We and our and not I and mine." What spirit of life and source of truth guided that desire?

February 20. Although Walter enjoyed pointing out exactly how God was helping the farmers escape the grasshopper epidemic, Margaret was not impressed. In what ways do natural and nonmiraculous explanations of how things come about enhance or undermine your sense of God?

Victor Cousin is credited with the saying: We need religion for religion's sake, morality for morality's sake, art for art's sake. What complementarities among these might Margaret have seen in light of her comments on Milton's "On His Blindness" and Wagner's "Wedding March"?

Freeing Unifying Religious Truths from Their Partisan Entanglements

*I*n his letter on February 5, Walter commits a common God-yes logical fallacy in writing that God must exist because a prevailing scientific theory (evolution) cannot explain what is needed to "create this world … and then keep the whole thing in order." A couple of weeks later in her letter on February 20, Margaret commits a common God-no logical fallacy when she is neither surprised nor thankful that God evidently used the cold front that Walter had expected would stem a predicted grasshopper epidemic. Instead she dispassionately observes, "Probably the grasshoppers were frozen to death."

Both fallacies loomed before me years later when I asked Dad what he thought of evolution. Both were averted when he responded, "Should God have wanted to create the world through evolution, he certainly could have." My sense of God and my interest in evolution were thereby broadened.

That doesn't always happen. Several years later, I joined my brother, James; his wife, Ruth; and their three young daughters for the two-day trip back to Denver from Phoenix. I was looking forward to getting to know my nieces on one level and touching base with James and Ruth on another. My nieces invited me to sit with them in the back of the van. After we had solved a riddle or two, Amy, the oldest, abruptly changed the subject by asking, "How can you believe in evolution and the Bible at the same time?"

Fortunately, James had just stopped to fill the van with gas. I got out and mentioned the question to Ruth, who was homeschooling her children. She felt that Amy would be confronting believers in the theory of evolution, and she would rather have that person be someone who at least believed in God. With Ruth's OK, I climbed back into the van, looking forward to learning how Amy saw her world. Thus began a delightful two-day conversation in which we shared our disparate views on a number of issues raised by the Creation Institute. Nothing was resolved. Amy would later marry and go on to homeschool her children. I expect she committed a God-no logical fallacy each time she thought that the theory of evolution, if it were true, contradicted the creative power of God and the truth of the Bible.

In the book *Evolution: Scripture and Nature Say YES!*,[1] Denis Lamoureux relates a tortuous struggle stemming from his God-no logical fallacy. He writes, "My first biology course in the first term of college involved evolution. ... The basic message was quite obvious. ... Since evolution is true, then the Bible must be false and Christianity a lie. ... I had no idea there was an intellectually respectable middle position between atheistic evolution and six day creation."[2] He lost his faith, left the church, and went on to become a dentist, "believing that happiness was to be found in a self-serving lifestyle."

Eventually, he became "fed up with living a selfish and filthy lifestyle ... and wanted God in his life." When he ran across Duane Gish's book *Evolution: The Fossils Say No!*,[3] he felt the Lord calling him "to become a creation scientist in order to attack evolutionists." He decided to equip himself for the battle by getting PhDs in both theology and biology. Toward the end of one of his courses, a professor he deeply respected asked, "Denis, if you gave up your belief in six day creation, would you also give up your faith in Jesus?"

Denis writes, "Wow! That was one question I was not expecting. ... I stepped away from this science and Christianity class still believing in six day creation. But for the first time, I began asking myself ... is it possible for a Christian to reject the assumption that God has revealed basic scientific facts in the Bible?"

Stephen Jay Gould, in *Rocks of Ages: Science and Religion in the Fullness of Life*,[4] notes that the potential conflicts between science and religion reflect basic misunderstandings concerning the nature of these two sources of truth. He writes, "Science tries to document the factual character of the natural world, and to develop theories that coordinate and explain the facts. Religion ... operates in the equally important ... realm of human purposes, meanings, and values." In "enunciating the Principle of NOMA, or Non-Overlapping Magisteria," he wants us to see science and religion as dealing with "two distinct subjects, each covering a central facet of human existence," and that each magisterium is "a domain of authority ... where one form of teaching holds the appropriate tools for meaningful discourse and resolution."[5]

Gould's claim is appealing in that we certainly need peacemakers. However, whether the claim stands depends on how science and religion function as sources of truth. When he writes, "This magisterium [religion] of ethical discussion and search for meaning includes several disciplines traditionally grouped under the humanities — much of philosophy, and part of literature and history," he raises doubts regarding the unique significance of religion. Moreover, he adds a caveat to his characterization of religion by viewing "as fundamentally religious all moral discourse on principles that might activate the ideal of universal fellowship among people," a view he attributes to D. H. Huxley.[6]

However, Gould's implication that religion's inherent interests are not intimately linked with material fact undercuts the sincerity of historical religious positions regarding the roundness of the earth, the earth's movement about the sun, the material origins of life, and the spans of creative time. More seriously, his suggestion also overlooks a religious counselor's essential interest in personal material facts when comforting and guiding someone struggling with the loss of a job, cancer, or the death of a child.

More fundamentally, something is amiss with the suggested complementarity of science and religion. If fact has a complement, it is not "purpose, meaning, or value" but, rather, feeling or fantasy. Although neither feeling nor fantasy is mechanistically linked to the external world in a scientifically explicable manner, they can be coordinated by artists in creations that can hold us spellbound, set us dancing, make us laugh, and bring tears to our eyes. Even when consisting entirely of imagined fact, artistic creations can dramatically change the world in which we live. Legend has it that Abraham Lincoln, on being introduced to the author of *Uncle Tom's Cabin*, asked, "Is this the little woman who wrote the book that started this great war?"

Art is a magisterium in which truth comes across not in demonstrable facts but in a wide array of experienced feelings. In the case of instrumental music, there is often little if any agreement on the material facts that a listener brings to a performance and that shape his or her interpretive experience. On hearing Beethoven's "Moonlight Sonata," one listener may be watching the motions of the pianist or concentrating on the chord progressions, another may be recalling an evening with a lover or picturing a moon rising over a quiet lake, and another may simply be lost in the sounds.

To suggest art is another independent magisterium is one thing. To distinguish its focus, the nature of its truths, its methods and tools, and its evaluative criteria from those of science and religion is quite another. Assuming for the moment that such distinctions exist, a brief reflection on how we arrived at art as an independent domain of truth reveals a fourth and equally productive truth domain.

The notion of complementarity was fundamental. If there is a left, then there must be a right; if a male, then a female; if a member, then a nonmember — simple illustrations of pure reasoning applied to notions of handedness, sex, and inclusion. Pure reasoning has given us the austere disciplines of logic and mathematics, with their exact definitions, formal axioms, and incontrovertible deductions. Philosophers take over when cold, logical reasoning is applied to the terms and assumptions governing our broadest categories of social endeavors. The Declaration of Independence and the Constitution of the United States are two widely accepted and consequential embodiments of philosophical assumptions and arguments.

We have only to turn to the mental complement of philosophical reasoning to get to the heart of the magisterium of religion where material fact and personal feeling are inextricably linked.

So what changes when the facts and feelings associated with an event cannot be separated? Everything. It is one thing to have heard or read about mothers who have carried and given birth to a baby; it is entirely different when it is your own. It will change how you talk about birthing a child. Should you be a scientist studying childbirth, birthing your own will reprioritize your facts. Should you be a writer conveying birth experiences, birthing your own will enrich the feelings in your narratives. Should you be a philosopher interested in family and marital relationships, birthing your own will influence and substantiate your choice and weighing of terms, assumptions, and claims.

The list of life events has no end. Someone being abused by a parent or a spouse is one thing; it is entirely different when you are directly involved. Someone experiencing a failure or a success is one thing; it is entirely different when you do. Someone losing or finding meaning in life is one thing; it is entirely different when you have.

These telling experiences are grafted into our identities. They fill our memories, color our thoughts, and seed our conversations. They shape how we feel about ourselves, how we see our world, and how our world sees us. We share our experiences through endless gestures, words, and actions, both consciously and unconsciously. The better ways should be taught in our schools. To see why the better and established ways will come from the magisterium of religion, we must clarify each magisterium's means of finding and establishing truth so that we can better discriminate the nature of the truths flowing from the different domains.

* * *

We note first some eminent names from each magisterium: Plato, Aristotle, Bacon, Descartes, Hume, Kant, and Russell, among others, in philosophy; Homer, Shakespeare, Leonardo da Vinci, Beethoven, Austen, Whitman, and Rodin, among others, in the arts. Galileo, Harvey, Kepler, Newton, Mendel, Darwin, Pasteur, and Einstein, among others, in science; Moses, Lao Tzu, Confucius, Buddha, Jesus, and Mohammed, among others, in religion. We may more naturally call founding leaders in the last group "spiritual leaders," but that in no way implies that the founding leaders in the other three disciplines were not spiritually centered, committed, and expressive.

For the most part, the leaders in the first three groups were trained and tutored in the fields in which their contributions were later recognized. That is not the case for those in the fourth group. Moses was a shepherd. Lao Tzu may have kept the archives in the royal court during the Zhou dynasty, although his life is largely surrounded in mystery. Confucius was a government official. Buddha was a prince who left the throne in search of freedom from suffering. Jesus was a carpenter's son; Mohammed, a merchant.

The essential differences in these four realms of truth emerge when contrasting some of the typifying contributions of a few of the early leaders, the features of our world that interested them, the forms of their expressions, their methods of discovery, their criteria for judging validity and accomplishment, and the disciplines and institutions that eventually arose as a consequence of their efforts.

Turning first to philosophy, we have the following conversation in one of Plato's dialogues. Socrates is discussing his upcoming trial on a capital charge of impiety with Euthyphro, a self-proclaimed theologian.

> *Soc*. Remember that I did not ask you to give me two or three examples of piety, but to explain the general idea which makes all pious things to be pious.

> *Euth.* I remember. … Piety, then, is that which is dear to the gods, and impiety is that which is not dear to them.
>
> *Soc.* Very good, Euthyphro; you have now given me the sort of answer which I wanted. But whether what you say is true or not I cannot as yet tell, although I make no doubt that you will prove the truth of your words.[7]

In the guise of Socrates, his teacher, Plato (ca. 400 BC) guides our understanding of philosophical truth. Clarification and claims regarding general concepts are central — in this case, piety. Examples, factual or contrived, illustrating the concepts and claims can be helpful, but they remain anecdotal and always replaceable. Emotional considerations are also set aside. Socrates has been accused of being impious. He will be convicted and sentenced to death. Yet, rather than seeking sympathizers opposing the charge against him, he is trying to understand exactly what we mean when we say some action or endeavor is or is not pious.

The early Greek philosophers were interested in virtually every broad issue related to how we examine our world. The following categorization in the *Great Books of the Western World* of the writings of Aristotle (384 – 322 BC), a student of Plato, illustrates that breadth: "Logic" (including "Categories," "On Interpretation," "Prior Analytics," and "Posterior Analytics"), "Physical Treatises" ("Physics," "On the Heavens," and "Meteorology"), "Metaphysics," "On the Soul," "Biological Treatises," "Nicomachean Ethics," "Politics," "The Athenian Constitution," "Rhetoric," and "On Poetics."

Aspects of Aristotle's interest in verbal clarification come through in the first sentence of his discourse on interpretation: "First we must define the terms 'noun' and 'verb,' then the terms 'denial' and 'affirmation,' then 'proposition' and 'sentence.'"[8]

Descartes, one of the fathers of modern philosophy, initially struggled with what he could indubitably know to be true. His answer, shared in an expression in his *Discourse on the Method of Rightly Conducting the Reason and Seeking for Truth in the Sciences,* reveals an essential source and method of establishing philosophical truth:

> Since all the same thoughts and conceptions which we have while awake may also come to us in sleep, without any of them being at that time true, I resolved to assume that everything that ever entered into my mind was no

> more true than the illusions of my dreams. But immediately afterwards I noticed that whilst I thus wished to think all things false, it was absolutely essential that the "I" who thought this should be somewhat, and remarking that this truth *"I think, therefore I am"* was so certain and so assured that all the most extravagant suppositions brought forward by the skeptics were incapable of shaking it, I came to the conclusion that I could receive it without scruple as the first principle of the Philosophy for which I was seeking.[9]

Note the interest in grounding premises and principles, the centrality of thought, reasoning as a method of ascertaining truth, consistency as a requirement of truth, and contradiction as a valid argument in dispelling false premises and claims.

The essential nature of truth in this realm is starkly revealed in the disciplines of mathematics and formal logic. Although mathematical truths have been endlessly suggested and illustrated through experience, the underlying definitions, assumptions, and proofs are solely constructs of the conscious mind. When introduced to algebra and geometry, we soon appreciate the severe constraints of rigorous reasoning.

Philosophy relaxes somewhat the definitional and reasoning rigor of mathematics in its attempt to formalize the concepts and ideas that underlie ordinary discourse and to develop rules by which we organize ourselves and our understandings. In *Leviathan,* Thomas Hobbes (1588 – 1679) argued for kingly rule based purely on society's protective self-interest. In *Treatises on Government,* John Locke (1632 – 1704) argued for the separation of the judiciary, executive, and legislative offices. Such works have given rise to the field of political science. Adam Smith's (1723 – 1790) *The Wealth of Nations* and Karl Marx's (1818 – 1883) *Das Kapital* contain assumptions and arguments from which our schools of economics arose. Saint Augustine's (354 – 430) *The City of God* and Saint Thomas Aquinas's (ca. 1225 – 1274) *Summa Theologica* are forerunners of many of the understandings in Christian theology that have been reasoned from narratives of experiences and understandings recorded in the Bible.

The treatises of Aristotle on physics and biology convey the deep interest early philosophers had in the question: What is materially going on in our world? For centuries, Aristotle's answers were definitive. That began to change in the sixteenth and seventeenth centuries. General axioms, unsubstantiated claims, and reasoning alone were blocking the progression of physical truth. In a couple of fascinating passages from *Advancement in Learning* and *Novum Organum,* Francis Bacon (1561 – 1626) captured the need for and nature of the change:

> For as water will not ascend higher than the level of the first springhead from whence it descendeth, so knowledge derived from Aristotle, and exempted from liberty of examination, will not rise again higher than the knowledge of Aristotle.[10]

> There are and can exist but two ways of investigating and discovering truth. The one hurries on rapidly from the senses and particulars to the most general axioms, and from them, as principles and their supposed indisputable truth, derives and discovers the intermediate axioms. This is the way now in use. The other constructs its axioms from the senses and particulars, by ascending continually and gradually, till

it finally arrives at the most general axioms, which is the true but unattempted way.[11]

The first passage heralds the departure of science from authoritative claims regarding authoritative truth. The second heralds the oncoming grounding of science in sensible and measurable facts. From such intuitions, a new realm of truth emerged. It was anchored not in assumptions and mental constructs but in physical facts.

* * *

The publication of Newton's (1642 – 1727) three laws of motion in *Mathematical Principles of Natural Philosophy* gave, for some, a positive answer to the challenging question in Job 38:33 (NIV): *Do you know the laws of the heavens?* Included in those laws were the motions of the planets. Shortly before Newton was born, Kepler (1571 – 1630) had mathematically described their elliptical orbits using Tycho Brahe's (1546 – 1601) accurate measurements of their changing positions relative to the sun. From his three laws of motion, Newton derived Kepler's mathematical descriptions. Alexander Pope (1688 – 1744) poeticized a feeling of the time, "Nature and nature's laws lay hid in night: God said, Let Newton be! And all was light."[12]

Newton's discoveries were one of many events leading up to the Enlightenment of the 1700s that epitomized an emerging interest in, and the significance of, a body of understanding based solely on those assertions that could be confirmed or rejected by measurement and observation. Galileo's (1564 – 1642) popularization of and improvements on the telescope brought the heavenly bodies close enough to see that they were different than we thought; later improvements put the stars farther from us than we had ever imagined. Leeuwenhoek's (1632 – 1723) work on magnifiers opened a new world of microscopic creatures (bacteria) inhabiting our food and bodily fluids; later improvements revealed another world of even smaller creatures (viruses) inhabiting the food and cellular fluids of bacteria. But it was James Hutton (1726 – 1797), a retired medical doctor, farmer, and natural philosopher, who dramatically extended our sense of time:

> If … we employ our skill in research, not in forming vain conjectures; and if *data* are to be found, on which Science may form just conclusions, we should not long

remain in ignorance with respect to the natural history of this earth, a subject on which hitherto opinion only, and not evidence, has decided.

Upon the supposition that the operations of nature are equable and steady, we find … means for concluding a certain portion of time to have necessarily elapsed.

We find the marks of marine animals in the most solid parts of the earth, consequently, those solid parts [fossils] have been formed after the ocean was inhabited by those animals, … therefore we … have some means for computing the time through which those species of animals have continued to live.

But when fire bursts forth from the bottom of the sea, and when the land is heaved up and down, so as to demolish cities in an instant, and split asunder rocks and solid mountains, there is nobody but must see in this a power, which may be sufficient to accomplish every view of nature in erecting land.

> To sum up the argument, we are certain, that all the coasts of the present continents are wasted by the sea, and constantly wearing away upon the whole; but this operation is so extremely slow. ... But, in order to produce the present continents, the destruction of a former vegetable world was necessary; consequently, the production of our present continents must have required a time which is indefinite. In like manner, if the former continents were of the same nature as the present, it must have required another space of time, which also is indefinite, before they had come to their perfection as a vegetable world. ... The result, therefore, of our present enquiry is, that we find no vestige of a beginning, no prospect of an end.[13]

The first paragraph emphasizes the role material observations play in his theory. The second discloses Hutton's operative supposition that would become the principle of uniformity in geology.[14] The third addresses science's core interest in mechanistic understandings by providing the explanatory reasoning underlying his emerging sense of geological epochs whereby (1) marine organisms die in the ocean, (2) their shells are mineralized into fossils, and (3) the fossils are eventually lifted up to form new mountain ranges. The fourth provides material evidence for the powerful forces needed to reposition once deeply buried marine fossils atop our current plains and mountains. The last paragraph conveys Hutton's reaction on encountering the geological unconformity of rock formations at Siccar Point in Scotland where gently dipping layers of the Old Red Sandstone formation lay atop layers of a steeply dipping Silurian greywacke (a darker, clayey sandstone) formed in a much earlier epoch.[15]

Roughly two and a half centuries after Hutton grasped the time scales implied by his mechanistic explanations of the unconformity at Siccar Point, I hiked there and placed my fingertips on the sandstone and my palm on the greywacke while trying to imagine the times and forces by which mountain ranges and oceans would have had to have been formed and then swept away for that unconformity to come about.

Hutton's work clearly illustrates how the validity of a scientific assertion or general hypothesis is ultimately judged by the concordance of its various reasoned implications with observable facts. However, in *An Introduction to the Study of*

Experimental Medicine, Claude Bernard (1813 – 1878) notes that even "If the hypothesis is not verified and must be abandoned, the facts which it will have helped us to discover will remain as undeniable results in our investigation."[16] Promising scientific theories concur with the concomitant facts across diverse sets of observations arising from reasoned implications. The basic assertion stands and is treated as "scientifically true" until new observations discount the overall concordance or undermine its relevance to further investigations. The truly revolutionary ones become the scientific paradigms that largely constrain how scientists see and explain the material behavior of our world.[17]

That said, it remains a simple fact that the original expressions of scientists, when preserved, get buried in research notebooks and manuscripts or are archived in research libraries largely for patent or historical interest. For example, Hutton's original work "Theory of the Earth; an Investigation of the Laws Observable in the Composition, Dissolution, and Restoration of Land upon the Globe" resides in the *Transactions of the Royal Society* of Edinburgh, 1788, volume I, part II. Dedicated specialists in the relevant disciplines read, study, and cite these original expressions. The basic understandings and most definitive data are eventually summarized and explicated in our scientific textbooks and class lectures. Even so, the cerebral expressions, the unfamiliar terms, and the data tabulations soon glaze a lay reader's eyes unless linked with human feelings and familiar concerns.

We turn now to another source of truth where original expressions are valued, many are cherished, and a few eminently prized. Here the focus of truth turns from methods of objectively sensing, measuring, and explicating the physical facts of our world to methods of creating, conveying, and sharing the vast realm of feelings about our world. But first it helps to have a clear sense of what science can and cannot tell us about our brain.

* * *

The human brain is an intricate and dynamic organization of roughly eighty-five billion highly interconnected nerve cells and an equivalent number of supporting glia cells. To get a sense for the size of that number, a person with a yearly income of $85,000 would need not a hundred or a thousand years but a thousand times a thousand years to earn $85 billion.

A nerve cell can be less than a tenth of an inch to over a yard long. Each comprises a dendritic tree of antennae covered with thousands of synapses through which it sends and receives molecular signals. Some can send up to a thousand signals per second, with some signals moving at speeds that can traverse the length of the body in a fifth of a second.[18] Yet, most of us go about our day without giving this astoundingly complex dynamic a moment's thought.

Tools such as electroencephalography (EEG), magnetic resonance imaging (MRI), and positron emission tomography (PET) are giving us illuminating glimpses of how the brain functions and the different contexts in which its various groups of interlinked neurons "light up." But these advances have yet to invalidate Joseph Henry Woodger's (1894 – 1981) claim, "You can learn more about a man's mind by talking to him for ten minutes than by looking at sections of his brain for ten years."[19] An updated version regarding what science can tell us about another person's thoughts has been cogently summarized by Bear, Connors, and Paradiso: "While analysis of an EEG cannot tell us *what* [emphasis mine] a person is thinking, it can help us know *if* a person is thinking."[20]

So what might we like to know more about with regard to what goes on in our brains for which the tools and terminology of science may always fall far short? The list is endless: our feelings and reactions to both real and imagined events; our hopes and motivations; our imaginations and our dreams; our musical rhythms, tunes, and harmonies, to name a few.

The rudiments for sharing such things formed before we left the womb and largely developed before our teens. Most of us can make up and hum a catchy tune. Composers translate their tunes along with enriching chord progressions into musical compositions that orchestras then play. Most of us can draw interesting images. Visual artists create paintings exhibited in museums. Most of us can dance. Ballerinas captivate an audience as they grace the stage. Most of us can share passable anecdotes. Novelists craft books that hold their readers spellbound.

Our artists have always been with us. Homer (ca. 800 BC) unveiled in the *Iliad* and the *Odyssey* the many types of feelings, imaginations, and events that excited the early Greeks. Sophocles (496 – 406 BC) memorialized in his play *Oedipus the King* the tangled feelings that can arise toward one's parents now known as the Oedipus complex. In his painting *Mona Lisa,* Michelangelo (1475 – 1564) captured the mystery that can be conveyed in a human face. With but a few words, "To be or not to be, that is the question," Shakespeare (1565 – 1616) weighed in *Hamlet* the depth of an existential concern to which someone can be driven. On hearing Beethoven's (1770 – 1827) "Moonlight Sonata," the listener is transported into a tonally moving moonlit night. In Jane Austen's (1775 – 1817) *Pride and Prejudice,* the reader is taken into a young woman's developing mind as it works through her desires for life while encountering the cultural constraints of her time.

Through their coordination of our feelings and imaginations, artists enhance and shape how we experience and share our inner worlds. Take a simple case, Auguste Rodin's (1840 – 1917) sculpture *The Thinker*: no introductions, no explanations, no words are given, yet *The Thinker*'s solidity and musculature arrest and hold our attention. He is seated, motionless, his muscles defined but relaxed. While one arm forms a pedestal for his head, he blankly stares over his knuckles, on which his jaw is jammed, oblivious to our presence. Our eyes move about his features as this image of the weight and loneliness of deep thought is sculpted into our own minds as we ponder what is occupying *The Thinker*'s thoughts.

The Thinker vividly conveys the experience of being lost in thought. Later we may have at one time assumed a similar posture when thinking or wanting others to think we were.

Like so many works of art, Rodin's sculpture conveys the profound role wordless gestures play in interactions among humans, animals, and even plants. It satisfies a fundamental criterion of good art: it arrests and holds our attention. When my wife says a painting "makes her eyes dance," I know that work captured her imagination. It may or may not capture mine, for, as we all know, "Beauty is in the eye of the beholder."

The diversity of tools, the media, the gestures, the metaphors so characteristic of the magisterium of art comes across in the following excerpt from Nat Hentoff's profile of Bob Dylan in the October 24, 1964, issue of *The New Yorker*. The excerpt reveals the synergistic appeal of his words, his sounds, and his behavior.

> The second — and more influential — demiurge of the folk music microcosm is Bob Dylan, who is twenty-three. Dylan's impact has been the greater because he is a writer of songs as well as a performer. Such compositions of his as "Blowin' in the Wind," "Masters of War," "Don't Think Twice, It's All Right," and "Only a Pawn in Their Game" have become part of the repertoire of many performers, including Miss Baez,

who has explained, "Bobby is expressing what I — and many other young people — feel, what we want to say. … Bobby's songs are powerful as poetry and powerful as music. And, oh, my God, how that boy can sing!" Another reason for Dylan's impact is the singular force of his personality. Wiry, tense, and boyish, Dylan looks and acts like a fusion of Huck Finn and a young Woody Guthrie. Both onstage and off, he appears to be just barely able to contain his prodigious energy.

Although the social force of Bob Dylan's songs, like many of the folk songs of the sixties, was sourced in whole gestalts of material facts, specificities are difficult to pin down. That's the power of metaphor. Consider the first two lines of *Blowin' in the Wind*:

How many roads must a man walk down
Before you call him a man

Your mind is free to choose the "man." It could be yourself, another man, even another woman. It is also free to choose the road. It could be a road you've walked, maybe a time in which you struggled, or somewhere you linked hands and marched with others. Moreover, the "How many" is only suggestive — a couple of times, many times, a life of times, generations of lifetimes? Your memory and imagination are free to wander until settling into a compelling resolve.

The source of artistic truth and its metaphoric link to materiality come across in two brief excerpts from Flannery O'Connor's work. The first comes from her short story "Good Country People."[21]

> The boy's astonished eyes looked blankly through the ends of her hair. "Okay," he almost whined, "but do you love me or don'tcher?"
>
> "Yes," she said and added, "in a sense. But I must tell you something. There mustn't be anything dishonest between us." She lifted his head and looked him in the eye. "I am thirty years old," she said. "I have a number of degrees."
>
> The boy's look was irritated but dogged. "I don't care," he said. "I don't care a thing about what all you done. I just want to know if you love me or don'tcher?"

and he caught her to him and wildly planted her face with kisses until she said, "Yes, yes."

"Okay then," he said, letting her go. "Prove it."

She smiled, looking dreamily out on the shifty landscape. She had seduced him without even making up her mind to try. "How?" she asked, feeling that he should be delayed a little.

He leaned over and put his lips to her ear. "Show me where your wooden leg joins on," he whispered.

This second excerpt, taken from her essay "Writing Short Stories,"[22] conveys the source of the truth for her gripping masterpiece.

Early in the story, we're presented with the fact that the Ph.D. is spiritually as well as physically crippled. She believes in nothing but her own belief in nothing, and we perceive that there is a wooden part of her soul that corresponds to her wooden leg. Now of course this is never stated. The fiction writer states as little as possible. …

If you want to say that the wooden leg is a symbol, you can say that. But it is a wooden leg first, and as a wooden leg it is absolutely necessary to the story. It has its place on the literal level of the story, but it operates in depth as well as on the surface. …

Now a little might be said about the way in which this happens. I wouldn't want you to think … [that] I sat down and said, "I'm going to write a story about a Ph.D. with a wooden leg, using the wooden leg as a symbol for another affliction." I doubt myself if many writers know what they are going to do when they start out. When I started writing this story, I didn't know there was going to be a Ph.D. with a wooden leg in it. I merely found myself one morning writing a description of two women that I knew something about, and before I realized it, I had equipped one of them with a daughter with a wooden leg. As the story progressed, I brought in the Bible salesman, but I had no idea what I was going to do with him. … But when I found out … what was going to happen, I realized that it was inevitable. This is a story that produces a shock for the reader, and I think one reason for this is that it produced a shock for the writer.

Although Flannery O'Connor started writing about "two women that she knew something about," she quickly descended and maybe got lost in her imagination when "a daughter with a wooden leg" and "the Bible salesman" not only joined the story seemingly of their own accord but began interacting in a surprising manner. In saying "Before I realized it, I had equipped," O'Connor suggests that both a conscious and unconscious dynamic was at play as the story unfolded.

O'Connor notes that although the wooden leg resides at the literal level of the story, it also operates well below the surface of the story. These artistic devices that delve beyond the literal facts when communicating human experience are unavoidable. Even O'Connor's essay is filled with metaphors. "Level of the story," "operates," "below," and "the surface" are all metaphors. A story does not have levels physically separated by height. Neither does it have physical surfaces. Although the "wooden leg" pictured in your mind may operate in the mind in a mechanistically defined manner, you can easily imagine what it means to have one. The images in metaphors, as products of the mind, are not subject to the laws of physics. That freedom underlies their strength for vivifying the depth and complexity of human experience.

Just as scientists can explore truths concerning material fact without explicitly taking existing human feelings into account, artists can explore truths concerning human feeling without explicitly taking existing material facts into account. This critical distinction comes across in this excerpt from "How to Tell a True War Story"[23] by Tim O'Brien, a veteran of the Vietnam War.

> You can tell a true war story by the questions you ask. Somebody tells a story, let's say, and afterward you ask, "Is it true?" and if the answer matters, you've got your answer.
>
> For example, we've all heard this one. Four guys go down a trail. A grenade sails out. One guy jumps on it and takes the blast and saves his three buddies.
>
> Is it true?
>
> The answer matters.

You'd feel cheated if it never happened. Without the grounding reality, it's just a trite bit of puffery, pure Hollywood, untrue in the way all such stories are untrue. Yet even if it did happen — and maybe it did, anything's possible — even then you know it can't be true, because a true war story does not depend upon that kind of truth. Happeningness is irrelevant. A thing may happen and be a total lie; another thing may not happen and be truer than truth. For example: Four guys go down a trail. A grenade sails out. One guy jumps on it and takes the blast, but it's a killer grenade, and everybody dies anyway. Before they die, though, one of the dead guys says, "The fuck you do that for?" and the jumper says, "Story of my life, man," and the other guy starts to smile, but he's dead.

That's a true story that never happened. …

In the end, of course, a true war story is never about war. It's about the special way that dawn spreads out on a river when you know you must cross the river and march into the mountains and do things you are afraid to do. It's about love and memory. It's about sorrow.

It's about sisters who never write back and people who never listen.

* * *

We turn now to truths where what happens is relevant. Here is one from my life.

I had spent another Friday afternoon studying in the library before finally heading across campus to the Rainbow Cafe where I could get an inexpensive but basic meal. After crossing the main campus drag where fellow students in cars were yelling and waving at their friends as they headed into a weekend of fun, I took my usual seat at the counter, ordered a hot roast beef sandwich, and slowly ate my meal, occasionally talking to the cashier, a friendly lady who gave me the last piece in her pie cabinet on her way to flipping the sign on the door from open to closed. I thanked her, forked it in, said goodbye, and headed home to contemplate the lonely wilderness I had come to call my life.

Home was an inexpensive upstairs bedroom rented from Mrs. Kolath, an older lady who spent her entire evenings downstairs watching TV. I flopped down on the bed, stared at the ceiling for a while, then got up and pawed through my small record collection. Nothing stood out except a record my brother, Paul, had given me a couple of years earlier. I put the record on the turntable, hit play, flopped back down on the bed, and returned to what it was about myself that kept me from having fun like everyone else. A cymbal started tapping out a fast-marching beat. It was soon joined by the other members of a Dixieland band. *Joined* is hardly the word. A trumpet, trombone, and sax suddenly started playing all at once and in every which way but quiet. They were playing "Muskrat Ramble," and like everyone else, they were having a ball.

I was about to get up and put the record back in its cover when they somehow sensed my mood and started playing a blues arrangement of "Ballin' the Jack."[24] In muted tones, the trombone began exuding slow, mournful notes that spoke to me, "Wait a second. This guy's in trouble, and it ain't right." The melody expressed how I was feeling while the background instruments sympathetically affirmed the moan. I began thinking, *These musicians know how I feel — dejected, alone, pointless.* A few moments later, the trumpet nudged the trombone aside and began crying out one of the saddest soliloquies I had ever heard. *These musicians understand.* As the trumpet faded away, the sax took up the strain and reiterated my mood in mellower yet equally understanding notes.

As it turned out, they had brought along a piano and a bass that started up a new tune just for me, "Synthetic Blues," with chords and rhythms on the same track. My mind began following the improvised chords as they rolled off the keyboard, and shortly I was humming along with them. *I am among friends.* By the time the song ended, my mood had lifted.

With "Billboard," their parting piece, they returned to the lively Dixieland beat by which they had entered. *I am with them now.* As we marched along, I was chuckling and thinking, *Maybe I'll wade through another chapter or two in the lives of* The Brothers Karamazov.

I don't know why I put on that Dixieland record. I was not into Dixieland music and totally unacquainted with Dixieland blues. That musical genre never was and never became my "thing." Yet, in my later college years when I was dejected and anticipating a lonely weekend, by playing that particular sequence of musical arrangements, those friends would again take notice much as I mentioned and would soon lift my spirits.

But what if I lied? What if it was all made up to gain your attention or to prove a point or to simply mislead you? Philosophers cannot prove we should tell the truth without there arising debatable issues regarding their underlying assumptions and assertions. Scientists disown those who knowingly falsify their data, but they have no scientifically established explanations for justifying that action. Artists celebrate works of fiction as long as they are marketed as such. It is in the magisterium of religion that we encounter the injunction, "You shall not bear false witness against your neighbor" (Exodus 20:16 RSV).

* * *

Our religious pathfinders are known, some largely through legend, for the lives they lived and the understandings they shared. What we know about their lives and teachings constitutes our most cherished and enduring expressions of life and its reward.

Moses gave us the Ten Commandments to guide our relationship with the creator of the universe and with each other. We received the key elements of the life and teachings of Confucius in his Analects or "aphorisms." Siddhartha Gautama, known to us as the Buddha, "the awakened one," gave us his Four Noble Truths and his Eightfold Path. The teachings of Lao Tzu come to us in the *Tao Te Ching* ("the way"+"great book"). The life and teachings of Jesus are recorded in the Four Gospels. (*Gospel* derives from an Old English translation of the Latin word *evangelium,* meaning "good story"). The five pillars of Islam (an Arabic word with connotations of submission and peace) arose out of Mohammed's recitations collected in the Quran.

The teachings and lives of these and other pathfinders have captivated different groups of us for centuries: Moses for 3,000 years among Jews, Christians, and Muslims; Siddhartha

Gautama, Confucius, and Lao Tzu among Buddhists, Confucianists, and Taoists for 2,500 years; Jesus among Christians and Muslims for 2,000 years; Mohammed among Muslims for 1,500 years.

We know very little about how Lao Tzu came upon his understandings. We know more about Confucius from his Analects. Here is a relevant sampling:

> Book 1, Chapter 1. The Master said, "He who exercises government by means of his virtue may be compared to the north polar star, which keeps its place and all the stars turn towards it."

> Book II, Chap. IV. The Master said, "At fifteen, I had my mind bent on learning. At thirty, I stood firm. At forty, I had no doubts. At fifty, I knew the decrees of Heaven. At sixty, my ear was an obedient organ for the reception of truth. At seventy, I could follow what my heart desired, without transgressing what was right."

Book II, Chap. XI. The Master said, "If a man keeps cherishing his old knowledge, so as to be acquiring new, he may be a teacher of others."

Book VII, Chap. I. The Master said, "A transmitter and not a maker, believing in and loving the ancients, I venture to compare myself with our old P'ang."

Book VII, Chap. XVI. The Master said, "If some years were added to my life, I would give fifty to the study of the Yî [I Ching], and then I might come to be without great faults."[25]

The first chapter of the second book reads, "The Master said, 'He who exercises government by means of his virtue may be compared to the north polar star, which keeps its place and all the stars turn towards it.'" Although I expect some recognized that "north polar star" in Confucius at an early age, unlike many of our pathfinders, he does not point to a time when he was gripped by an overwhelming revelation of who he was and what he was to be about. Contrast that with Siddhartha

Gautama's description of the revelation that overwhelmed him the night that ended his ascetic search for enlightenment.

> I thought: "Suppose I practice entirely cutting off food." Then deities came to me and said: "Good sir, ... If you do so, we shall infuse heavenly food into the pores of your skin." ... So I dismissed the deities, saying: "There is no need." ... So I took very little food, a handful each time ... Because of eating so little my limbs became like jointed segments of bamboo stems. ...
>
> I thought: "This is the utmost ... but by this racking practice ... I have not obtained ... any distinction in knowledge or vision worthy of the noble ones. Could there be another path to enlightenment?"
>
> I recalled that ... while I [as a young prince] was sitting in the cool shade of a rose-apple tree, quite secluded from sensual pleasures ... I entered upon the first jhana, which is accompanied by applied and sustained thought, with rapture and pleasure born of seclusion.

> I considered: "It is not easy to attain that pleasure with a body so excessively emaciated. Suppose I eat some solid food — some boiled rice and porridge." ... When I had ... regained my strength, then quite secluded from sensual pleasures, secluded from unwholesome states, I entered upon and abided in the first jhana.[26]

During the first watch of that same night, Siddhartha "entered upon and abided in" three higher jhanas (states of mindfulness) after which he "recollected his manifold past lives." In the second watch of that night, his "divine eye" saw "beings passing away and reappearing ... according to their actions." Here he describes what happened during the third watch of that night:

> When my mind was thus purified, bright, unblemished, rid of imperfection, malleable, wieldy, steady and attained to imperturbability, ... I direct knew ... "This is suffering." ... "This is the origin of suffering." ... "This is the cessation of suffering." ... "This is the way leading to the cessation of suffering."[27]

While Siddhartha was consciously meditating that propitious night, his description suggests that his mind cascaded down a sequence of local mental equilibria before finally settling into a sea of understandings summarized in his Four Noble Truths.

Mohammed (Quran 96:1 – 7, 97:1 – 5) describes an equally gripping experience for the source of his understandings that commenced roughly a thousand years later:

Read in the name of thy Lord who creates —
Creates man from a clot,
Read and thy Lord is most Generous,
Who taught by the pen,
Taught man what he knew not.
Nay, man is surely inordinate,
Because he looks upon himself as self-sufficient.

Surely We revealed it on the Night of Majesty —

> And what will make thee comprehend what the Night of Majesty is?
>
> The Night of Majesty is better than a thousand months.
>
> The angels and the Spirit descend in it by the permission of the Lord — for every affair —
>
> Peace! It is till the rising of the morning.[28]

Although Mohammed purportedly could neither read nor write, on that Night of Majesty, his mind, too, settled into a new and lasting understanding of a source of power and peace for which he used the term *Lord*.

The same term was used in Exodus 3:1 – 6 for the source of understandings in an equally dramatic revelation given to Moses — but roughly fifteen hundred years earlier:

> Moses ... drove the flock into the wilderness, and came to Horeb, the mountain of God. An angel of the Lord appeared to him in a blazing fire out of a bush. He gazed, and there was a bush all aflame, yet the bush was not consumed. Moses said, "I must turn aside to look at this marvelous sight; why doesn't the bush burn

> up?" When the Lord saw that he had turned aside to look, God called to him out of the bush: "Moses, Moses!" He answered, "Here I am." And He said, "Do not come closer. Remove your sandals from your feet, for the place on which you stand is holy ground. I am" He said, "the God of your father, the God of Abraham, the God of Isaac, and the God of Jacob." And Moses hid his face, for he was afraid to look at God.

The Judeo-Christian scriptures are filled with revelatory experiences that changed the lives of their recipients. Here are four more:

> *Isaiah*: In the year that King Uzziah died, I beheld the Lord seated on a high and lofty throne; and the skirts of his robe filled the temple. Seraphs stood in attendance of Him. … One of the seraphs flew to me, with a live coal … He touched it to my lips and declared, "Now that this has touched your lips, your guilt shall depart and your sin be purged away." Then I heard the voice of my Lord saying, "Whom shall I

send? Who will go for us?" And I said, "Here am I; send me." (Isaiah 6:1 – 8)

Jeremiah: The word of the Lord came to me: "Before I created you in the womb, I selected you; before you were born, I consecrated you; I appointed you a prophet concerning the nations." I replied, "Ah, Lord God! I don't know how to speak, for I am still a boy." … The Lord put out his hand and touched my mouth, and the Lord said to me, "Herewith I put my words into your mouth. See, I appoint you this day over nations and over kingdoms: To uproot and to pull down, to destroy and to overthrow, to build and to plant." (Jeremiah 1:4 – 10)

Jesus: In those days Jesus came from Nazareth of Galilee and was baptized by John in the Jordan. And just as he was coming out of the water, he saw the heavens torn apart and the Spirit descending like a dove on him. And a voice came from heaven, "You are my Son, the Beloved; with you I am well pleased."

And the Spirit immediately drove him out into the wilderness. He was in the wilderness forty days, tempted by Satan; and he was with wild beasts; and the angels waited on him. (Mark 1:9 – 13)

Paul: Now as he journeyed he approached Damascus, and suddenly a light from heaven flashed about him. And he fell to the ground and heard a voice saying to him, "Saul, Saul, why do you persecute me?" And he said, "Who are you, Lord?" And he said, "I am Jesus, whom you are persecuting; but rise and enter the city, and you will be told what you are to do." (Acts 9:3 – 6)

How are we to understand these revelations? They are neither philosophical assumptions nor reasoned arguments. Rather, they are figurative descriptions of personal experiences.

Whether materially factual or metaphorical, the descriptions present moments when our pathfinders were touched by an awesome power and understanding that preceded and overwhelmed their prior conscious thoughts. Their descriptions suggest the touch was unexpected and intensely personal. It changed who they were, what they were about, and the world they saw. Out of these revelations flowed our enduring scriptures, scriptures that have spawned and sustained diverse religious identities that have cut across and superseded national, cultural, racial, even political identities.

Our religions grew up around the desire for and exhilaration of that touch — gestalts of songs and dances, rituals and celebrations, symbols and sanctuaries, postures and practices, prayers and meditations, doctrines and recitations, teachings and exhortations. Testimonies of changed lives confirm the effectiveness of the resulting religious gestalts — resurrected drug addicts and alcoholics, lives newly filled with meaning and purpose, joys discovered in the midst of material suffering, relationships miraculously changed, newfound peace even when facing death.

These gestalts — once birthed — grow and evolve, bud and divide. Sometimes they wither and die; they seldom, if ever, merge. Although they are the living means of their practicing communities for propagating the needed and unifying understandings, their embodiment can be foreign to outsiders, alien to those filled with fear and insecurity, and mortally threatening to those blinded by hate.

The differences in our religious gestalts are all too apparent. Yet, those religious gestalts that have endured grew up around some surprisingly basic and common understandings flowing out of a universal spirit of self-worth that overwhelmed our pathfinders and lit up the world they saw.

But how are we to understand what our pathfinders experienced and beheld? For example, how are we to materially clarify the words, *"Ehyeh-Asher-Ehyeh"* in Exodus 3:14, variously translated as "I Am That I Am," "I Am Who I Am," and "I Will Be Who I Will Be"[29] — the answer Moses received when questioning that which called to him from that flaming bush? Or, how are we to materially clarify the opening of the *Tao Te Ching*: "The Tao that can be told of is not the Absolute Tao; the Names that can be given are not the Absolute Names. The Nameless is the origin of Heaven and Earth; the Named is the Mother of All Things"?[30]

For that we need teachers. Consider how, centuries ago, a few of our teachers fixed into the minds of their listeners a simple but gripping narrative describing the moment a fleeing people found themselves trapped between the army of their enslavers and a seemingly impassable sea. First the narrative from Exodus 14:10 – 14:

> As Pharaoh drew near, the Israelites caught sight of the Egyptians advancing upon them. Greatly frightened, the Israelites cried out to the Lord. And they said to Moses, "Was it for want of graves in Egypt that you brought us out of Egypt? Is this not the very thing we told you in Egypt, saying, 'Let us be, and we will serve the Egyptians, for it is better for us to serve the Egyptians than to die in the wilderness'?" But Moses said to the people, "Have no fear! Stand by, and witness the deliverance which the Lord will work for you today; for the Egyptians whom you see today you will never see again. The Lord will battle for you; you hold your peace!"

The story is easy to remember, but how does it remain relevant? That was the issue for some rabbis looking at the text some centuries after the story was scrolled. Here is what they said:

> There were four groups among the Israelites at the sea.
>
> One said, "Let us throw ourselves into the sea."

One said, "Let us return to Egypt."

One said, "Let us make war against them."

One said, "Let us yell at them."

To the group that said "Let us throw ourselves into the sea," it was said, *Stand by, and witness the deliverance which the Lord will work for you today.*

To the group that said "Let us return to Egypt," it was said, *For the Egyptians whom you see today you will never see again.*

To the group that said "Let us make war against them," it was said, *The Lord will battle for you.*

To the group that said "Let us yell at them," it was said, *You hold your peace.*[31]

By using more general metaphors easily transferred to any time and culture, those rabbis gave life and meaning to that ancient event and its narrative by addressing some timeless concerns in their listeners' minds. Each concern was answered with a memorable phrase from the revered text.

Although we may not have the visionary experience of life that our pathfinders were privileged to behold, we can still join in what they saw taking place. And even if we don't identify with any or all of the religious gestalts that grew up around their teachings, we can learn from their understandings.

Consider their understanding of *universal self-worth*. From China circa 500 BCE, we read:

> Confucius said, "From the man bringing his bundle of dried fish for my teaching upwards, I have never refused instruction to anyone." (Analects VII:7)

From the Middle East circa 50 CE, we read:

> And they were bringing children to him, that he might touch them; and the disciples rebuked them. But when Jesus saw it he was indignant, and said to them, "Let the children come to me, do not hinder them; for to such belongs the kingdom of God." (Mark 10:13 – 14)

Returning to China circa 500 CE, we read:

I paid homage to the Patriarch and was asked where I came from ... I replied that I was a commoner from Sun-chow in Kwang-tung ... and then said, "I ask for nothing but Buddhahood."

The Patriarch replied: "So you are a native of Kwang-tung, are you? You evidently belong to the aborigines; how can you expect to become a Buddha?"

I replied: "Although there are Northern men and Southern men ... North and South make no difference in their Buddha-nature. An aborigine is different from your Eminence physically, but there is no difference in our Buddha-nature." (Autobiography of Hui-Neng in the Sutra Spoken by the Sixth Patriarch)[32]

Or consider the *joy* that can be found when joining in their vision:

The kingdom of heaven is like a treasure hidden in a field, which a man found and covered up; then in his joy he goes and sells all that he has and buys that field. (Matthew 13:45 – 46)

> He who lives a hundred years not perceiving the deathless state, a life of one day is better if a man perceives the deathless state. (Dhammapada VIII:15)[33]

Or look at their views on the *spirit of play* that characterizes those at home with their vision and its joy:

> I will give you a new heart and put a new spirit into you: I will remove the heart of stone from your body and give you a heart of flesh; and I will put My spirit into you. Thus I will cause you to follow My laws and faithfully to observe My rules. (Ezekiel 36:26 – 27)

> In embracing the One with your soul, can you never forsake the Tao? In controlling your vital force to achieve gentleness, can you become like a new-born child? (*Tao Te Ching* X)

> Yoga is the cessation of the turnings of thought. When thought ceases, the spirit stands in its true identity as observer to the world. (Yoga Sutra 1:2 – 3)[34]

> Let us live happily then, hating none in the midst of men who hate. Let us dwell free from hate among men who hate. (Dhammapada XV:1)

> Blessed are the poor in spirit, for theirs is the kingdom of heaven. Blessed are those who mourn, for they shall be comforted. Blessed are the meek, for they shall inherit the earth. Blessed are the pure in heart, for they shall see God. Blessed are the peacemakers, for they shall be called sons of God. Blessed are those who are persecuted for righteousness' sake, for theirs is the kingdom of heaven. (Matthew 5:2 – 10)

And look at their criteria on *recognizing leaders* who will not lead us astray in seeking the needed spirit of play:

Jesus said, "The good shepherd lays down his life for the sheep." (John 10:11)

Confucius said, "There was Shun. He indeed was greatly wise! Shun loved to question others, and to study their words, though they might be shallow. He concealed what was bad in them, and displayed the good. He took hold of their two extremes, determined the Mean, and employed it in his government of the people. It was by this that he was Shun [the sage-emperor]. (Doctrine of the Mean, Chap. VI)

And look at the importance they place on the *consequences of our thoughts, words, and deeds,* both individually and corporately, as we go about this play:

The Master said, "Yû, have you heard the six words to which are attached six becloudings?" Yû replied, "I have not." "Sit down and I will tell you. There is the love of being benevolent without the love learning — the beclouding here leads to foolish simplicity. There is the love of knowing without the love of learning — the beclouding here leads to dissipation of mind. … The love of being sincere without the love of learning … leads to an injurious disregard of consequences. … The love of straight-forwardness without the love of learning … leads to rudeness. … The love of boldness without the love of learning … leads to insubordination. … The love of firmness without the love of learning … leads to extravagant conduct." (Analects XVII:8)

God, speaking through Moses, said, "If you follow My laws and faithfully observe My commandments, I will grant your rains in their season so that the earth shall yield its produce and the trees of the field their fruit. … You shall eat your fill of bread and dwell securely in your land. … You shall lie down untroubled by anyone. … But if you do not obey Me and do not observe all these commandments, … I will set My face against you … your foes shall dominate you. You shall flee though none pursues. … Your land shall not yield its produce, nor shall the trees of the land yield their fruit." (Leviticus 26:3 – 20)

Our pathfinders knew that we would be encountering endless choices whose consequences would draw us either toward or away from the spirit of their joy. Although they came from vastly different cultures and times, they are surprisingly consistent when directing our attention to the nature of the choice. They point us toward spirits that flow from an encompassing holistic spirit that we can trust to bring us into a vibrant harmony with one another and away from spirits that flow from a countering egotistic spirit focused principally on personal gratification. The context of our choice often gives rise to general pairings our pathfinders frequently addressed.

Unity versus Division:

> If you love those who love you, what credit is that to you? For even sinners love those who love them. … But love your enemies, and do good, and lend, expecting nothing in return; and your reward will be great, and you will be sons of the Most High; for he is kind to the ungrateful and the selfish. Be merciful, even as your Father is merciful. (Luke 6:32 – 36)

Tsze-chang asked what constituted intelligence. The Master said, "He with whom neither slander that gradually soaks into the mind, nor statements that startle like a wound in the flesh, are successful, may be called intelligent indeed ... may be called far-seeing." (Analects XII:6)

Self-Insistence versus Selfishness:

Fame or one's own self, which does one love more? One's own self or material goods, which has more worth? Loss [of self] or possession [of goods], which is the greater evil? ... The contented man meets no disgrace; Who knows when to stop runs into no danger — He can long endure. (*Tao Te Ching* XLIV)

It will be like a man going on a journey, who called his servants and entrusted his wealth to them. To one he gave five bags of gold, to another two bags, and to another one bag, each according to his ability. Then he went on a journey. The man who had received five bags of gold went at once and put his money to work and gained five bags more. So also, the one with two bags of gold gained two more. But the man who had received one bag went off, dug a hole in the ground and hid his master's money. (Matthew 25:14 – 18)

And whoever strives hard, strives for himself. Surely Allāh is Self-sufficient, above [need of] [His] creatures. And those who believe and do good, We shall certainly do away with their afflictions and reward them for the best of what they did. (Quran 29:6 – 7)

Truthfulness versus Deception:

The Master said, "I do not know how a man without truthfulness is to get on. How can a large carriage be made to go without the cross-bar for yoking the oxen, or a small carriage without the arrangement for yoking the horses?" (Analects II:22)

He who testifies faithfully tells the truth, but a false witness, deceit. There is blunt talk like sword-thrusts, but the speech of the wise is healing. Truthful speech abides forever, a lying tongue for but a moment. (Proverbs 12:17 – 19)

Humility versus Superiority:

The Sage puts himself last, and finds himself in the foremost place; regards his body as accidental, and his body is thereby preserved. Is it not because he does not live for Self that his Self achieves perfection? (*Tao Te Ching* VII)

Pride goes before ruin, arrogance, before failure. Better to be humble and among the lowly than to share spoils with the proud. He who is adept in a matter will attain success; happy is he who trusts in the Lord. (Proverbs 16:18 – 20)

Self-Responsibility versus Faultfinding:

Not the unworthy actions of others, not their [sinful] deeds of commission or omission, but one's own deeds of commission and omission should one regard. (Dhammapada IV:7)

Why do you see the speck that is in your brother's eye, but do not notice the log that is in your own eye? (Matthew 7:3)

Generosity versus Greed:

The Master said, "The superior man thinks of virtue; the small man thinks of comfort. The superior man thinks of the sanctions of law; the small man thinks of favors which he may receive." The Master said, "He who acts with a constant view to his own advantage will be much murmured against." (Analects IV:11 – 12)

Come, look at this world, resembling a painted royal chariot. The foolish are sunk in it; for the wise there is no attachment for it. (Dhammapada XIII:5)

Send your bread forth upon the waters; for after many days you will find it. Distribute portions to seven or even to eight, for you cannot know what misfortune may occur on earth. (Ecclesiastes 11:1 – 2)

If you give in charity openly it is well, and if you hide it and give it to the poor it is better for you. (Quran 2:271)

Service versus Dominance:

Let the greatest among you become as the youngest, and the leader as one who serves. For which is the greater, one who sits at table, or one who serves? Is it not the one who sits at table? But I am among you as one who serves. (Luke 22:26 – 27)

Victory brings hatred; the conquered dwells in sorrow. He who has given up [thoughts of both] victory and defeat, he is calm and lives happily. (Dhammapada XV:5)

Immortality versus Mortality:

The evil doer grieves in this world, and he grieves in the next; he grieves in both. He grieves, he is afflicted, seeing the evil of his own actions. The righteous man rejoices in this world and rejoices in the next; he rejoices in both. He rejoices and becomes delighted, seeing the purity of his own actions. (Dhammapada I:15 – 16)

Jesus answered, "Truly, truly I say to you, unless one is born of water and the Spirit, he cannot enter the kingdom of God. That which is born of flesh is flesh, and that which is born of Spirit is spirit. (John 3:5 – 6)

The life of this world is only sport and play. It is surely the home of the Hereafter that will be life extended and new, if only they knew! (Quran 29:63)

In what sense might these understandings of our pathfinders be true? When it comes to philosophical understandings, we gravitate to those that can be argued from initial concepts and assertions that appeal to us. Similarly, when it comes to religious understandings, we gravitate toward the spirits of those who appeal to us. The choice reflects how we see ourselves and others. If we are drawn to those seeking a fuller life for others via inclusive associations, we gravitate to the encompassing spirits of our pathfinders. If we are drawn to those getting what they can for themselves via exclusive associations, we drift away to possibly attractive but ultimately divisive spirits. The nature of our peace and joy and the truths and consequences of our lives flow from the spirits that attract and guide us.

Our pathfinders tell us that, for better or for worse, an eventual reckoning comes to all. While we live, we can always choose to enter the lasting joy into which the inclusive doors open. By the time our options cease, tragedy awaits those who find themselves forever locked away from the many welcoming spirits their self-interest has imprisoned, ignored, or locked out. John Newton captured how dramatic our sense of that truth and its consequences is when he wrote, "Amazing Grace! How sweet the sound that sav'd a wretch like me! I once was lost, but now am found, was blind; but now I see."

* * *

One world — four distinct types of truths and understandings. The magisteria of science and art are poles apart with respect to the elements they coordinate and their means for doing so, yet in their material creativity, they complement and enliven each other. The magisteria of philosophy and religion are also poles apart, yet in their communal teachings, they, too, complement and enrich each other. Scientists, artists, philosophers, and religious leaders dedicate much of their lives to the truths at the poles of these two complementary axes of truth. Most of us meander about the political crosshairs where we forge our world views of who we are and what we are about.

As parents, we are responsible for guiding the choices and lives of our children prior to the age where the community holds them personally accountable for their actions. Naturally, both parents and children seek assistance and support in this guidance. Although that help is variously instituted, the equivalent of a high school education is required for science, art, and philosophy because of the universality of the personal need for knowledge, the inevitability of communal judgment of our actions, and the individualistic and often limited nature of parental training. That educational requirement is equally valid when it comes to our most basic religious understandings.

Our students need a grasp of how the spirits that guide their thoughts are fundamental to how they will come to see and experience life. They need to know the spirits that underlie fulfilling and lasting relationships. They need to see that they are valued and have a meaningful and lasting part to play. Tragedy brews every time we fail and a student graduates feeling worthless or seeing a hopeless road ahead, even a life of crime or a suicidal end. Of course, self-worth, honesty, and fair play can and often are conveyed in our schools and athletic programs, but seldom is that the central focus. But when students are struggling with their sense of self-worth, their relationships with their peers, and their hopes for a meaningful role to play, they need classes where they can anticipate an encounter with helpful understandings and empathetic discussions.

With that in mind, I'd like to venture some thoughts on how our most fundamental and unifying religious truths can be taught to high school students without violating the establishment clause of the First Amendment or undermining their appreciation of science, art, and philosophy. Effectively doing so will further their sense of self-worth, their desire for a cooperative spirit in their personal interactions, and their search for rewarding professional pursuits.

The basic idea is to enhance their consciousness of the spirits at play in the many choices they will be making as they go about their lives. They don't need to be taught how to distinguish the spirits. The basics were learned by the time they entered preschool. Rather, they need telling examples of the immediate and the less obvious long-term consequences of words and actions that flow out of the spirits they choose to follow.

Take one of our most fundamental of choices: whether to be guided by a spirit of unity or a spirit of division. The possible long-term divisive consequences of even a single word is well illustrated in Countee Cullen's poem "Incident." By having students read and discuss this artistic testimonial of a lived event, they become aware of the concern raised by both Confucius and Jesus without referring either to the Confucian expression "statements that startle like a wound in the flesh" or to its counterpart in Matthew 5:22, "Whoever says, 'You fool!' shall be liable to the hell of fire." The contrast between the two spirits is equally apparent when distinguishing healthy competition (in which students hone many of the skills needed for later life) from destructive fighting. In between lie all shades of gray that students can productively discuss and later apply to adult life in communities and nations.

Most students are keenly aware of the negative consequences that can take place even among friends when selfishness reigns. Many may not have seriously discussed the importance of self-insistence. Yet from that spirit flows our instinct to live, our innate feeling of self-worth, and our desire and essential need to develop and express our individual talents. The importance of rules may be well known, but few have contemplated how the spirit of play emerges from notions of unity and self-insistence or how the spirits of division and selfishness get entwined with those seeking to "game the system." Nor may a self-insistent student seeking overall unity know what to do when encountering individuals or groups guided by a selfish and divisive spirit. A discussion of Rosa Park's simple insistence on her inherent freedom to take an open seat in the front of the bus rather than being relegated to the back would be revealing and inspiring.

Although students may wonder whether they are being self-insistent or selfish, they are almost always fully aware of their truth or deception. Their choice reflects their personal assessment of the pros and cons of the envisioned consequences. They could greatly benefit by sharing some of their assessments of those consequences in the contexts of taking tests, building short-term and long-term relationships, playing games, reporting events, and making promises to others — and to themselves.

Every student is engaged in numerous group endeavors: families, classes, sports, musical groups, cheerleading teams, and drama clubs, to name a few. All have an acute sense of the relative success of the group endeavors with which they identify. All have a sense of their performance relative to the performances of the other participants. The possibilities are endless for discussing the choices between two pairs of contrasting spirits that inevitably come into play. They may enjoy discussing how an air of humility versus an air of superiority on the part of one individual can change the nature of the banter that follows a successful group event. However, they may benefit more by comparing how an air of faultfinding versus an air of self-improvement can change the banter following a disappointing group endeavor. Two scenarios could prove interesting: one in which each person focuses on someone else's mistakes, and the other in which each person focuses on where they could have done better.

Our students will naturally anticipate their participation in the game of life as adults when they will have greater responsibility over resources and opportunities. Various pairs of conflicting spirits may come into play as they increasingly come in contact with others. They are likely to be aware of some adults enjoying and being guided by a spirit of generosity while others seem captivated by a spirit of greed. A discussion of how their notion of fairness arises and how it reflects their sense of who they are and those with whom they identify would be revealing. They may enjoy comparing how these two spirits work in largely capitalistic versus largely socialistic economies. They will also be well aware of the distinction between the spirit of service and the spirit of dominance. In an open and spirited discussion, they may be surprised how their inclination to choose one or the other in various contexts also reflects their sense of who they are and those with whom they identify.

Our students need safe and nonjudgmental formats to sort out the lasting from the transient pros and cons of the many choices they will make while pursuing their desires. So much depends on how they identify with the consequences of their words and actions. They may not see that the choice of seeking an immediate pleasure rather than a lasting joy largely flows from following a spirit of mortality. A discussion of the statement "Give me liberty or give death!" attributed to Patrick

Henry may clarify the subtlety of the issues. A probing discussion of what each student could not forget about a best friend or person no longer physically present could greatly aid them in sorting out their own priorities.

Our students need a grasp of how the spirits that guide their thoughts are fundamental to how they will come to see and experience life. They need to explore the spirits that underlie fulfilling and lasting relationships. They need to see that they are valued and have a meaningful and lasting part to play. These understandings would be emphasized in a class in which unifying religious understandings are taught and discussed. We would all benefit.

HOW ELSE COULD I KNOW IT WAS LOVE?

Readers of the *Washburn Leader* learned on February 18 that a Nazi military shake-up was bringing war much closer and on February 25 that Austria was jumping to Hitler's command. Readers of the *Greeley Tribune* learned on February 28 that federal agents were searching for military spy suspects, on March 8 that workers were seeking cash for three million jobs, and on March 11 that German troops had crossed into Austria.

February 22 [Postmarked February 22, 4:30 p.m.]

Dear Margaret:

"I will never forget thy precepts; For with them thou hast quickened me." Psalm 119:93

I was asked to read scripture and lead in prayer at the evening service of the Colorado district Luther League Midwinter rally, held at Loveland, Colorado, last Sunday afternoon and evening. Rev Fritchell of Our Saviours Lutheran Church in Greeley spoke and had as his theme "Youth in a Changing World." Therefore I chose to read the 35 verse of Matt. 25 [For I was hungry and you gave me food, I was thirsty and you gave me drink, I was a stranger and you visited me] *and this portion of the 119th Psalm 89 – 96. It tells of God's Word, which is everlasting as well as quickening. It is certainly the only foundation upon which any youth can build securely for time and eternity. …*

Margaret, you said that I should tell you or get after you if you are too stingy. You know, I am really glad that you are and have learned to be economical. It is a virtue. I know that you will willingly render unto God what is God's, will you not? To save and be careful in order to render more to Him should be our goal. I want to do my work well, but my spare time I feel should go to God's work; at least the biggest part of it. …

Have you heard that the cattle prices have advanced steadily for the last two weeks? I surely hope I can get a fair price for my cattle. I may ship my cattle about the 10 of Mar., or I may buy a little more feed and keep them until Apr the 1st. …

Thank you also for the excellent Bible verses. They are certainly good. You must be pretty thorough in your reading to see them as you go along. It is certainly a help to me and, for that matter, to all true Christians to know that there are others who know Christ and experience definite answers to prayer. …

Yours in Christ,

Walter

Feb. 24 [Postmarked February 26, 8:30 a.m.]

My Dear Margaret:

Give ear to my words, O Jehovah

Consider my meditation. …

I am sorry that you froze your nose but glad that you were able to relieve it immediately with the snow. We had plenty of snow when I froze my cheeks, but I had no one to tell me that they were freezing. I did not know of it until a day or two later. …

You mention making plans for our wedding. We should do that; in fact, I plan as fast as possible, but until a little later, after I have sold my cattle and potatoes, it will be hard for me to make any definite plans. They are both looking better, and perhaps I will get a good price for both of them. As soon as I sell them, I will write and tell you my financial standing, and then we can discuss and make definite plans. …

Margaret, I wish you could be here now. The temp is about 40° above zero with a breeze in the air. It feels like a soft caress upon your face. A few rays of the sun filter thru the soft gray clouds in the sky. On the whole, very springlike. This is the time of the year which I love. New life coming into the plants with the birds coming back again.

Just a moment ago I was down at the cattle corrals, watching them. All were lying down and looked so contented. I wish you might have seen them. I believe you will like the farm because you love nature and all God's creation. Now there is a freshness in the air, which you will love. I would so much like to talk with you this afternoon. …

It must be quite a sight to stand upon the banks of the Missouri River and watch it flow ceaselessly on its way. I am glad you take such walks. I am going to take one right now, as soon as I finish this letter. I wish you might go with. We would walk out to the haystacks and go to the south side, out of the wind, and sit down, for a while, in the sunshine. I feel an intense desire to do this this afternoon, and since it may be my last chance for some time, I am going to do it. …

May God haste[n] *the day when we will be united in Christian Love.*

Walter

Walter's stopping to enjoy one of life's moments reminds me of a time my brothers and I were playing with some sparrow hawks. We had caught them shortly before they could fly and kept them alive on a diet of grasshoppers. They soon learned to fly a few feet, land on our hands, and eat the grasshoppers that we held in our fingers. One morning right after breakfast we decided to let the hawks go. They flew a few yards before landing on some nearby fence posts. When we held up some grasshoppers, they briefly stared at us, lifted off and silently glided over, fastened their talons on our gloves, and tore into the grasshoppers with their hooked beaks.

Pretty soon Dad came striding over. "Why aren't you out in the fields by now?"

"Hey, Dad, watch this!" We held up some more grasshoppers. Again the sparrow hawks lifted off their perches, glided over, gripped our gloves, and devoured the tasty morsels.

Without further comment, Dad joined the fun, watching the hawks glide toward his outstretched glove with their fierce focus on his hapless offerings. The fun ended a half an hour later with his words, "We've got to get to work if we hope to get anything done today."

February 26 [Postmarked February 28, 3:00 p.m.]

Dear Walter,

"Jehovah is nigh unto all them that call upon Him,

To all that call upon Him in truth." Ps. 145:18 …

Walter, I am just a little lonesome for you. I just wish that you weren't so far away. I don't know how I am going to stand it until September. If I could sit in your lap right now, I would be so happy. You just don't know how much. I can hardly wait to come and spend the twenty-fours of each day with you. Won't it be fun to live in our home together? I never realized to be loved and to love a man would be so wonderful. God, I believe, has given that as an additional gift to his children. …

Walter, I am so happy that you are praying for me. I pray that I might be a true Christian wife to you always. God truly answered my prayer for a Christian husband in sending you. I am very glad that you do not smoke or chew; that was one thing that I prayed God that if He would sometime give me a husband that he would be one who was a Christian who did not smoke tobacco and chew it. I am glad that I am not awfully much older than you; also, I am glad that we plan to get married before I am thirty years old. …

Like Margaret, most of us can specify desirable attributes in the partner "meant for us." On entering college, I wanted an attractive Lutheran with long, dark hair and who enjoyed music. Even though I was willing to give a little on that strange combination of attributes, none in that restrictive set of coeds was particularly attracted to me during my undergraduate years.

God must have decided, possibly with a chuckle, to answer my desires when I entered graduate school. At the opening fall get-together of the Lutheran Student Association, in walked a striking first-year coed with long, dark hair. Later that evening, we sat together on a piano bench while she played Beethoven's "Moonlight Sonata." I don't know why she fell in love, but I knew why I had.

We enjoyed making out from the start. A heady two months passed quickly. We were already quite serious when she invited me to meet her parents, who lived a few miles from mine. I arrived Friday afternoon an hour before dinner. After briefly greeting her mother, she took my hand and led me to her church. She was one of the organists — and she had a key.

We entered through the heavy door and climbed the stairs to the choir loft. She adjusted the bench, turned on the organ, and began setting the tonal stops. I sat down beside her, lost in the ancient silence of the church. As she began to play, I was alone with all my desires — her presence, the music, the church.

Dinner came all too soon. The food was good; the spirit … unsettling. Her parents shared so little of their day. They must have asked me some questions, but I don't recall. Shortly after dinner ended, we got in the car and drove to a secluded place where we could be alone together for a couple of hours.

Later that night as I tried to fall asleep, uneasy thoughts began swirling through my mind. Like the two of us, her parents must have been "in love" before they married. Yet, they seemingly ended up with little feeling for each other. Could that happen to me? Could I wake up one day and not enjoy seeing the woman across the table?

The next evening, we double-dated with my brother and a friend of hers. I found myself watching her and her friend chat away while I wondered about some of our seemingly mutual interests. She played the piano and I played the trumpet, but we never played together. We were both Lutherans, but we didn't discuss what it meant to be a Lutheran or even a Christian. We were both in college but had never really discussed our educational and vocational interests. I think she and her friend had a good time. I didn't. That night, I struggled with what was going amiss in what I desired. By morning, the attributes that colored the girl I sought had faded, and her physical touch had lost its appeal.

A few days later I apologetically handed back her class ring. She was taken aback and justifiably angered, accusing me of finding someone else. I left confused and disillusioned as to what I was seeking in this basic choice in life. God had brought into my life an answer to my desires, but what good was that answer when my desire was out of sync with my heart's reality?

So the cattle prices are going up! I can just see you feeding the stock. It seems now I notice the diamonds of the married women, and they just sparkle. A diamond is certainly a beautiful gem with its brilliant myriads of colors. May God help and make me worthy of the gift. …

Some time ago you asked me to discuss a number of Sunday School questions. The first question: Do miracles happen today? I believe they do. It's a miracle that we are going to be married since I know that it was done through God's guidance, but please don't misunderstand me. Mother said not so very many years ago there was a field missionary in South or North Dakota who got lost in a blizzard.

All at once he saw a lighted window. He knocked at the door, and a lady opened the door. He found shelter there. This lady was without flour and had but a half loaf of bread. This missionary was with this family and was given the loaf of bread until the weather was such that he could walk safely. Every time the lady cut from the loaf, it remained still a half loaf. This missionary said that that was a miracle. Evodia can tell this story better than I, and maybe I have not told it all as it was, so it would be well for you to ask her. Someway or other when I relate episodes I add and subtract to them, altho I do not do so intentionally. The third question: Why do we end our prayers by saying "In Jesus Name and for His sake"? I think that it is because Jesus says to His disciples, "Verily, verily, I say unto you. If ye shall ask anything of the Father, he will give it to you in my name: ask, and ye shall receive, that your joy may be made full. In that day ye shall ask in my name: and I say not unto you, that I will pray the Father for you; for the Father himself loveth you, because ye have loved me, and have believed that I came forth from the Father." St. John 16:23b, 24, 26, 27. The fourth: What was the purpose of Christ's coming upon the earth? To save us from our sins and cause us to be redeemed and justified before God that we might inherit eternal life in heaven. John 3:16. Why did he have to die to save us from our sins? Because only through Christ could we be made alive since thru Adam all sinned and died but by man, that is, Christ, shall all be made alive. By man came also the resurrection and life. We all sinned thru Adam, and no one but a sinless sacrifice was acceptable in the sight of God. He was the spotless lamb of God that willingly offered up himself to redeem us. I think the hymn no. 114, "My Crucified Savior Despised and Condemned," answers the question fully. I love that hymn. I hope to memorize it during Lent. I almost know it, but I need to do some refining. The second question: Is prayer answered in dreams and visions? I don't believe God uses [them] *much today because we have the whole Bible, which in Old Testament times and even New Testament times they didn't. However, I am sure God still uses it to call. Some ministers have dreamt that certain persons were in need and have followed out the dream and found it to be true. I think that God sends dreams and visions if He needs to but it is seldom necessary. …*

I don't discount dreams. Whether you see the brain as a creation of God or the result of the daunting time frames of evolution, its operational structure must reflect a deep harmony with creation itself. The mind coordinates the rhythms, mystical images, and experiences of childhood. It organizes the massive informational inputs of daily life of which only a select few are consciously entertained. Who knows what is laid aside, reorganized, or brought to the fore while we sleep? Here is a dream that spoke to me when my two children were in high school.

I was an elder at a church that emphasized prayer. Our meetings with the pastors and deacons ended with our praying in small groups for members with special needs.

It was a transition time for the church. The head pastor of the congregation had been called to another congregation. The youth pastor was taking over the reins. He greatly desired the prayers of the elders and deacons, and he suggested that we meet at a restaurant for prayer on Tuesday morning at seven. We could have breakfast and break in time for work. Attendance was optional.

That week I struggled with the issue. I wanted to support the youth pastor. The early hour was no problem. I had already set aside that time for exercising, meditating, and walking to work — an energizing and creative hour and a half that I hated to give up even for one day.

The night before the first prayer breakfast, I climbed into bed still undecided. In a dream that night, I was lying in bed thinking that I should attend the early prayer group. On hearing my alarm, I reached over and hit the alarm button. It kept ringing, so I hit the alarm button again and again, but it kept ringing. Then I woke up, hit the alarm button on the bedside clock, dressed, and went to the first of the many weekly Tuesday-morning prayer breakfasts I enjoyed as an elder.

Walter, I believe you must be quite active in church if you were at a meeting of the board of trustees, Luther League rally & party, and taught Bible class. I just love to go to church, and I know you do. May God always keep that longing for temple worship to be within us and granted.

This letter has gotten too long, so I hope that you have stopped ever so often to get a little recreation while you please after reading a few pages.

Now it is time to go to bed, so I guess I will say good night and may God bless you and keep you for Himself and for me also.

Yours in Christian love,

Margaret

What is a miracle? It is miraculous that a single fertilized human cell barely visible to the human eye has the knowledge and skill to grow and go forth from its mother's womb and become an independent being. And if a baby's being able to grow into an adult is not a miracle that should fill our hearts with joy and for which we should give thanks and sing praise, what is?

Margaret says that she believes miracles happen today. She points out, "It's a miracle that we are going to be married." Although the circumstances under which two people fall in love are less predictable than the development of a human life from a sperm and egg, many rewarding marriages stem from seemingly fortuitous encounters. Margaret recognizes that if she calls her fortuitous encounter with Walter a miracle, then the miraculous again becomes commonplace. She ends up answering the question with a secondhand story that apparently defies our naturalistic assumptions and mechanistic understandings.

Although it is difficult to define a miracle, each of us has a sense of the term and has possibly experienced one. Here's one that happened to me.

I was joining my friend, Bill, for our weekly Thursday morning coffee together at work. He was a biochemist interested in science and philosophy. I was a statistician interested in science and religion. On our weekly coffee breaks, we were often among the first to sit down and the last to leave.

This particular coffee break held the usual promise. At the checkout counter, I reached into my wallet to pull out a dollar bill to pay for my coffee and donut. But instead of there being a few dollar bills in my wallet, there was an unending number. I was rich beyond all possible need. At least that was the experience. At the same time the following story in II Kings 4:1 – 7 flashed through my mind:

> Now the wife of one of the sons of the prophets cried to Elisha, "Your servant my husband is dead; and you know that your servant feared the Lord, but the creditor has come to take my two children to be his slaves." And Elisha said to her, "What shall I do for you? Tell me; what have you in the house?" And she said, "Your maidservant has nothing in the house, except a jar of oil." Then he said, "Go outside, borrow vessels of all your neighbors, empty vessels and not too few. Then go in, and shut the door upon yourself and your sons, and pour into all these vessels; and when one is full, set it aside." So she went from him and shut the door upon

> herself and her sons; and as she poured they brought the vessels to her. When the vessels were full, she said to her son, "Bring me another vessel." And he said to her, "There is not another." Then the oil stopped flowing. She came and told the man of God, and he said, "Go, sell the oil and pay your debts, and you and your sons can live on the rest."

Naturally, I puzzled over what had happened. Speaking as a scientist, the miracle must have involved different types of neuronal and biochemical interactions in my brain responsible for my elation and surprise. Maybe I fell into a pleasant and more stable region in mental space. Maybe an unconscious understanding of what the story of Elisha and the poor widow meant for me was unleashed. Who knows how the mythic stories in scripture work their wonders in our minds?

I eventually came to see the experience as an inauguration of a new way of counting what is in my "wallet." Previously, my quick and easy tallies always raised worrisome questions. Do I have enough? Where am I in the financial pecking order?

Now my counting takes my life into consideration. Dollars are counted when pulled from my "wallet" to pay for a need.

The totaling never stops. When counting that way, my monetary concerns fade, and I am free to concentrate on other things.

That was then, and this is now. As I see it, a miracle remains a curiosity until it brings about a change in your view of life. In opening my wallet and seeing an endless number of dollar bills coming out, I fell back on God's providential trampoline and exhilarated in the experience, knowing that God had always cared for my needs and always would.

March 2 [Postmarked March 3, 8:30 a.m.]

Dear Margaret

"And the spirit of Jehovah will come mightily upon thee, and thou shalt prophecy with them, and shall be turned into another man." I Sam. 10:6

"And it was so, that when he had turned his back to go from Samuel, God gave him another heart: and all those signs came to pass that day." I Sam. 10:9

Thank you, Margaret, for the verses which you sent, for the answers to the questions which I sent, and for the whole letters. It was not a bit too long. I never paused once until I had read it all.

A few days ago, I came across the above verses as I was reading. To me it is a good answer to the question: Do we have to be born anew, and what does it mean? Don't you think so? …

Margaret, do not worry about your inability to do personal work. When God wills it, He will provide opportunity, grace, and strength to do it; of that you may be sure. As you walk daily before your pupils and fellow teachers, your life is doing a personal work in these fellow men that you are unaware of. You may be sure that a pleasing, smiling greeting does not go unnoticed, nor any kind acts, even tho very, very small. …

If just a letter from you lifts up my spirits, "it actually makes me feel I could move mountains barehanded" and draws me closer to Christ, think what it will mean to me to be able to come to you at any time. Margaret, I mean every word of this. Letter writing is not easy for me. I would never sit here and write just to be kidding you. In fact, I hope you do not care for it because I do not like it nor can I do it. I write because I miss you. …

You mention some things in me which you were glad for. I too am glad, first that you are a Christian woman and that you want to go to Church, that you do not smoke nor drink, that you do not care for shows nor dancing, that you actually like to work, and I am sure you like and want a home and children. For all these I am glad and happy.

I am praying for you always, Margaret, and for the day to haste when we may be united in Christian love.

Yours in Christ,

Walter

I like Walter's words, "your life is doing a personal work … that you are unaware of." As he wrote these words, he and Margaret were trying to find time and ways in their busy lives to witness to what God had done for them. As they struggled with these issues, they were compelled to write letters demonstrating their faith. No — it was their joy to dwell on not only what God was doing for them but also how they viewed it. Yet they seem to be completely unaware (at least they don't comment on it) of the opportunity they have been given for the very witness they desire and how naturally they have taken advantage of it.

March 3 [Postmarked March 4, 7:00 a.m.]

Dear Walter,

"Heal me, O Jehovah, and I shall be healed; save me, and I shall be saved: for Thou art my praise." Jeremiah 17:14

This is one of the verses from my evening's devotions. Poor Jeremiah; he is always ready to burst into tears. I guess he saw the awful or terrible sinfulness of sin committed by the people of his day.

Thanks for your work of today. I can just imagine that you are having the good tired feeling that makes one rest easily. I haven't done much in the line of grading examination papers, but teaching nevertheless saps some strength. Marie was so tired this noon that she was provoked at everything; she even felt like crying. Mildred was so nervous the other day that her hands just shook. She said at four o'clock (right after dismissal) if anyone had pointed his finger at her, she would have started to bawl. Her father is still very ill. I am thankful that I do not feel that much on edge. …

It is true, as you mentioned, [that] *it is better to make plans for our wedding this summer rather than now. This summer will be such a different one for me. I hope God will make it very profitable for both of us.*

You asked me about my spring vacation. We have only one day off, and that is Good Friday. … I would enjoy being with you this spring, but I don't see how it could work out.

The district basketball tournament is being held here. The first game was played this evening. I plan to watch only the games in which our team competes. It's just this way; I want to grade papers and figure out the six weeks' marks for the pupils on Friday, tomorrow. Then on Saturday I will be able to plan my next week's assignments.

This evening I got my knitted skirt and the yarn for my sweater. I will enclose a sample so that you might see the color and texture of the yarn. The skirt fits well. It will take quite a while to knit the sweater, but Helen has promised to help me. I have not picked out a pattern yet.

Tomorrow we are supposed to receive our monthly salaries. It will be fun to put away another thirty dollars. Some of the teachers saved nothing from last month's check but are planning to do so this month.

You asked if I receive letters regularly from my folks. Yes, I do when I think over it, but I am very slow in answering. … Father used to write very often. I miss his interesting fatherly, Christian letters. …

I haven't been on a single walk since last Saturday. The snow had been melting so that the walk would be too muddy. Then this afternoon we have had a change of weather. The wind began to blow, and then snow began to come just in torrents if that were possible. I am sure that the farmers appreciate the added moisture. …

Walter, I surely would enjoy seeing you sometime in the near future, but how can we manage?

Yours in Jesus,

Margaret

2

Who are the Evodia Singers? I haven't heard of them? It would have been fun to have listened to their program.

It is true, as you mentioned, it is better to make plans for our wedding this summer rather than now. This summer will be such a different one for me. I hope God will make it very profitable for both of us.

You asked me about my spring vacation. We have only one day off and that is Good Friday. Last year school closed on the twenty-eighth of May. This year, I presume, it will be the twenty-seventh. We have but two more six weeks' periods. I would enjoy being with you this spring but I don't see how it could work out.

The district basket ball tournament is being held here. The first game was played this evening. I plan to watch only the games in which our team competes. It's just this way; I want to grade papers and figure out the six weeks' marks for the pupils on Friday, tomorrow. Then on Saturday I will be able to plan my next week's assignments.

March 6 [Postmarked March 8, 3:00 p.m.]

Dear Walter,

"May Thy rich grace impart,
Strength to my fainting heart,
My zeal inspire;
As Thou has died for me,
O may my love to Thee
Pure, warm, and change-less be
A living fire."

Now I just returned from the song fest at church. There were quite a few people present. The junior choir sang quite well, but oh, I wish that I could direct them better. There is too much "sameness" in their singing. The above stanza was the one I sang while the others in the senior choir hummed. …

While in Bismarck Saturday I bought some things. Among them was a purser perfume bottle, as they called it. I'll put some of it on this page so that you can have some of the fragrance too. …

Walter, I appreciate that you dislike teasing. I don't like it either. There are so many wonderful things happening in the world that one can talk about, and then I think speaking more of God and His gifts to us that one will not wish to spend time in a useless stream of nonsense talking. …

Dad and Mom seldom uttered "a useless stream of nonsense talking." We children delivered a stream of teases, tomfoolery, one-upmanship, and zingers that always tried Mom's patience.

Mom did, however, have one anecdote she loved to share and could not do so without first chuckling. It seems that in college, a friend of hers was attracted to a young man who worked in a general store that carried, among other things, various nuts and candies. Her friend hoped to start up a conversation with him by using the introductory excuse that she wanted to purchase some pecans. She wanted to confirm the pronunciation, *peaKHANS* or *PEAcans*. Mom obliged, and her friend set off for the store.

A few minutes later she burst back into the room. "You told me they were pronounced PEAcans and when I asked for some, he brought down from a high shelf a pee can [a large, bedside bucket]. I was so embarrassed I had to leave, and it's all your fault."

"No, it's not. I said *peaKHANS*!" With that, Mom's face would light up, and she would start laughing all over again.

Now the time is continuing to fly. Soon you will have sold your cattle. I wish that you could come here to put that ring on my finger rather than to get it thru the mail. It will mean so much more. Maybe your cattle will bring so much that you can. You know what is best, however. May God guide you in your business transactions and in other affairs. …

How is Mr. Brown overcoming his liquor-drinking habit? I hope that he will come to the Savior and He will care for that problem. I get rather afraid when I think of having a drunkard so close by, but they are near even now. Last night the ones who refereed the games had been to a dance the night before; one of them had become drunk. Marie had danced with him; she didn't know that he was drunk. Now the news is out about it, and she is quite worried. She said she can't tell that a man is drunk unless he can hardly stand up. Oh, that our government would prohibit the sale of liquor! …

Last Saturday I went to the Bismarck City Library. They have a very nice one. I presume the reason Greeley's isn't as good as it might be is that the college has such a large one. Have they started building the new library they promised us last summer? I hope that you and I can do quite a lot of reading. There [are so many] *instructive and well-written books that I hope we can get a hold of them if by no other means than by checking them out from some library. I have a number of books. Maybe we can classify them like the Dewy Decimal System advocates. That will be quite an interesting project, don't you think? I know that you have quite a number of books also. It is fun for me to visualize what our home will be like after about a half-year's period of living together helping one another. …*

There is a spot on this letter right here that Helen happened to make when she was putting up her hair for the night. This sounds as though she had a wig. …

May He ever bind us close in Christian love and fellowship.

Margaret

This letter has so many errors, but I hope that you will overlook them. I am glad that you love [me] *altho I can but give myself (with all my faults, but hopes and prayer to be rid of them) to you.*

March 12 [Postmarked March 12, 3:00 p.m.]

Dear Walter,

"Oh send out Thy light and Thy truth; Let them lead me:

Let them bring me unto Thy holy Hill, And to Thy tabernacles." Psalm 43:3

This is Saturday morning. I am sitting by my desk in my classroom. I should, perhaps, be at home, but Miss Foster, or Helen, is still sleeping, so I thought I would disturb her less by doing my writing here. …

I haven't heard any market reports over the radio. I am glad that they have improved in price for cattle. Mr. Thorson handed us a questionnaire regarding our desires of being reelected. I said I would. There was a question if we would come back for the same salary and I wrote no, but I plan to speak to him about it and tell him I would. It hasn't been decided if we get rehired or not. I don't know if the contract may be broken after having signed it. …

The weather is grand: the air is balmy; the sun, shining; the birds, singing; and I am happy. I just heard that there were about three inches of water above the ice, so the river should soon go out.

I will be glad to get your picture. Have you had it taken yet? I hope it looks just like you. The ring maybe will reach me before Easter. Walter, sometimes when I think about all what has happened and what will happen if God wills us to be united next fall, I feel sort of weak but happy. I hope you aren't regretting what happened last Christmas; maybe I led you to do that which you regret, but your letters don't sound that way. I love you so much, but I am afraid that I can't do the planning, work, and be of help like a farmer's wife should. If you can be satisfied with below-average work in regard to speed, completeness, and quality, I will be glad to be your wife. I wish that I were better for you. I am afraid I won't be able to help you make both ends meet like you would want your wife to do. I have earned some money teaching, but I am afraid housekeeping is much different. I know that God can make me and mold me after His will while I am patient, quiet, and still, so with His power and your help my incompleteness can and will be overcome. I don't believe you want to get married next fall, and maybe one of the main reasons is because you aren't certain if I am the one whom God wishes you to marry, or is it just because of money? I guess I don't understand it all. Sometimes I long so for you that I can hardly wait till next fall, but if that longing can't be satisfied, I guess God means for me to do something else, then. I still believe you love me, but I just don't understand it all.

I haven't written before because I was waiting for a letter from you. It came last night. I guess you are busier than I realize, and so when I wait for a letter, I forget that there are many more urgent things than to write letters. I know I have wanted to write many times, but I felt that maybe I led you on, altho I didn't mean to and didn't realize that it would turn out as it did last fall, so I just haven't written. Walter, if you don't want to spend your money for a ring or don't want to get married next fall, I wish you would say so. I don't want to have you disappointed in marriage; however, I don't know how I can stand to live without you. Maybe God just sends these times to me to try me. …

I am glad that you didn't shoot well on that Sunday. I know you don't believe in misusing that holy day. Time that He gives us for worship and rest from toil is a gift from Him. I have sinned on that day so much that I imagine that that is the reason why I have not grown in grace as a sturdy plant should have done. I guess God sends us to do His will even tho we think we are going in the opposite direction. …

Unfortunately, the letter Margaret says "came last night" is missing. None of Walter's previous letters mentions shooting on Sunday. Margaret responded on March 6 to Walter's last letter, which was postmarked on the fourth. In her January 16 correspondence in the *Courtship Letters,* Margaret playfully says, "You can burn this letter if you like." It is almost unimaginable that she burned the missing letter. It is also unlikely that, of the ninety-three letters Walter wrote, she accidentally lost the particular one she was waiting to receive before wanting to write again. Maybe she was disturbed and distracted, but still?

I wish you were here, Walter, and then we could converse about certain problems. I regret very much not getting to spend that last night with you at home, but I know that God intended it to be as it was. Now you are so far away that I can't even see you. …

You asked me if I have a chance to practice. I don't have. It seems when I get to school in the mornings I have to prepare my lessons. At home everyone is busy doing other things. I don't understand where the time goes. …

I hope you'll like the pictures and that you don't regret having come to Minnesota. I just feel that it was God's plan, and I wish that I could be with you now. I wonder if other people who are engaged feel like I do. This molding is not an easy process, is it? I guess I feel that I need you too much, and God is showing me that you can easily get along without me and for me to just cast myself on Him, and He'll carry me through. That's what I am going to do, and it'll all turn out fine because He loves us both and wants to give you and me just what is best, so if He wants to withhold you from me, He knows how to do it and when to do it, and He will supply all you need and all I need in His own time. May God bless and keep you in Him always.

With much love through Christ,

Margaret

The importance of not giving up one's renewal time, like Margaret's chance to practice, was impressed upon me at a professional meeting early in my career. Professional meetings were a maze of colleagues, presentations, and displays vying for one's attention — enjoyable but hectic. Having stayed up late Sunday night with some friends from graduate school, I was not looking forward to the 8:00 a.m. presentation my supervisor had requested I attend.

The room alarm brought the upcoming day into focus all too soon. Time didn't permit my usual morning ritual of exercising, reading one or more passages in a world scripture, and meditating on their relevance to the day ahead. I got up and headed for the sink. While shaving, the words of Jesus in Luke 10:42 swept over me, "Martha, Martha, you are anxious and troubled about many things; one thing is needful. Mary has chosen the good portion, which shall not be taken from her." In essence, I was being asked by something deep inside me, "Why are you giving up the most rejuvenating moment of your day?"

I put down the shaver. I enjoyed my morning ritual. I walked to the restaurant and ordered a big ham, egg, and hash brown breakfast with coffee, toast, and jam. I took my time browsing the abstracts of the presentations that interested me. After paying my bill, I walked to the meeting contemplating the morning interruption and the slower pace I would set for my participation in the meeting. From start to finish, the meeting was a surprisingly pleasant and informative affair.

Upon returning to work, I was prepared to share with my supervisor how it was that I missed the presentation he wanted me to attend. He never asked. Maybe had I gone and reported back on what I had learned, my performance evaluation would have improved, at least temporarily. Who knows? In any case, since that time, I have chosen to walk, and occasionally jog, rather than run through life. When I get too busy, I often hear those words again, "one thing is needful," accompanied by the understanding that I can give up my renewal time but that it won't be taken from me.

March 13 [Postmarked March 14, 6:30 a.m.]

Dear Margaret:

"And he took bread, and when he had given thanks, he broke it and gave to them, saying, This is my body which is given for you: this do in remembrance of me." Luke 22:19

We had communion service in Greeley today and a very good sermon with it. There it was pointed out to us that we are to do this in remembrance of Him who died for us. Then I heard Dr. Maier, over the Lutheran hour, point out the same truth, and it came to me in a new and fuller light. We suffer sickness, war, trial, and many troubles here on earth, as a result of sin. Nor do we in any way pay for all our sins thru earthly suffering. Else Christ would never have needed to die for us. Would he? So it seemed to me that we are to be reminded of Christ's immeasurable suffering as well as be spiritually strengthened by this Holy Sacrament. ...

Whether or not I can come to put the ring on your finger is hard to say. If it is His will, I should like to. The cattle market & potato market both look even better. Margaret, I know you are praying with me and for me, and God will help us and lead us in that manner. I long for the day when I can speak instead of write, but I shall let you know the minute the cattle are sold and keep you informed of my financial standing all along. If you can, try to learn the cost of the kind of a wedding you should like to have. Then we can decide whether to use the 50 dollars it would cost me to come up there for coming or for something else. …

And now may He haste[n] *the day when we may be united.*

Yours in Christian love.

Walter

I can agree with Walter that we "suffer sickness, war, trial, and many troubles here on earth" due to ignorance, greed, and any number of narrow interests, and if you want to group them together by calling them "sins," that's fine with me. In that sense, we pay for our sin. And sometimes we pay dearly and many times over because suffering does not stop the negative consequences of sin; forgiveness and the desire for forgiveness can.

Jesus encouraged forgiveness. In Matthew 18:21 – 22 he was asked, "How often shall my brother sin against me, and I forgive him? As many as seven times?" and Jesus replied, "I do not say seven times, but seventy times seven." And we see it in an action of Jesus's. When being crucified on the cross for his teachings, Jesus pleads in Luke 23:34, "Father, forgive them; for they know not what they do."

You would only want to forgive someone who had wronged you if you valued your relationship with that person. The needed feelings and the underlying love often arise in a healthy relationship between a parent and a child. But if forgiveness is ever to get to the root of sin, an even deeper relationship is involved and must continually be set right. Maybe it is something vague within oneself, or one's conscience, or a teaching one reveres. For me, it is my relationship with God, and as Margaret so cogently writes in her November 6 courtship letter, once that relationship is set right, the "veil" that can keep one from freely communing with God "is broken."

March 14 [Postmarked March 15, 4:30 p.m.]

Dearest Margaret:

"Come unto me, all ye that labor and are heavy laden, and I will give you rest." Matt. 11:28

Margaret, there is so much I want to write about. I received your last letter today. I want to first of all thank you for it, the pictures and the paper [and] *also the news from Minn. I am returning the paper and pictures. I should like to have some pictures when you get others, and it will not be much trouble for you to send them again, will it? As for me, they are indelibly imprinted in my very poor memory. I shall never forget those days, nor cease to thank God for them.*

My Dear, I cannot help but feel that you were and have been much worried of late. I certainly want to apologize for not writing oftener and making myself clear. I am a poor letter writer, always in a hurry and taking too much for granted. Now for the first thing that I want to say: As I told you once while we were together in Minn., I have never said one word which I should care to retract or change. I love you more than ever. It may seem that to you that you led me on, but you did not. God led me, and I do thank him for that leading.

As far as being sure whether you are the right one or not, of that I am now positive. That was why I would not take you in my arms until I was at least quite sure; in fact, I wanted your promise to be my wife before I did that. How else could I know that it was love and not desire or passion on the part of either one of us? As far as I have gone in seeking a helpmate, God has answered every prayer. Those tender and beautiful moments that every young couple experience are ours to look forward to and not to look back upon. Not only that, but with God's sanction and blessing, they will be abiding and will not become timeworn. Without God, this cannot be.

When I wrote asking whether or not you could get your contract and then break it, I was not putting your love to a test or you upon probation but merely looking forward and preparing for all emergencies. I do not remember telling you of them, but we have had hail storms which did not leave a single leaf upon the large trees, nor a green stalk in the fields. Should this happen to me this summer, I would have a very hard time to make ends meet, and I could not ask you to share a debt which it might take some time to pay. In spite of all, marriage cannot thrive only on love. It does take some money, altho I do think if it be true love, the true love of God in each lover, that it would have to be hard indeed if they could not be happy anyway.

But all this ‸misunderstanding is all my fault, for not making myself clearer.

Margaret, believe me when I say that I love you and long for your companionship and help; I will keep you informed, absolutely correct[ly], *on all money matters. I think it right that you should know them. And please remember and believe this, that everything I do will be done to haste*[n] *the day when we may be united in Christian love and marriage. If God should provide and will it, I should like to be married before fall. It would give you more time to get accustomed and get things arranged in the way you should like to have it. There is much work to do in the fall. I am glad for the last part of your letter where you say you will cast yourself upon God's mercy and that He loves us and will help us. That is true.*

It is absolutely necessary to be prepared and to be in Christ. We may and we may not see the end of all things, but the signs of the times are certainly evident. I suppose you read of Hitler's seizure of Austria. This and many other events point toward the last days. May we ever be found in Him. ...

For me it is not necessary to plan an elaborate wedding; in fact, I am inclined to like simplicity in all things. My requirements are not great, and it may be that yours are not either, and in that case we would not need such a vast sum of money. Let us together take our problems to God even tho we are so far apart. Surely He will provide for us.

I read an article by Elsie Robinson, quite a well-known columnist and philosopher. (Do you know of her?) In that article, she told of the psychological value of prayer. That it is not necessary to be religious or to call upon any special name for help. She said the psychological effect of praying helps to heal sick minds; in fact, she told of a friend who became mentally and physically well thru the effect of prayer.

If this is true, how much more can we not expect, who having a living God to pray to and come to with our burdens? I think it will all work out for us, Margaret. I, too, have blue moments, but I am so busy that I have little time to think of them. Perhaps that is God's way of helping me.

May God bless and keep you, in Christ always.

Yours in Christ,

Walter

A Glimpse Back

February 22. Walter opened a youth gathering on the theme "Youth in a Changing World." Whom would you quote, and what thought would you share, if opening a similar gathering on that theme today?

February 24. It was a winter day. The thought occurred to Walter while writing this letter to "walk out to the haystacks and go to the south side, out of the wind and sit down, for a while, in the sunshine." How would you picture the weighing of priorities leading up to his decision?

February 26. Margaret prayed for a Christian mate who didn't smoke or chew. What would you tell someone to look for when seeking a lifetime partner?

Margaret viewed her anticipated marriage with Walter as a miracle because "it was done through God's guidance." Why do you think she followed that remark on miracles with the qualifier "but please don't misunderstand me"? How would you have answered the question: Do miracles happen today?

March 2. Walter says a "pleasing, smiling greeting" and "kind acts, even tho very, very small" do not go unnoticed. What significance do you attach to these small acts of kindness?

March 6. On January 16 of their courtship letters, Walter writes, "though Mr. Brown is an atheist and drinks more than any man I know, yet he and the whole family ... are fine people. ... They are almost a 2nd home to me." On February 14 he writes, "Mr. Brown is a rank atheist and has lived a hard life, so it is hard to talk with him." In this letter, Margaret fears living next door to a "drunkard." What do you feel underlies the differences in these three views of Mr. Brown?

March 12. Margaret shares numerous discouraging feelings in this letter. Although we know little of what was in Walter's missing letter, in what ways might her response have helped her and her relationship with Walter? In what different issues addressed in her letter do you see faith playing a role? In what way is her understanding of God essential to her faith?

March 13. In what ways might cruel and unusual punishment, outlawed in the Eighth Amendment, be seen as excessive payment for breaking a law? How do you reconcile your answer with Walter's claim that "We do not in any way pay for all of our sins thru earthly suffering"?

March 14. What do you make of Walter's apology? How might it have been better or worse for their relationship if he had pointed out how Margaret would have been less distraught had she read his letters more carefully?

Walter is concerned that "those tender and beautiful moments … will … become timeworn" if he first takes Margaret in his arms because of desire or passion rather than love. How do you see the interplay between love and desire when it comes to the duration over time of "those tender and beautiful moments"?

IF WE ARE DRAWING NEAR THE END

Readers of the *Greeley Tribune* learned on March 15 that Hitler reduced Austria to a German district, on March 17 that bombs jarred the American embassy in Barcelona, and on March 26 that President Roosevelt offered safety for European refugees if other countries agreed. On March 21, the Greeley paper reported that heifers sold between $6.75 and $8. Readers of the *Washburn Leader* learned on March 25 that a wave of suicides was spreading over Austria.

March 14 [Postmarked March 15, 7:00 a.m.]

Dear Walter,

"But unto you that fear my name shall the sun of righteousness arise with healing in its wings;" Malachi 4:2

Walter, this evening I finished reading the Old Testament. It has been very interesting, but parts I couldn't understand. Maybe we can understand them after we get a chance to read and study them together.

Walter, I just heard over the radio a talk by a speaker of the Farmer's Union. He said if a certain bill passed Congress it would mean the president could enlist all men between the ages 26 [and] *31 in waging warfare. I do hope it doesn't pass. I can't stand to think of you're fighting. It almost makes me feel like crying or else [writing] to the president to tell him that he can't have you. I know that I can bring it to God in prayer, which I have already done.*

I have read over several of your letters, and I realize that the reason you are undecided about our being married this fall is because of maybe a lack of funds. I know that you are trying hard with God's help to make the money that you have stretch to the nth degree, and you are praying that the cattle and potatoes may bring you enough so that you will have enough money to buy a ring, pay for a picture, and to supply you with running expense money during the summer. I know that you love me, and I know that you long for the time when we may be together in a home of our own. I am sorry that I wrote the way I did in the last letter. Walter, you have already done so much for me that I don't know how to thank God for sending you to me. I know this much that you came to me and God sent you. I didn't do anything to make you interested in me except that I prayed for someone to take me home from that Luther League picnic. I believe, too, that you love me more than you did at Christmas, not because of my merits but because God works in your heart to make that love stronger. …

Last Saturday afternoon I received a letter from Bernard. He said there is quite a stir at Bethany. "Uhe, violin instructor and orchestra director, was forced to resign." He said, "The whole system needs to be revamped. Pihlblad will have to get out but with the board back of Pihlblad and Uhe, it will be a fight, but conditions cannot go on this way any longer and be called a Christian school." Doesn't that sound sad? I thought when I attended that there was a certain element that was not Christian, and it looks as though it has gotten worse. …

Figure 1. Margaret's graduation photo.

Yesterday, Sunday afternoon, Helen and I walked about a mile and a quarter out of town along the river. It was beautiful to see the ice on the river and the water flowing all around it. Tomorrow I plan to go to Asbury Park to see the river at another place. Helen can't always go along, and the other teachers don't care much about walking, so if they don't feel inclined to go, I shall go alone. I am alone yet not alone because I pray at the same time as I walk. …

I can sympathize with Margaret walking alone to "see the river at another place." In undergraduate school I enjoyed intramural sports, played in the bands at sporting events, and enjoyed discussions in the Lutheran Student Association. I didn't enjoy sitting around drinking and smoking and vying for attention at parties. Although I enjoyed playing a variety of sports, sports talk was often boring. I liked to dance, but I disliked the numbing loudness of disco music.

These limited social activities pretty much died out with graduate school with the exception of golf and intramural softball. During the day, I enjoyed being with colleagues who shared my growing interest in statistics, but when evening came, they went home to their wives. Although practicing my trumpet could sometimes lift my spirits when I was alone, life often turned dark and meaningless at night.

Walter, I am glad that you are going to write more often because it gets kind of lonesome not to get letters on certain days. I don't know why it should make such a difference not to get letters, but it does. I am so happy that I can read that you pray for me. When I am in the midst of teaching, I get more ambition to instruct with love for my pupils when I recall that you intercede for me.

Walter, I am sorry for some sentences that I wrote in the last letter. I have prayed God to forgive me. I wish that you would too. I mentioned something about maybe you didn't want to buy me a diamond, but I know last Christmas you said that you would like to have had the money to buy even then. And now you have been working so hard to keep your cattle until prices are better. If you don't think we should get married yet because of lack of money in sufficient amount, I think we had better not too. I don't know if I will be rehired or not, but I can easily join an agency, and I believe they can get me a teaching position nearer home. I need to help pay on debts too. We have some family debts that would not be if those who owe us would do so. I have helped some to pay off the amount, but I should and would like to pay more. We have land that if we could get a good price for that would help much to lessen the sum if we would sell. I don't suppose you're in debt, and I would hate to cause you to get into such a dreadful enemy to happiness. …

Walter, I will be so glad to hear from you, and I want you to forgive me for what I wrote. You would please me much if you would burn my last letter to you. … Harold Klebs must have been home lately because he and Ruth rode down to Minneapolis together. I just wonder how this is going to turn out; maybe if we wait there will be a double wedding. "All the Way Our Savior Leads Us."

Yours in Christ,

Margaret

March 17 [Postmarked March 18, 8:30 a.m.]

Dear Margaret:

John 10:17,18 (to save space; I have only one sheet of paper). …

Thank you for the last letter, Margaret. You need not worry about forgiveness. You had good reason to believe as you did, and the fault was mine. I am so glad that you took it to God and that He revealed the truth to you. It was so good to know that God answered my prayer for peace of mind and heart for you. Margaret, you need never fear in that respect again. You are the only girl I want, and each letter I get adds to my certainty. I am so glad, so glad, that you are a Christian girl, and I think you will have peace of mind & heart from now on. I hope, though, that you will always have a longing for me, and I am sure you will. I, too, long exceedingly much for the day when we may share all things. …

I am working quite hard now. I began cleaning my horse corral today. I will have about 200 loads of manure to haul. I plan to do it myself; in fact, I have to, for I have no money with which to hire help.

It was warm and beautiful today. I saw several robins. Tonight the wind is whistling around the corners, though. We have some pretty hard winds out here.

You certainly have been getting along with your reading. I am only in 1st Chronicles. I will not be able to spend so much time reading now. My spare time will have to go toward the S. S. I have to do most of my reading in the winter. …

As this is all the paper I have, I must again wish God's peace and blessing for you. …

In Christ,

Walter.

I wish I might walk on the banks of the muddy Missouri with you. I should so like to see you, speak with you, and hold you close, for I do love you. May God always help me to be worthy of your love.

March 19 [Postmarked March 21, 3:00 p.m.]

Dear Walter,

"But He was wounded for our transgressions, He was bruised for our iniquities, and with His stripes we are healed."

This morning I finished reading the gospel of St. John. It is much easier to understand the New Testament than the Old. …

The farmers around here are glad about the river being overflowed. Some say it assures them of good crops for at least two years. [The] *Larsons took Dorothy, Ruth, and me out to where the river had flooded a farm home and had flooded part of the highway. The water is sinking eight inches hourly here, so after a while, the river while will have its normal amount of water. …*

The selection "It Was for Me" came last night, which was too late for the Lenten service, so I sang "Take My Life and Let It Be." I surely do enjoy singing. The senior choir is giving a cantata on Palm Sunday. I get to sing the part that Mary says, "They Have Taken away my Lord and I know not where they have laid Him" and where she recognizes Jesus as her master. …

John wrote me of a vacancy at Eagle Bend. He didn't know what subjects were to be taught, but he knew that one was music. I haven't heard anything from this school board. None of us teachers has heard yet. It would be much easier to teach here, but I am so far from my dear ones. I haven't applied at Eagle Bend yet. ...

Last Thursday the juniors had a dancing party. They invited all the teachers except me. I think they were very considerate of my wishes. They are busy learning to dance for the prom this spring. I wish that they wouldn't have one, but it seems I can't do anything about it. I haven't remembered the social functions of the school in my prayers for a long time. ...

Walter, I don't plan for you to pay for our wedding. My sisters, Clara and Evodia, paid for theirs. I don't think that our wedding needs to be elaborate. I imagine that we can be married in the beautiful church at Clarissa. That in itself makes a beautiful setting,

I am so glad, Walter, that you say that you are sure that you want me. I understand now fully that it was because of finances that you weren't sure if it would be wise to be married this fall. Farming must be a vocation that is dependent on many outside forces. I am glad that you are a good farmer so that if God sends the moisture and favorable weather and directs the market, all will turn out well. ...

Walter, last Saturday night I read through about twelve of your letters, and I cannot understand how I could get the impression that you no longer wanted us to get married this fall. I know that you love me, but I guess I felt pretty blue when I got to thinking I might have to teach another year and not be with you.

This is the time of the year that I love. Almost every evening before supper I have walked to the river. It has had more water in it this spring that record has it for over sixty years. The ice has flowed down the river in such large cakes and so swiftly that it was a marvel to me to see it. …

Walter, I am so happy that you want me and I want you. Could we get the plaque someday for our home that states "Prayer Changes Things?" It has changed much for me. …

May God watch over you always and guide you in your various undertakings, and may He grant that I may someday be with you.

Yours in Christ,

Margaret

Loneliness can take destructive turns. Not long after entering a PhD program in North Carolina, I began entertaining suicidal thoughts. It's not like I didn't enjoy my classes and research. I did. It's not like I didn't make new friends. I did. It's not like there were not parties or events to attend or dates to enjoy. There were. But all too often, my involvements and surroundings would lose their appeal, and I would end up alone, confiding with myself. What difference did it make if I proved a great theorem in statistics? No one cared. And even if they did, what good was that when all you had to hug at night was a lifeless pillow?

It is hard to know how meaningless life can become at times until it does. Somehow, I was carried through those times. My self-destructive thoughts always got weighed against the hurt to my parents and the waste of my life. But as the months wore on, it took longer and longer for the depth of that hurt and the relevance of the waste to stop me from contemplating the easily loaded answer standing in the corner of my closet.

March 20 [Postmarked March 22, 8:30 a.m.]

Dear Margaret:

May God's peace and assurance be yours today.

Some time ago I mentioned that I cared very little for teasing and jesting. Today in our Epistle text "3rd Sunday in Lent Eph. 5:1,14, [Let there be no filthiness, nor silly talk, nor levity, which are not fitting; but instead let there be thanksgiving] *We have proof that it has no value." Paul, must of thot jesting and foolish talking to be a wrong use of the glorious gift of speech. ...*

If the cattle sold extra well, could we arrange to be married before Sept.? If you are afraid of your housekeeping ability, I think I would like to take the chance. Though I know you have been away teaching most of the time, yet I am sure that you are not entirely incapable of the duties of housework. Are you? If you must learn by experience (everyone else does), why not with me? I hate to think of the long summer without you. Anyway, this batching business does not appeal to me very strongly. It would probably mean cutting down considerably on the honeymoon, but to me, to be anywhere with you would be a honeymoon. May God grant and help us make our whole life together a lifelong honeymoon. ...

Work is progressing well on these Colorado farms. I will have to cut down on my reading now for a few months. Aside from preparing my S. S. lesson each week, I will have little time for any reading. …

Yours in Christ,

Walter

March 23 [Postmarked March 24, 3:00 p.m.]

Dear Walter,

"Jesus, and shall it ever be a mortal man ashamed of Thee?"

I just returned from a Lenten service. Rev. Berg had as his theme, On the Auction Block. It does seem as though Judas asked, "How much am I bid?" He said that many of us sell Jesus for other things than money. …

Last night the school board met. While it met I had a prayer session. … Well, the result of the meeting is that all of us teachers are rehired. We know nothing about our salaries, however. I am certainly grateful to God that I was rehired. I rather like it here, and I think that next year it would be especially easy to teach, but whatever God wants us to do may He be glorified in the tasks He gives us.

Walter, you said something about getting married before fall. I would prefer that too, because I think summer is more suitable for weddings. … My mother's birthday is the twenty-ninth of July. Would that be too early? …

The music contest is to be held April the thirteenth at Turtle Lake. My groups are gradually learning their numbers. They seem to learn very slowly; it seems I do not get the results that I used to, but maybe I expect too much and do not prepare enough. I presume it is my fault.

Will you pray that I might improve? One girl has her costume finished except for sewing on three buttons on the back. …

My watch just keeps gaining time and then ever so often decides to rest. I haven't decided what to do with it. It cost a little over four dollars. I bought it last fall. The guarantee is no longer valuable. What would you do, if you were in my place?

Now I must retire because it is rather late. …

Yours in Christ, Margaret

March 23 [Postmarked March 24, 8:30 a.m.]

Dear Margaret:

"And they that know thy name will put their trust in thee;

For thou, Jehovah, hast not forsaken them that seek thee." Psalm 9:10

This afternoon as I sat on the rake (I was raking thistles in a stubble field), the words of one of our most beautiful hymns came to my mind. Not only that God has not forsaken us but that He is actually cheering for us, hoping that we will win the crown of life. The words are from the hymn (All the way My Savior leads me).

"Cheers each winding path I tread."

I do not have a hymnal over here at my place so I cannot look to see if those are the right words or not, but it is something like that.

They say that the cheering of the spectators is a great help to athletes in any contest. It made me feel good this afternoon to think that God is cheering for you and [me].

This song was first mentioned on March 14 when Margaret raised the possibility of a double wedding with her sister Ruth. The song must have been resonating in Walter's mind as he mounted the rake harnessed to his horses, rode out to his field, and then guided his horses up and down the field, periodically pushing down a lever to release the growing pile of thistles caught in the long and curved raking tines. Here's the second verse of the song he was probably humming:

All the way my Savior leads me,
Cheers each winding path I tread;
Gives me grace for every trial,
Feeds me with the living Bread.
Though my weary steps may falter,
And my soul athirst may be,
Gushing from the Rock before me,
Lo! A spring of joy I see;
Gushing from the Rock before me,
Lo! A spring of joy I see.

Margaret; sometimes the uncertainty of so many things kind of bothers me. It is without doubt best this way, but I should like to know what my cattle will bring and the potatoes and whether or not it will be enough to make possible our marriage in the near future.

I am glad that God's word and all things pertaining to His kingdom are certain and sure. It must be awful for the atheist when the uncertainties of this world overwhelm him. I do not know what I would do if I could not turn to God.

I wish I could say for a certainty that I would have enough money to buy the things we would need so that you would not need to look for a teaching contract. It must be God's will, though, for He has been very good to us.

Let us put our trust wholly in God and seek His will, thru prayer. He will teach us how to pray and give us the desire and strength to come to Him often.

It is hard to write what I wish to tell you, for the words seem empty. I cannot write words which tell you how glad I am that you are a Christian girl. Margaret, you may not believe it, and it may sound funny, but as I think about it (I often do), I cannot help but feel that you are just the kind of girl I have always wanted. I have told you this before, that I prayed to God often to lead me and help me find a Christian girl in order that we might have a Christian home. I believe that God did lead us and that if we come to Him in prayer for help, that all will go well. May His will be done. …

It was nice of the juniors to respect your wishes by not asking you to the dance. I wish I had a lot of time to help young people find worthwhile things to do. If God wills it, I hope to do well enough farming so as to hire some work done and allow me some time to work with young boys especially. Please pray for this, Margaret. …

We now have meadowlarks, robins, bluebirds (a little red-headed gray bird; I think it is a bunting), flickers, magpies, crows, sparrows, and many wild ducks. …

Yours in Christ,

Walter

Walter senses some uncertainties stirring in his metamorphic grounding. Otherwise, why would he try to imagine what life is like when seen through an atheistic metaphor?

"Trying to imagine" is as far as Walter can go. Had he actually been able to look through the metaphoric eye of an atheist, he would have been wondering how one could possibly believe in, much less experience, a guiding spirit underlying the twists and turns of an evolving world. That, Walter cannot do. That's not what he sees going on. On February 5 he writes, "It has always seemed very strange to me that anyone could walk upon this wonderful earth and … deny God."

The way we feel about our world is the way we end up seeing it. Once we start feeling the world may be different from how we see it — well, you can see the problem. We become tentative and no longer sure of our interpretations. We may even sense unwanted tremors in our grounding beliefs.

March 26 [Postmarked March 28, 3:00 p.m.]

Dear Walter,

"I am the vine, ye are the branches: He that abideth in Me, and I in Him, the same beareth much fruit: for apart from me ye can do nothing." St. John 15:5

This was one of the verses in my Bible reading this evening. ... I haven't read as much as I usually do but I still have some more time. ... I wish that we would always abide in Him, for He loves us.

You mentioned in the letter which I received this afternoon that you had seen several birds. While Blanche Holtan and I were out walking, we heard and saw a meadowlark. Its singing was so clear and jubilant that I wish that you could have heard it. I have seen a robin, but I have not heard its song this year. ...

Last night the Power Plant gave the goodwill supper which I wrote to you about. Helen and her club served 228 people. She is a very competent organizer and planner, so she didn't do any worrying about it. I wish you could have seen the large owl that some of the employees had made. It was six or eight times as large as a real owl. It was made of paper that was made into a kind of paste and then painted. Its eyes were very large. Each eye had an electric light bulb in it. These were made so that it could close and open. The bill moved as the speaker within the owl spoke thru a microphone to the audience. The men from the broadcasting station at Bismarck hooked up the owl so that the speaker's voice was amplified. The owl's head moved either around or up or down. Mr. Larson, the manager of this plant, gave the owl to the home economics department. A club in Bismarck wants to rent it, so perhaps they will receive some extra money.

Tomorrow we have cantata practice. I do enjoy singing in it. The two solos that I have are very short but very beautiful when sung with expression. I hope that God will teach me how to sing it to His honor. …

I found out that none of us teachers got a raise in salary. I guess funds are getting quite low for educational purposes. If it is so that I am to teach here another year, that will be all right because I enjoy it here. I enjoy teaching, too, but I would rather be with you. May God's will be done.

Goodnight,

Margaret

Sunday evening

Walter, I am so glad that I haven't spent a single penny at the beauty parlor since I came to Washburn after Christmas. It takes more time and patience to do the work oneself, but I am sure that I have saved at least two dollars. We have penny banks to fill, and I can just imagine that I am spending my hair money for missions instead. …

It seems that you are still sleeping in our home. I don't know how you will be able to get used to my being around there. I am glad that you would put up with an inexperienced housekeeper. I hope that I can get your meals on time and be waiting for you when you come in from your work. It seems that I have a time keeping things in order just in my room; how will it work in a whole house? I'll just get the power that I need through prayer, and if He wills that I get my work done on time and in the right way, I will do so; otherwise, Walter, I am afraid you'll always have to be ashamed of the house and its keeper. Will you remember me in this way too? I need you, Walter, more than you realize, because I am not what I should be. It is true that I should know how to work even tho' I have spent much time in teaching, but I am afraid you will have much cause to be ashamed of me and my actions, but won't you help me overcome my faults? One thing is sure, I know your advice will be Christ speaking thru you. May God ever fill you with His Spirit.

Yours in Christ,

Margaret

Although we sometimes hesitated to invite friends over because of untidy rooms, dusty furniture, worn-out linoleum, dirty windows, and unswept floors, neither Dad nor we children were ashamed of the housekeeper. My feelings are enshrined in a memory of a visit by one of Mom's sisters. During a break while helping us pick up and clean some rooms, she said our mom was a fine person but a poor housekeeper. My youngest sister, Anna, a preteen at the time, found the words for which I was struggling, "Yes, and we love her just the way she is."

March 27 [Postmarked March 27, 10:00 p.m.]

Dear Margaret:

"Grace to you and peace from God our Father and the Lord Jesus Christ." Paul's salutation to Philemon and my sincere greeting and wish for you. …

Margaret, I have several things for which I wish to ask you to pray for. First, I am going to lead in a Bible study of Paul's letter to Philemon; at L. L. [Luther League], *May 13. … Then I had planned until a few moments ago to ship my cattle Tues. (Mar 29) and sell them Wed. I have asked God to direct me in this matter, and I know you have. As I sat milking the cow, a plan came to me whereby I could keep them until after Easter. "I am selling some seed potatoes to a young friend (for a decent price 80¢ per 100 lbs). If he is able to pay for them immediately, I would probably get enough money to buy feed until after Easter. If he is not able to, I will have to sell my cattle." May God's will be done in either case.*

Congratulations upon receiving notice of your retirement by the school board. I do so hope that this coming May will be the last which you will spend as a teacher in public schools. …

I wish I had more time to read. You are certainly reading a great deal. I am glad you can and do. It is a problem in my mind. I have so much farm work to do; I cannot afford to hire it done, and yet I would like to read more. Now I only am able to study my S. S. lesson, do a little devotional reading, and glance at the daily paper. I have to get some sleep. Of course there is some time in the winter. …

Should I ship my cattle Tues., I will go to Denver Wed. Then, God willing, I shall be able to shop for a thing which I have longed to shop for a long time. If it be God's will and He provides enough money, I will be tempted to bring it to you or, better yet, come to see you and get your help. We could go to Bismarck, could we not? I shall send word to you immediately as to what I did with the cattle. …

Yours in Christ.

Walter.

March 29 [Postmarked March 30, 8:30 p.m.]

Dear Margaret:

"But seek ye first his kingdom, and his righteousness; and all these things shall be added unto you." Matt. 6:33

I do hope that the true spirit of prayer will help me to make this my prayer and help me to utter my prayers to this end always.

I have loaded my cattle today, and tomorrow I will go to Denver to see how they sell. We send them to commission houses at the stockyards who take them over and sell them, charging a commission for the service.

Elmer Nelson (Helen Nelson's brother) helped me drive them to Eaton where we loaded them on a freight car. It was chilly and windy today and no fun to ride a horse, but we had no trouble aside from freezing a little.

Walter will drive the sixty miles to Denver through several small towns fronting the Rockies. On his arrival, he will unload his cattle, obtain his lot number, join the chattering crowd of buyers and sellers, and head to the commission house for his check. If the stock market is down that day, it will be a long trip back while he contemplates how to put a positive spin in his next letter.

I am also sorting potatoes now and working in the field. The price on potatoes is up a little, so they will help to pay some of the expenses. The way it looks now, according to my books, I would have been $500 to the good if I had not farmed at all this year. But last year was good, and next year may be, so I cannot kick.

You should see my little reading table; with 3 big volumes of helps in Bible study, it looks very impressive, but I hope to make a good study of Paul's letter to Philemon at the L. L. meeting I mentioned. I visited Rueben & Evodia last Sunday evening after church. We had an interesting visit and pleasant time. … He suggested and loaned me these helps. …

You probably do as I do, hear rumors of war and talk of war. Please do not worry too much about it. Margaret, we are not sure of anything now, it seems, except one thing: If we are in Christ then no harm can befall us. Of course there will be dark moments and even times of oppression, perhaps. This will be especially true if we are drawing near to the End, and though we do not know for sure, yet the times seem to me to be pointing that way. The persecution of the Jew is certainly almost an unmistakable sign. Then the rising of the dictatorships will also bear watching. You know, Jesus admonishes us to watch, pray, and be ready, for no one knoweth the hour. When the break comes, we have much reason to believe that it will come suddenly. For we are also told that the end will come as a thief in the night.

Walter is contemplating prophecies such as the following from Matthew 24:6 – 8:

> And you will hear of wars and rumors of wars; see that you are not alarmed; for this must take place, but the end is not yet. For nation will rise against nation, and kingdom against kingdom, and there will be famines and earthquakes in various places; all this is but the beginning of the birth-pangs.

I do not write this to frighten you, not at all. Because it is not frightful. I shall be glad when the day comes when I may meet my Lord and Savior, though I am so unworthy. So I write to remind you and hope to help you. We do not think of this too often, and it should certainly not frighten us or make us blue but rather give us joy to know that tho they may destroy this body, yet they cannot take us from Jesus. … Oh, that I might be a powerful example of Christian living, thinking, speaking, and teaching in order that I might lead not only my dear ones but many, many, to the Rock of Ages.

So be of good cheer always, Margaret. I know that you are a Christian, but I also know that much of the fault and blame for the chaos in the world today rests upon us because we say too often, "It is too bad that so and so does not come to church and that so and so is not a Christian" and not nearly often enough "God have mercy upon me, a sinner." God can only use the time we give Him. The time we give to the devil, God cannot use. And any time not used at all or improperly used is time given to Satan, Margaret; I cannot tell you or make clear to you or anyone else how hard this awful condemnation comes upon me.

So again, I say, go to God often; pray for me, Margaret, and if it be God's will that we be united in this world, may we walk in His way together, and tho things may arise which will prevent our union, it will still be my wish to find you in Heaven when I get there. There is only one thing right now that I want more than you, in marriage; that is that I find first you, then all our near and dear ones in the Heavenly Mansions which are already prepared for us by our Dear Christ.

Now, Margaret, as I write this to you, I am not in the least bit sad or blue but instead so unutterably happy in the knowledge that you are seeking first the kingdom of God and His righteousness. And so I wish you to be happy as you finish reading it. It is not meant to be idealistic, for I know moments of doubt and fear do arise, but when they arise, remember that many are praying for you and then go to God yourself, for yourself and them.

Now may God give you Grace and Peace and keep you always in Christ Jesus.

Yours in Christ,

Walter.

Please be assured that you are not less dear to me as I write this but more dear than ever before.

It's 1938. The horrors of the Great War and the Great Depression are still on the country's mind. Another deep depression looms. Fascist and Communist ideologies are on the rise. Japan is at war with China. A civil war rages in Spain, with Europe taking sides. Hitler's troops are in Austria. Many Jews are returning to Jerusalem due to wide-ranging religious and economic persecution. If such events don't signal the end of the world as predicted in the Bible, what would? Walter thinks they might.

They didn't. Instead, machine guns, tanks, submarines, ships, and planes rained terror across the European, Asian, and African continents. The war ended seven years later when an atomic bomb devastated Hiroshima, followed three days later by a larger atomic bomb that devastated the neighboring city of Nagasaki. Many of the immediate survivors suffered slow cancerous deaths caused by the radioactive fallout.

The devastation of those two bombs led world leaders to reconsider a more powerful version of the defunct League of Nations that emerged as a reaction to the Great War. Many sought a world governing body with the power to control the testing of atomic weapons. But the nuclear arms race had commenced, and a much weaker governing body resulted — the United Nations.

We were well into the arms race by the time I entered grade school. I was shown film clips of the mushrooming aftermath of a nuclear explosion. More bombs, an order of magnitude more powerful, were under development, along with the B-52 Stratofortresses and intercontinental ballistic missiles needed to deliver them. Newspapers and magazines explained the need for and construction of bomb shelters. There was a real possibility that the human race would be destroyed in an all-out nuclear war. Although Dad looked forward to the Second Coming of Christ, I don't recall his mentioning the possibility of nuclear war as a forewarning of such a time. I, on the other hand, feel we are nearing a change in the world order and am among those concerned about the spirit of that new order.

A Glimpse Back

March 14. How do you explain the literal contradiction in Margaret's expression "I am alone yet not alone?" What is the nature of the implied presence, and where might that felt presence be materially manifest?

Margaret ends this letter by suggesting that Walter burn her previous letter on the twelfth that questioned his interest in marriage. How do you see the privacy issues regarding how Walter should honor her request? What about those facing her children or you?

March 17. Walter's words "The fault was mine" suggest that he is seeking his responsibility in the issues surrounding Margaret's apology for questioning his interest in marriage. In what way does that decrease or increase your impression of Walter's character?

March 19. The juniors "invited all of the teachers except [Margaret]" to the Thursday-night dancing party. If you were in her shoes when meeting those students and teachers the next day, what thoughts would you be having?

March 20. Walter writes, "If you must learn by experience … why not with me?" How might that expression build Margaret's faith in their relationship?

March 23. When pointing out to Margaret that "God … is actually cheering for us," Walter mentions a hymn that precipitated his thought. How would you characterize the material presence of the hymn, its author, and God accounting for his experience? How would you characterize the material presence of the entities and understandings that cheer you on?

Walter feels that if he and Margaret "come to [God] in prayer for help, that all will go well." How might their praying to God for help awaken them to their partner's unspoken needs?

March 26. Margaret responds to the "cheering" metaphor in Walter's letter with a verse in which Jesus says, "I am the vine, ye are the branches." In what ways might she experience those metaphors as true both in fact and feeling?

What role do you feel Margaret's self-critical comments on her housekeeping play in the development of their relationship?

March 29. Walter feels that "much of the fault ... for the chaos in the world today rests on us" because of how we use our time. Which of your many choices, actions, and efforts do you feel touch on the long-term harmony or chaos in our world today?

Visions of the Oncoming World Order

Each of us has probably entertained a scenario of ultimate outcomes regarding life at one time or another. Some scientists see a universe now expanding but eventually collapsing. The sun is expected to engulf our world in the distant future. Scientists have discovered evidence of a meteoric strike or a volcanic eruption of such a magnitude that life on earth as we know it would end in a suffocating blanket of dust. But why speculate on catastrophic changes that are out of our hands when we are engaged in pervasive changes that are much more fundamental to who we are and what we are about?

The letters my parents exchanged during their year-long courtship prior to World War II provide a feel for the rate of change over the past century. When these letters were written, the world's population consisted of roughly two billion people. Today that number has quadrupled. Due to the consequences of concurrent technological advances, we globally alter the air and water essential to life. In the 1980s we had destroyed the ozone layer — which blocks the sun's most harmful ultraviolet rays — to the point that the use of our initially synthesized refrigerants and aerosols were banned by international agreement. According to the National Aeronautics and Space Administration (NASA),[35] carbon dioxide levels have very slowly fallen and risen four times in the past 400,000 years in a fairly stable pattern with the four highs being roughly 60 percent higher than the four lows. They last bottomed out 25,000 years ago before slowly edging back up. When these letters were written, the levels were again 60 percent higher than the previous lows. Today, they are more than 200 percent higher — and we are not concerned with the escalating use of coal and other fossil fuels.

When these letters were written, the food Walter and Margaret ate, the clothes they wore, and the machinery and tools they used were largely made in America. Now the manufacture, assembly, marketing, financing, and delivery of a single appliance entail the efforts of individuals dispersed throughout the globe. Should that global cooperation disintegrate, an economic collapse could easily ensue.

When these letters were written, war was personal for the combatants. People fired guns, drove tanks, flew bombers, spied on enemies, and photographed enemy positions. Now bombs are delivered by remote-controlled missiles. Neighborhoods are scanned by cameras, and terrorists are targeted by drones. Some of us have envisioned dystopian worlds controlled by computers and robots.

When these letters were written, the recorded information on most persons was largely limited to pictures stored in photo albums and few official records sequestered in filing cabinets. Now our pictures, emails, blogs, tweets, buying preferences, banking and investment accounts, and medical records can be easily retrieved by anyone who attains, legally or otherwise, the required access codes. Shortly that will be true for our genotypes as well.

For the most part, this information is being used and mined to find interesting and helpful behavioral and physiological trends and predispositions. However, the same information can also be manipulated, copied, locked up, destroyed, and weaponized by clandestine hackers and foreign agents.

When these letters were written, the needed connections between the lines carrying a telephone conversation resided solely at complicated switching boards. A long-distance call entailed verbal exchanges between multiple switchboard operators before all of the needed connections could be established. Consequently, for most Americans, mail was the only practical means of long-distance communication. This "snail mail" has given way to telephone calls, emails, texts, snapchats, and tweets on personal computers and mobile phones. We are notified of events, news, and opinions coming from friends, commentators, solicitors, and politicians via sounds, flashes, and vibrations on our desks, in our pockets, and on our wrists. The information that comes streaming in may be real, or it may be spun or fabricated to suit a purveyor's interest. When we solely advocate — rather than discuss — political positions, truths get slanted, half-truths are encouraged, and outright lies assume an air of truth within the party of believers that spawns and shares them.

When these letters were written, alliances were meticulously negotiated between heads of states. Now voices adept at coordinating the thoughts and minds of others can organize groups within a matter of weeks, recruit followers from around the globe, and interactively coordinate their efforts in conversational time frames. These voices may be driven by personal and factional greed or guided by a universal concern for one another. Greed will play upon minds sown with seeds of advantage and connivance. Universal concern will guide minds sown with seeds of fairness and hope.

As we vie for the same earthen resources, our relational distances shrink, our interactive times shorten, and our interdependencies grow at an ever-increasing rate. A more centralized coordination and governance is coming. Its nature should concern us all.

* * *

Contemplations of the future inevitably incorporate both historical accounts and the futuristic narratives of others. I'll be reflecting on understandings in seven highly acclaimed books that have influenced me. Three are written by eminent historians with a decided interest in clear and objective reasoning about how our past may portend our future. Three are unpromising scenarios for those seeking a free and meaningful life for all in the coming order. A more encouraging scenario arises in the seventh book. What follows are some of the issues raised in these books that are critical to the choices we will be facing in the future.

In his insightful book *Sapiens: A Brief History of Mankind,* Yoval Noah Harari writes, "What we should take seriously is the idea that the next stage of history will include not only technological and organizational transformations, but also fundamental transformations in human consciousness and identity." He ends by noting, "Since we might soon be able to engineer our desires too, the real question facing us is not 'What do we want to become?' but 'What do we want to want?' Those who are not spooked by this question probably haven't given it enough thought."[36]

Our spiritual pathfinders have given that question a lot of thought. From the Abrahamic tradition, which I follow, the gift of our world and our role in it comes through in Genesis 1:29: "Be fruitful and multiply, and fill the earth and subdue it; and have dominion over the fish of the sea and over the birds of the air and over every living thing that moves upon the earth." The next two chapters address the gift by which that dominion would be achieved. The gift came when we ate of the fruit from a forbidden tree in the Garden of Eden with the words of the serpent ringing in our ears, "be like God, knowing good and evil."

The serpent's ancient words proved partly true. When making decisions, we probably all have a sense of what is good for us and what is not. But to "be like God" is both insidious in its appeal and false in its promise. The control we might seek over our lives and those of others always turns out to be a mirage. Even should our envisioned power at times be great, we are mortal.

The concerns and consequences addressed in these experienced metaphors typify and prefigure many of the concerns inherent in the empirical observations compiled in Harari's book. He notes our uniqueness by saying, "Sapiens can cooperate in extremely flexible ways with countless numbers of strangers. That's why Sapiens rule the world, whereas ants eat our leftovers and chimps are locked up in zoos."[37] He points out that "the real difference between us and chimpanzees is the mythical glue that binds together large numbers of individuals, families, and groups."[38] He sees religion as "the third great unifier of humankind, alongside money and empires."[39]

The consequences of humankind's alienation from the creator of the universe are prefigured in the story of Noah and the Ark in Genesis 6 and 7. Briefly, when "all flesh having corrupted their way upon the earth," God told Noah and his family to build an ark and to bring "two of every sort into the ark … also take with you every sort of food that is eaten." After Noah did what he was commanded, it rained "forty days and forty nights," and the "waters prevailed above the mountains, covering them fifteen cubits deep. And all flesh died that moved upon the earth."

Some, who do not see the narrative as a metaphor somehow grounded in facts and orally transmitted through many generations, will argue over the details of its factuality. In doing so, they might easily overlook the wholesale catastrophic destruction of species described by Harari when he writes, "The historical record makes *Homo sapiens* look like an ecological serial killer … The First Wave of Extinction, which accompanied the spread of foragers, was followed by the Second Wave of Extinction, which accompanied the spread of farmers, and gives us an important perspective on the Third Wave of Extinction, which industrial activity is causing today."[40] They might, just as easily, discount the construction of another "Noah's ark" by concerned scientists that hopefully will float above these destructive human tides by identifying and taking measures to preserve rare plant seeds, protect endangered species, and to continue to issue clarion calls to protect and preserve our environment.

Noah can be viewed as just another concerned man on earth, but his story suggests that humankind's being out of step with Mother Nature can have climatic consequences. They are already under way — a huge hole in the ozone layer over the Antarctic, a rise in the acidity and temperature of the oceans, the rise of carbon dioxide levels in the atmosphere, and global warming, to name a few.

Noah's story ends on a hopeful note: "Behold, I [God] establish my covenant with you … and with every living creature that is with you." God promises in the covenant that "Never again shall there be a flood to destroy the earth" and signs it, "I shall set my bow in the cloud" — which we sometimes see as a rainbow arching over the horizon.

However, it's not another apocalyptic flood that should worry us. Rather, it's a different concern prefigured in the Tower of Babel as described in Genesis, chapter 11. In the story, humankind presumptuously attempted to build a city having a tower "with its top in the heavens." When "the Lord came down to see the city and the tower," the Lord grew concerned and confused their language so that "they did not understand one another's speech." Consequently, they were "scattered … over the face of the earth, and they left off building the city."

Human optimism must have pervaded the builders as the tower rose above the surrounding buildings. A much later but similar optimism is described by Norman Davies in his international best seller *Europe: A History*: "There is a dynamism about nineteenth-century Europe that far exceeds anything previously known. Europe vibrated with power as never before: with technical power, economic power, cultural power, intercontinental power."[41] He then adds that in the last third of that century, "Europe entered a period of intense rivalry, aggravated by diplomatic realignments, military rearmament, and colonial competition. Forty years of unequalled peace could not restrain the growing tensions which in August 1914 were permitted to pass into open conflict."[42]

Permitted? In what factual sense might that word come to mind? Davies continues, "In a climate of growing unease, serious thought was given to the task of minimizing international conflict. … Military staffs … accelerated their preparations for war, assembling huge arsenals and training vast conscript armies, whilst carefully avoiding conflict decade after decade."[43] While some of the military staff may have wanted war, I doubt they were saying, "Let's start one, and here is how we're are going to do it."

In any case, even if some military staffs did want war, their "permission," to use Davies's word, assuming they granted it, was not heeded. Instead, on June 28, 1914, the heir to the Austrian-Hungarian throne visited Sarajevo, Bosnia, during a Serbian National Festival — a "calculated insult" according to Davies. When the heir's driver made a wrong turn, he was assassinated by a local discontent, Gavrilo Princip. Davies goes on to say, "Within four weeks, the gunshots of Sarajevo brought Europe's diplomatic and military restraints crashing to the ground."

Yet, I doubt Gavrilo had any sense of "getting permission to start" the resulting world war. Davies raises other possibilities — "forty years of unequalled peace" and "growing tensions" — but these are cultural conditions and states, not permissions or freedoms to act.

I like to think the underlying permission was granted ages ago and that the ongoing consequences of that horrific war were prefigured in the rise and fall of the Tower of Babel. Exactly when and how permission was given will never be known. Whether it came instantaneously or took thousands of years is beside the point. For me, the essence of that prescient moment is described by what transpired in the Garden when the freedom to acquire knowledge was bestowed and we exercised that freedom. Moreover, we consciously feed the fruit of that tree to our children as soon as they leave the womb and begin their schooling. Of course, the yet-to-be-deciphered genetic coding for desiring and digesting that fruit is in place long before any child is born or even conceived.

Our problem is not the creator of that tree. Neither is it the gift of the fruit — in any case, we can't reject the gift and go back to the Garden, for we read in Genesis 3 that our entrance is blocked by a flaming sword. Nor should we want to go back. Even though the products of science and technology made possible the global scale and terror of WWI — transport ships, machine guns, explosives, barbed wire, mustard gas — to reject the means for gaining that needed knowledge for those products is to reject the material basis on which life as we now know it depends. It is how to use that knowledge and what we choose to build based on that knowledge that should concern us. In other words, we are back to Harari's question: What should we want to want?

* * *

Hopefully, most of us don't want war or, more appropriately, don't want contexts that breed war. We have plenty of possibilities from which to choose given the freedom we sometimes grant our leaders to discount and vilify persons of another party — and even applaud them when they do — while attempting to unify us with rallying cries.

All of the spirits previously discussed come into play in one form or another with complex synergies that wax and wane over varying periods of time. War was intermittent and gradual for roughly four centuries when land – and opportunity-seeking Europeans dislodged and decimated most of the indigenous cultures of what are now the Americas. Economic abuse led to uprisings among the underprivileged, who participated in the French, Russian, and Chinese revolutions. Aggressive belief in an ideology spirited the Napoleonic Wars and World War II. Freedom from outside dominance propelled the American Revolution and India's break with England. Deep economic and social divides spurred both the American Civil War and the more recent Vietnam War.

An encouraging note that war (as we know it) could one day end is found in a *New York Times* bestseller, *The Better Angels of Our Nature: Why Violence Has Declined.* In it, Steven Pinker documents the decline in violence with extensive facts, charts, and arguments. He grew up during what he terms the Long Peace that followed the Second World War. He "knew that ... the Long Peace and the New Peace were also decades of progress for racial minorities, women, children, gay people, and animals." But he "had no idea that in every case, quantifiable measures of violence — hate crimes and rape, wife-beating and child abuse, even the number of motion pictures in which animals were harmed — would all point downward."[44]

In searching for explanations of the downward trend, Pinker encountered four "better angels" in our nature: empathy, self-control, morality, and reason — all working together. But these are not drivers for a new world order, not if one sympathizes with the words of Joseph Roux, a priest and poet: "Reason guides but a small part of man, and the rest obeys feeling, true or false, and passion, good or bad."[45]

With Roux's words in mind, it's worth looking at four probing scenarios that have been envisioned by writers regarding a dramatic change in the world order. One can view the scenarios as arising from four different spirits that guide our passions. To better know these spirits, we must contemplate how they reveal themselves. How would they steer our sympathies and associations? How would they guide the justifications of our thoughts and actions? What types of leaders would they lead us to heed and follow? From what types of contravening voices would they turn our ears?

Brave New World was written by Aldous Huxley six years before these letters were written. During his time, the concepts of Mendelian genetics and Darwinian evolution were coming together into a unified theory of evolution that his brother, Julian Huxley, popularized a decade later in the book *Evolution: The Modern Synthesis.* The physical and biological sciences were advancing on all fronts. The pharmaceutical industry promised a new world of man-made drugs. Motion pictures brought life-size entertainment to increasingly large audiences.

Aldous Huxley's brave new world is populated by cloned and pliant humans, chemically programmed and verbally indoctrinated into preselected classes and roles. Life is "good" — no war, an intellectual elite, preordained jobs for the working classes, perfectly formed babies, facilitated sexual gratification with no attending commitment, ready access to pleasure-inducing drugs, and even a peaceful and pain-free death — self-gratification at every turn.

Yet something is amiss. The consequences become evident when Savage, a stranger from an off-limits reservation with an individual bent, is accidentally brought into this Utopia. He is an immediate celebrity but is naturally puzzled and soon bored with the easy, uncontemplated, and passively accepted life of those he meets. Later, an attractive friend repulses him by the lack of emotional commitment in her sexual advances. He is torn and angered when his dying mother turns from him back to her drugged bliss. He ends up a self-imprisoned freak after he encounters the spirit of this strange world embodied in the Controller, a rational human like himself.

In a later forward, Huxley writes, "All things considered it looks as though Utopia were far closer to us than anyone, only fifteen years ago, could have imagined. Then, I projected it six hundred years into the future. Today it seems quite possible that the horror may be upon us within a single century."

We are not yet there, but we are finding ways to modify and clone the human genome, developing mind-correcting drugs, creating virtual realities, and building work-relieving robots. How we see the pros and cons of these evolving capabilities will reflect the spirit that guides our choices and weighs their consequences. These material improvements will broadly and lastingly benefit our lives if we focus on creating opportunities and means for all individuals to realize their callings and creative talents in mutually beneficial ways. However, should our focus be self-gratification, the brave new world Huxley envisioned may not be far off. Should we choose to follow that spirit, the path ahead will be increasingly lined with mind-grabbing distractions, soothing appeals, and addictive technologies. Once we accept blanket conformity, a life free of struggle, and manufactured happiness, our individuality and meaning in life will be lost along the way.

The novel *1984* was written by George Orwell shortly after the Second World War. This astute political writer and literary critic grew up during the years that Lenin and the Bolsheviks marshaled Russian discontents into a governing force. Orwell watched the world suffer through the Great War. Later, as a young man, he saw Stalin don Lenin's mantle during the Russian revolution. He saw Hitler voted into office in Germany and Mussolini in Italy. He heard the violent rhetoric of those dictators castigating the "enemies of the people," and he watched how they achieved totalitarian control and would later learn how they instrumented the murder of millions. Just before Christmas in 1936, he voluntarily fought in the Spanish Civil War against General Franco, who eventually became a Fascist dictator of Spain. Less than two years later, he saw Hitler and Stalin usher in the Second World War by ordering their military forces into Poland — first the Nazis from the West and, two weeks later, the Communists from the East. Before writing *1984,* he had no doubt read Sinclair Lewis's provocative American novel *It Can't Happen Here*.[46]

In Orwell's dystopia, telescreens watch and prompt you at work, at meals, on the streets, and in homes and apartments. Records of events are erased or modified to suit the interests of *Big Brother,* a center of leadership whose workings are conveyed through *newspeak,* hearsay, and innuendo but are not directly confrontable. The submissive acceptance of this imposed surveillance and altered records of events is maintained through repeated rallies demonizing a constantly proclaimed enemy of the people and praising the needed armament industry and *thought police*.

Winston, the protagonist, is charged with "updating" the records to conform with the "facts" broadcast by Big Brother.

When he chances upon a fact that clearly does not square with a critical, even though vague, childhood memory, he begins his search for the truth and soon finds, in Julia, a compatriot along the way.

Spurred by rumored hints that there is a group that has helped some find freedom, he feels opportunity lies in the rare but recurrent glances and suggestive gestures of O'Brien. Meanwhile, he and Julia find a hideout where they can enjoy moments of freedom away from Big Brother's watchful eye. Those moments come to an abrupt end when the formerly disinterested proprietor brazenly enters their rented room.

Guards hustle Winston off to an office, where he is greeted by O'Brien. When O'Brien dismisses the guards, shuts off the TV monitors, and begins questioning him as to what sacrifices he would be willing to make for his freedom, Winston's fading hopes brighten. Winston shares the depth of his willingness. O'Brien then summons the guards, and Winston soon learns that O'Brien's job is to "correct" his thought, and sessions of physical torture will be the means. The "correction" will be complete once O'Brien is convinced that Winston actually believes whatever O'Brien says is true. It is not enough for Winston to simply parrot back that two plus two equals five whenever O'Brien says that to be the case. The torture is ratcheted up until O'Brien is convinced that after telling him two plus two equals five, Winston actually thinks that to be the case.

How would we ever head down a path leading to Orwell's dystopia? Maybe something like a pervasive fear causing many to question their adequacy, their safety, their societal supports, and their future — a fear that there is something "out there" working against their interests. Should such a spirit of self-apprehension grow within us, we would naturally gravitate to groups sharing our concerns and may be drawn to charismatic voices boasting quick-fix solutions that obscure the complexity of the underlying issues. They would feed our fears, change and distort our facts, and discredit and mock our sources for truth. Should such groups coalesce and spur the movement, the underlying spirit of apprehension could easily morph into a spirit of aggression encouraged by these hypnotic "leaders." Should such a self-interested leader's contingent of power-seeking collaborators ever gain full political and military control, the resulting voice of a dictatorship would soon become the only voice openly heard and shared as dissenting voices are threatened and eventually silenced along the way.

Something similar happened in Germany under Hitler and in Russia under Stalin. Lewis would not have written *It Couldn't Happen Here* if he didn't see its possibility even in an established democracy. Lewis felt that the leaders of a similar movement in America would be primarily motivated by financial gain and, to cover up their actions, would seek ways to diminish the free press and disrupt gatherings expressing opposing views. Fortunately, Lewis's dystopian vision has not yet come to pass and won't — so long as America's belief in democracy as instituted in its Bill of Rights and the just rule of law remains strong.

But the concern is always there. A spreading spirit of self-apprehension arising from rapidly escalating global concerns would know no national dictate. Should such a spirit arise, there will be those capitalizing on it for greedy and power-seeking ends. An international coalition seeking autocratic power and offering quick-fix solutions might, with the increasingly powerful and intrusive tools of social media, attract a large following of people soon convinced that differing nationalistic notions of human rights and rule of law are irrelevant. Once in power, that coalition could readily impose its own universal set of "rights" and "law" — a capricious subset of convictable behaviors for its detractors, a publicly praised constitution for its followers, and an honorific set of "licensed" behaviors for the ruling cabal and its cohorts.

Universal indoctrination, narrowly circumscribing admissible behaviors and relationships, haunts both *Brave New World* and *1984*. Independent thinking is discouraged and punished. There is bliss in the first scenario and terror in the second — but no war. More importantly, there are no calls to sacrifice one's life for the common good. Without families and communities, identities are unlikely to extend much beyond physical existence, making calls for self-sacrifice meaningless.

In Hal Lindsey and C. C. Carlson's best seller *The Late, Great Planet Earth*, there is war — apocalyptic and close at hand. They wrote their book shortly after the Arab – Israeli War in 1967 when the two world superpowers at the time, America and the Soviet Union, were rapidly expanding their nuclear arsenals. Lindsey, a dispensationalist theologian, found prophetic utterances in the Bible related to ongoing current events, much like Walter did in his last letter. Unlike Walter, Lindsey evolved much more specific interpretations of biblical expressions that he felt roughly predicted the times and unfoldings of future events. For example, he prophesied that human government as we know it would come to a catastrophic end "within forty years or so of 1948"[47] — the year the State of Israel was proclaimed.

It didn't happen in the eighties and hasn't happened yet, but in 1947 a group of concerned atomic scientists drew attention to the Doomsday Clock,[48] which was ticking away the "minutes to midnight" — a metaphor for the relative number of lifelines within reach before the global political current carries us over a nuclear cataract. The clock was initially set at seven minutes to midnight. When Russia tested its first atomic bomb in 1949, it was reset to three. It was reset a minute closer when America tested the first hydrogen bomb in 1953.

Due to collaborative efforts between the United States and Russia, the clock was set back to seven minutes to midnight in 1960 and to twelve minutes to midnight in 1963 when the Partial Test Ban Treaty was signed. After the signing of the first Strategic Arms Reduction Treaty in 1991, the clock was reset to 17 minutes until midnight.

Since 1991, the clock has slowly crept closer to midnight, moving from fourteen minutes to nine in 1998 when India and Pakistan forcibly entered the club of countries with nuclear weaponry. It leaped from seven to five in 2007, shortly after North Korea detonated a nuclear device. By 2015, it was set at three minutes from midnight, largely due to America's efforts to modernize nuclear weaponry and America's refusal to address global climate change. It was reset a half-minute closer shortly after President Trump was inaugurated and another half-minute closer a year later.

Why would anyone in the world want to edge closer to that nuclear night? It must entail a spirit stronger than the desire for peace, more enduring than the thirst for mutual understanding, and even more powerful than the fear of global war. It's a spirit of nativistic greed — nativistic because war requires opposing parties that are unrelenting in their nationalism, tribalism, racism, or any other deeply separating "ism"; greed because conflict requires one or more parties thirsting for what the other has, whether that be its resources, location, influence, status, or dominance. So long as this spirit rules and convinces us of an ever-increasing need for armaments, can it be quieted before it unexpectedly sets off World War III?

The spirit of nativistic greed can take over our lives all too easily. It emerges out of competitive contexts that are mutually enjoyed. We rally to the "thrill of victory and the agony of defeat." All is fine when the activity is engulfed in a spirit of fair play. Competition is enjoyed, and skills are sharpened. Moments of notable play and sometimes even the rules of the game are later celebrated. Unfortunately, nativistic greed can seed and feed rival factions when the participants begin choosing the spirit of greed rather than the spirit of generosity and the spirit of division over the spirit of unity. We have seen the rich grab from the poor, the powerful exploit the weak, and ruling factions perpetuate their dominance. Naturally, fights have ensued and sometimes ended in a mutually destructive war.

Self-gratification, self-apprehension, and nativistic greed abound. They show up in our conversations and in our actions (or inactions) toward others. They frequent our social media and monopolize our news stories and political rhetoric. Their spirits beckon at the crossroads that lies ahead. Fortunately, there is a contravening and more fundamental spirit beckoning as well. It's the spirit that underlies the human-rights revolution discussed in chapter seven of Steven Pinker's *The Better Angels of Our Nature.* Like all the other spirits, it has been around a long time. It is the spirit of universal self-worth present in a scenario of the future described in Isaiah 2:1 – 4 excerpted here from the Jewish Study Bible:

In the days to come,
The Mount of the LORD's House
Shall stand firm above the mountains
And tower above the hills;
And all the nations
Shall gaze on it with joy. …
He will judge among the nations
And arbitrate for the many peoples,
And they shall beat their swords into plowshares
And their spears into pruning hooks.

The prophet also describes in Isaiah 11:1 – 5 the lineage and nature of the person who will embody the spirit of that kingdom and through his actions and words throw open the door:

But a shoot shall grow out of the stump of Jesse,

A twig shall sprout from his stock.

The spirit of the LORD shall alight upon him:

A spirit of counsel and valor,

A spirit of devotion and reverence for the LORD.

He shall sense the truth by his reverence for the LORD:

He shall not judge by what his eyes behold,

Nor decide by what his ears perceive.

Thus he shall judge the poor with equity

And decide with justice for the lowly of the land.

Roughly five centuries later, we find in Luke 4:16 – 21 an amazing story of a Galilean man returning from a forty-day fast in a nearby wilderness:

And he came to Nazareth, where he had been brought up; and he went to the synagogue, as his custom was, on the sabbath day. And he stood up to read; and there was given to him the book of the prophet Isaiah. He opened the book and found the place where it is written [Isaiah 61:1 – 2],

"The Spirit of the Lord is upon me, because he has anointed me to preach good news to the poor.

He has sent me to proclaim release to the captives

and recovering of sight to the blind,

To set at liberty those who are oppressed,

To proclaim the acceptable year of the LORD."

And he closed the book, and gave it back to the attendant, and sat down; and the eyes of all in the synagogue were fixed on him. And he began to say to them, "Today this scripture has been fulfilled in your hearing."

This man, Jesus, went on to describe the kingdom foreseen by Isaiah and the other Abrahamic prophets. The spirit of universal self-worth radiates in the beatitudes of Jesus found in Matthew 5:3 – 4, 7 – 10:

Blessed are the poor in spirit, for theirs is the kingdom of heaven.

> Blessed are those who mourn, for they will be comforted. …
>
> Blessed are the merciful, for they shall obtain mercy.
>
> Blessed are the pure in heart, for they shall see God.
>
> Blessed are the peacemakers for they shall be called sons of God.
>
> Blessed are those who are persecuted for righteousness' sake, for theirs is the kingdom of heaven.

Jesus felt that the kingdom of which he spoke would somehow materially arise from a spirit within us. In Luke 13:18 – 19, he says:

> "What is the kingdom of God like? And to what shall I compare it? It is like a grain of mustard seed which a man took and sowed in his garden; and it grew and became a tree, and the birds of the air made nests in its branches. … It is like leaven which a woman took and hid in three measures of flour, till it was all leavened."

When asked when this new world order would come, Jesus replied in Luke 17:20: "The kingdom of God is not coming with signs to be observed; nor will they say, 'Lo, here it is!' or 'there!' for behold, the kingdom of God is in the midst of you" — which puts the onus back on our search for that guiding spirit.

Jesus also wanted us to look forward to and work toward a beautiful, worldwide material realization of that kingdom. Consider what he taught us to pray as recorded in Matthew 6:9 – 13:

Our Father who art in heaven,

Hallowed be thy name.

Thy kingdom come,

Thy will be done,

On earth as it is in heaven.

Give us this day our daily bread;

And forgive us our debts,

As we forgive our debtors;

And lead us not into temptation,

But deliver us from evil.

Again, we catch the spirit of universal self-worth. It comes across in the words "Our Father," "our daily bread," and "as we forgive our debtors." Of this prayer, John Dominic Crossan writes in the prologue to his book *The Greatest Prayer*:[49]

> The Lord's Prayer is Christianity's greatest prayer. It is also Christianity's strangest prayer. It is prayed by all Christians, but it never mentions Christ. It is prayed in all churches, but it never mentions church. It is prayed on all Sundays, but it never mentions Sunday. It is called the "Lord's Prayer," but it never mentions "Lord."
>
> It is prayed by fundamentalist Christians, but it never mentions the inspired inerrancy of the Bible, the virgin birth, the miracles, the atoning death, or bodily resurrection of Christ. It is prayed by evangelical Christians, but it never mentions the *evangelium*, or gospel. It is prayed by Pentecostal Christians, but it never mentions ecstasy or the Holy Spirit.
>
> It is prayed by Congregational, Presbyterian, Episcopalian, and Roman Catholic Christians, but it

> never mentions congregation, priest, bishop, or pope. It is prayed by Christians who split from one another over this or that doctrine, but it never mentions a single one of those doctrines. It is prayed by Christians who focus on Christ's substitutionary atonement for human sin, but it never mentions Christ, substitution, atonement, or sin.
>
> It is prayed by Christians who focus on the next life in heaven or in hell, but it never mentions the next life, heaven, or hell. It is prayed by Christians who emphasize what it never mentions and also prayed by Christians who ignore what it does.

Crossan continues, "What if the Lord's Prayer is neither a Jewish prayer for Jews nor yet a Christian prayer for Christians? What if it is … a prayer from the heart of Judaism on the lips of Christianity for the conscience of the world? What if it is … a radical manifesto and a hymn of hope for all humanity in language addressed to the world?"

* * *

We discussed four different scenarios arising out of four very different spirits. But do we have to follow any of these spirits? Why can't things just go on as they always have, with some good times and some bad? An answer may lie within the lowly cells that make up our bodies. There are trillions of them, ranging from a microscopic red blood cell with life expectancies measured in days to nerve cells running the length of our backs that will live for years. Somehow, they get along together. Should we ever tease them apart, they would have no idea how to reorganize.

Not so with the cells of the lowly sponge, which, when teased apart, can go their separate ways, much like amoebae. But if kept together in just the right concentration, some of them will come back together in multicellular aggregates. In many cases, another sponge emerges.[50]

We don't have a Rosetta Stone to aid us in translating into human terms the molecular communications that take place between cells, but we can anthropomorphically infer what they might be communicating by watching what they do, much as we do when watching our pets play. I like to think the sponge cells that "choose" to join a newly forming sponge must somehow share an organizational thought along the lines, "Something great is going to happen if we get together, something that is better than our trying to make do by going our separate ways."

"Going their separate ways" is what the cells that make up the common garden slug are wont to do. In a fascinating book *The Social Amoebae: The Biology of Cellular Slime Molds*, John Tyler Bonner points out that this primitive organism starts out life as a solitary cell. Through repeated cell divisions, a population of these independent amoeboid cells keeps growing until it exhausts its food supply. Then in an amoebic panic, these formerly independent cells start linking up and eventually circumscribe themselves with a slimy film. Once united, the cells move together as a slug, a most primitive multicellular organism.

So what can these primitive cellular organizations tell us about the coming world order? First, they hold out the hope that we, too, can peacefully organize into a cooperative world order entailing highly differentiated and complementary roles. Second, the sponge analogically conveys a coming moment when our reorganization may begin its inexorable acceleration. The sponge will not emerge until a threshold concentration of cells is exceeded. Population growth is bringing about the needed concentration for us. Third, the emergence of the slug provides a warning. Its amoebic precursors usually come together when starvation threatens. It's difficult to know what an analogous panic might be for us. A catastrophic climate change? An ecological disaster? A perverse technological advance? A massive migration? A pervasive distrust? Hopefully we can reach a universal and informed consensus of what we should want to want before a general panic sets in.

* * *

Over twenty-five centuries ago, Lao Tzu suggested that the answer to what we should want to want lies hidden in the ways of children. In Lin Yutang's translation of strophe 10[51] of the *Tao Te Ching*, he says, "In embracing the One with your soul, can you never forsake the Tao? In controlling your vital force to achieve gentleness, can you become like the new-born child?" Jesus reiterates that understanding when he says, in Matthew 18:3 – 4, "Truly, I say to you, unless you turn and become like children, you will never enter the kingdom of heaven. Whoever humbles himself like this child, he is the greatest in the kingdom of heaven."

Stop and think for a moment. Who would not like the joy trusting children find in a loving environment? They are drawn to activities that encourage their talents and creativity. If they don't get bored or hurt, they will lose themselves in play with anyone. Their relational affinities come naturally, largely free of distinctions in race, status, religion, nationality, sex, and creed. They don't enjoy being left out, jeered, bullied, or otherwise treated unfairly, and they instinctively sense a negative spirit at play and shy from or ward off the offenders when that happens.

Although our conscious understandings, capabilities, and responsibilities dramatically change when we become adults, we are still drawn to activities that bring out our talents and creativity. We like to play and work hard without getting hurt. We don't want to be left out, jeered, bullied, or otherwise treated unfairly. When we are, we also sense a negative spirit at play, and in consequence, our natural interest in the activity fades. Some of us quit; others strike back. Not so when we sense a positive spirit at play. Natural interest grows, hands are clasped, and invitations for additional engagements are exchanged.

The spirits at play during childhood quickly wax and wane. As we mature, time frames lengthen, activities interlink, allegiances arise, and factions form. The attending spirits, both positive and negative, can reign over pursuits extending over months and years, even decades and centuries. Naturally, numerous words and understandings for sorting and pointing out the spirits at play have been put forth. Many are honored in our scriptures.

One relational understanding indicative of the presence of a spirit of universal self-worth holding us together is called the Golden Rule. It encompasses the possible breadth of one's identity that our pathfinders have experienced. Here are a few of its versions found in *World Scripture: A Comparative Anthology of Sacred Texts,* edited by Andrew Wilson:

Judaism: You shall love your neighbor as yourself.

Islam: Not one of you is a believer until he loves for his brother what he loves for himself.

Jainism: A man should wander about treating all creatures as he himself would be treated.

Hinduism: One should not behave towards others in a way which is disagreeable to oneself. This is the essence of morality. All other activities are due to selfish desire.

Confucianism: Tsekung asked, "Is there one word that can serve as a principle of conduct for life?" Confucius replied, "It is the word *shu* — reciprocity: Do not do to others what you do not want them to do to you."

Buddhism: Comparing oneself to others is such terms as "Just as I am so are they, just as they are so am I," he should neither kill or cause others to kill.

African Traditional Religions: One going to take a pointed stick to pinch a baby bird should first try it on himself to feel how it hurts.

Christianity: "Teacher, which is the great commandment in the law?" Jesus said to him, "You shall love the Lord your God with all your heart, and with all your soul, and with all your mind. This is the great and first commandment. And a second is like it, you shall love your neighbor as yourself. On these two commandments depend all of the law and the prophets."

When asked by a listener, "Who is my neighbor?" Jesus gave an unexpected reply by means of a parable recorded in Luke 10. In the parable, three people encountered a man traveling from Jerusalem to Jericho who had been left half-dead by robbers. The first two passed him by. The third, a Samaritan, aided him. (Today, that gesture would be the equivalent of a Palestinian helping an Israeli.) Following the parable, Jesus asked the instigating listener: "'Which of these three, do you think, proved neighbor to the man who fell among robbers?' He said, 'The one who showed mercy on him.' And Jesus said to him, 'Go and do likewise.'"

* * *

Is it likely that we will eventually assemble into a new order on earth with a spirit of universal self-worth? There is much to suggest the reality of its appeal. We would be organizing under an identity in accord with that of our birth. We would be in tune with our genetic commonality, so well stated by Francis Collins, head of the Human Genome Project, in his book *The Language of God*: "At the DNA level, we are all 99.9 percent identical."[52] This suggests we would also be in accord with the God of Abraham that, according to Jesus, Matthew 5:45, "makes his sun rise on the evil and on the good, and sends rain on the just and on the unjust."

When coming together under a spirit of universal self-worth, we, like the lowly sponge cells, cannot know what all the transformational changes will entail. We do, however, have the suggestive visions of our pathfinders. The following parable in Matthew 22:2 – 14 has both inviting and frightening metaphors. Slightly different versions without the frightening metaphors are given in Luke 14:15 – 24 and in the Gospel of Thomas 64.

> The kingdom of heaven may be compared to a king who gave a marriage feast for his son, and sent his servants to call those who were invited to the marriage feast; but they would not come. Again he sent other servants, saying, "Tell those who are invited, Behold, I have made ready my dinner, my oxen and my fat calves

are killed, and everything is ready; come to the marriage feast." But they made light of it and went off one to his farm, another to his business, while the rest seized his servants, treated them shamefully, and killed them. The king was angry, and he sent his troops and destroyed those murderers and burned their city. Then he said to his servants, "The wedding is ready, but those invited were not worthy. Go therefore to the thoroughfares, and invite to the marriage feast as many as you find." And those servants went into the streets and gathered all whom they found, both bad and good; so the wedding hall was filled with guests.

But when the king came in to look at the guests, he saw there a man who had no wedding garment; and he said to him, "Friend, how did you get in here without a wedding garment?" And he was speechless. Then the king said to the attendants, "Bind him hand and foot, and cast him into the outer darkness; there men will weep and gnash their teeth." For many are called, but few are chosen.

In an earlier quote from Luke 13:18 – 19, Jesus ecologically likened the coming world order to a tree in which fledgling birds thrive. This parable likens it to a celebratory feast in which food is abundant in a festive atmosphere filled with beauty and music.

The parable admits multiple interpretations from both personal and political perspectives. The invitations were first sent to those most expected to attend. Some felt their business interests more pressing. A few must have been politically threatened because they killed the messengers.

The retributive justice in the parable was equally violent. From one perspective, this is surprising because the author of the parable was a pacifist who is recorded to have said, in Luke 6:27, "Love your enemies, do good to those who hate you, bless those who curse you, pray for those who abuse you." From another perspective, major political change has always entailed violence — even when led by pacifists such as Mahatma Gandhi and Martin Luther King. When constructing and voicing this parable, Jesus may have foreseen his eventual crucifixion because of the kingdom he was proclaiming.

The parable continues. Messengers were sent out to find and invite everyone. Once those who chose to come had arrived, the celebration began. Shortly after, a man not wearing a wedding garment was cast out.

Should we eventually come together in a new world order under the spirit of self-worth, our celebration will also begin. All that is needed is for a critical proportion of us to see our neighbors as ourselves as we do our part while "keeping an eye out" for ways of helping others do theirs. Should that take place, an unfathomable celebration of the new and long-prophesied world order will begin. The doors will swing wide open — for a while; eventually, they will close once all who truly desire are in.

Why would anyone be cast out? Consider again the lowly sponge. As the teased-apart cells reaggregate, they return to their fitted roles and reap the joy and material rewards of their cooperative efforts. However, should some of the participating cells find themselves ill-tuned and developing interests running counter to the organizational spirit of the sponge, their expressions could come to be interpreted as parasitic or even cancerous.

The parable of the talents in the earlier discussion of the spirit of self-insistence as opposed to the spirit of selfishness ends with a comparable judgment when the master returns and settles the three accounts in Matthew 25:19 – 30. The first two servants bring the talents they were given plus a comparable amount they had earned in trade. The master praises each of them with the words, "Well done, good and faithful servant; you have been faithful over a little, I will set you over much; enter into the joy of your master." The parable ends with the third servant returning his buried talent only to be upbraided by the master for his slothfulness and being cast "outside, into the darkness, where there is weeping and gnashing of teeth."

The message is clear. Our "talents" are not ours, but gifts that can unfold and enliven our lives and those around us as we walk this earth. There is another message — a transitional voice that hopefully will resonate toward the end of that walk. It is a sentence integrating five individually worthy phrases, each meriting contemplation when thinking about the consequences of the spirit of one's words and actions: "You have been faithful over little," "Enter into the joy of your master," "Good and faithful servant," "I will set you over much," "Well done."

* * *

A defining crossroads is approaching. A new world order is coming about. The most important consequences to our lives will not fundamentally depend on our choice for a form of government or for an economic system but rather on our choice for a guiding spirit. Should we choose to be guided by a spirit of self-gratification, self-apprehension and aggression, or nativistic greed, an abiding peace and joy will evade us regardless of the governmental and economic systems we might institute. Should we seek to be guided by a spirit of universal self-worth, the understandings, technologies, and governmental structures for taking into account everyone's gifts, contributions, and concerns will naturally emerge — and in a manner in which we will find joy in our individuality, in each other, and in our harmony with the creator of the universe.

Neither the spirits nor the issues are new. The biblical scenario is old. *Brave New World* was written five years before Walter and Margaret met, and *1984* was written twelve years later. *The Late Great Planet Earth* was written roughly forty years after that. More than fifty years have since transpired.

Although the issues are not new, as they press more cogently each year, Walter's ending sentiment in his last letter will become increasingly relevant: "Now, Margaret, as I write this to you, I am not in the least bit sad or blue but instead so unutterably happy in the knowledge that you are seeking first the kingdom of God and His righteousness."

SO YOU HAVE SOLD YOUR CATTLE

A few of Walter's friends probably figured that Walter's cattle were responsible for the *Greeley Tribune* report on March 30 that a few heifers sold for $7.75 and probably speculated what that meant to him. Meanwhile, the headline "Czechs Crumbling Before Nazi Boring from Within" in the April 1 issue of the *Washburn Leader* would set its readers speculating on the significance of events in Europe. A week later they learned that Il Duce, the Italian dictator, would fight if France interfered in Spain. That same day, those with students in Margaret's choruses might have seen the *Leader*'s notice of an upcoming music contest in neighboring Turtle Lake.

March 30 [Postmarked March 30, 3:00 p.m.]

Dear Walter,

"What do ye, weeping and breaking my heart? For I am ready not to be bound only, but also to die at Jerusalem for the name of Lord Jesus." Acts 21:13

This verse makes me feel like I haven't borne the marks of Jesus branded upon my body as Paul did. I have finished the book Divine Upliftings, *which has helped me to see that Christ wishes to lift me so that I may bear fruit for Him. I surely thank you for sending me these books, and as soon as possible I shall return them. …*

Mr. Thorson had a faculty meeting this evening just before supper. We got our contracts. In the contract there is a clause that states it may be returned anytime before August the first. I signed mine. Maybe it will be best for me to teach one more year. I think that next year I would be a better teacher. He said that the board just didn't have the money to raise the salaries, but if the legislature helps the educational system more next year, the board will raise the salaries. …

In Hamlet *we have studied about the tragic death of King Hamlet. I can't understand how a brother could kill his brother. I guess jealousy must just grip a person until one can commit the most terrible sin. The Bible must have been little used in that palace.*

Walter, let's memorize the hymn "All the Way My Savior Leads Me." I know most of it, but I need to relearn it. I think that [it] *should be sung at our wedding whenever we have it, be it this year or next. I had never thought of it in the light that you mentioned, but I see that that interpretation could be made. …*

Walter, I feel sorry that you are having to work so hard and then are uncertain as to your gaining anything from selling your cattle and potatoes. I surely am glad you like the place where you work. Now, I am afraid it is because I have not prayed over this as I should have. I am not used to praying about the stock market. I always just took it for granted. …

Tomorrow my Eng. III has a final examination in As You Like It. *Have you ever read that Shakespearean drama? The pupils surely liked it. I think it is one of the easiest of Shakespeare's dramas to understand. Eng. IV pupils are memorizing a large number of quotations from* Hamlet.

Five of my girls [in] *glee club have their dresses finished. A number of them have just a little more to sew, and then they will be ready also. Speaking of costume sewing, I am sewing a choir gown for myself. It is white. The gown is to be worn on Palm Sunday. Helen has been kept busy cutting the gowns.*

Walter, I don't think we should need so much money to live on. We wouldn't need to have such expensive furniture. I believe you are the type that when you have the money, you would see to it that [it] *is used to the best advantage for the things that are needed. I think it would be fun to buy some furniture that is absolutely necessary and then look around for bargains and good material to be purchased when more money is on hand. We wouldn't be exactly penniless.*

It is one thing to say you don't need much money to live on and quite another to enjoy life when you don't. You can, of course, enjoy most of your time (your time at work, at meals, with family, and in bed) with a surprisingly modest income. You need only find ways to enjoy these times by appropriately aligning your wants and expectations with your means and circumstance, but this is possibly easier said than done.

Of course, if we wouldn't get married this summer, I could buy a flute in the very near future, and I do long for one. … You see, if ever we have some children, I want them to learn to play piano, flute, clarinet, and violin, and cello. I can teach them somewhat on the string instruments, but after they would reach my limit, they could take lessons from some competent instructor. The new flute would come in handy to have them learn on it. May God lead us in our plans for the future. I am glad that the future is veiled. I used to long to know, but God has led me thus far, and He will continue to do so if I but put my trust in Him and obey. ... I know that you do trust Him and do love Him. Walter, may God keep you in the holy keeping that He has been asked by His Son to do.

It is rather late, so I must get to bed. I presume that there is much to do in the morning, so I must [be] *up on time. I am glad that I have the privilege to work in the capacity of teaching.*

May God grant you His peace and grace always.

Yours in Christ,

Margaret

Margaret wrote the following addendum on a cross-ruled sheet torn from a three-by-five-inch notebook in time for the 3:00 p.m. time stamp on an envelope containing both letters.

Dear Walter,

"The Lord is my shepherd I shall not want."

This morning I received your letter. Thank you. I will be glad to have you come, if you can. ~~If you~~ Let me know in time so that I can cancel my vacation stay at Underwood in due time. We can attend Easter services up there. I think you would enjoy it.

This morning the boys sang very well. I do hope they will continue to do so.

Well, may God direct your plans.

Yours in Christ,

Margaret

March 31 [Postmarked April 1, 10:30 a.m.]

Dear Margaret:

"We are his people, and the sheep of his pasture.

Enter into his gates with thanksgiving

And into his courts with praise.

Give thanks unto him, and bless his name." Psalm 100:4

This assuring promise followed by a worthy admonition comes to me, or the thot does, as I write this.

For I have sold my cattle, and tho my prayer was that I might make money on them, yet I always asked that I might be given grace to say, Thy Will be done. And I find it not hard but thank God for the privilege. I am not worthy of His goodness and cannot forget all His benefits as it mentions in the 103 Psalm, I believe.

Although I stand to lose about 150 dollars on my cattle, yet they pay all I owe the bank with a little left over. My potatoes will help pay all other debts, and I believe I will have a little money left for running expenses.

Margaret: Do you suppose God uses this way to help me learn how to take care of money and myself? I have never run around much, "not that I boast of it," but if money comes easy, I am prone to spend it easily and quickly. Perhaps God is granting just enough to supply my need. I had planned, all the time, to do as much of the work as *possible myself this summer, but I guess God wanted to be sure I did just that. But nevertheless, He has been good. I do have plenty. I got a good sale for my cattle, under the circumstances. I lost about $6.00 per head, and some have lost as much as $25 per head. So I have much to be thankful for.*

When I am through with the potatoes, I am going to send you a letter showing what I have left over. I am going to pay every debt if possible, then go as far as possible on the balance if there is one. I can borrow all the money I need, but I want to borrow as little as possible.

I am quite well pleased as it stands. I know I can pay all my debts and yet have my equipment (what there is of it, 4 horses and some machinery), clear.

But now I only talk about myself, but I do think of a very dear little girl, just the same. I pray for her and hope that God may be near her and give her peace and grace for each day. Now that you are nearing the finish of this school year.

I cannot help but feel that all things will work out well yet and that we can carry out our plans. I will not quit. In fact, I only start when the going gets tough! I suppose that is a boast, but I feel that way. I have lost two times on cattle. The law of averages says I win next time.

You mention something about not understanding how I could get used to not having you around. Margaret, I do not believe you actually fear that this could be true, but if you do, I want to assure you that I long for nothing else, so much. You would certainly be [a] *big help now. I could teach you to drive the car, and you could run errands; besides, I would not have to cook or run home at mealtimes. It would have to be very plain, but I could provide enough. Please do not fear, at all. I will help you and know you will help me, and God will help us, to become accustomed to one another. …*

Yours in Christ,

Walter

April 3 [Postmarked April 4?]

Dear Walter,

"But now abideth faith, hope, and love, these three: and the greatest of these is love." I Cor. 13:13

"Ye are our epistle, written in our hearts, known and read of all men, being made manifest that ye are an epistle of Christ, ministered by us, written not with ink, but with the Spirit of the living God; not in tables of stone, but in tables that are hearts of flesh." II Corinthians 3:2,3

Last Saturday, yesterday, I had the thirteenth chapter of I Corinthians as a part of my Bible reading. I recalled last Christmas Eve when we read it together.

Here is what they read:

If I speak in the tongues of men and of angels, but have not love, I am a noisy gong or a clanging cymbal. And if I have prophetic powers, and understand all mysteries and all knowledge, and if I have all faith, so as to remove mountains, but have not love, I am nothing. And if I give away all I have, and if I deliver my body to be burned, but have not love, I gain nothing.

Love is patient and kind; love is not jealous or boastful; it is not arrogant or rude. Love does not insist on its own way; it is not irritable or resentful; it does not rejoice at wrong, but rejoices in the right. Love bears all things, believes all things, hopes all things, endures all things.

Love never ends; as for prophecies, they shall be done away; as for tongues, they shall cease; as for knowledge, it will pass away. For our knowledge is imperfect and our prophecy is imperfect; but when the perfect comes, the imperfect will pass away. When I was a child, I spoke like a child, I thought like a child, I reasoned like a child; when I became a man, I gave up childish ways. For now we see in a mirror darkly, but then face to face. Now I know in part; then I shall understand fully, even as I am fully understood. So faith, hope, love abide, these three; but the greatest of these is love.

Walter, I am so glad that you love to read from the Bible. The second quotation certainly is an astonishing truth. I am afraid that the epistle that I have been this year has many blurred pages. May God who writes the words have mercy on me. …

So you have sold your cattle! I hope all went well for you. Now maybe I will soon see you. That will be fine. How do you plan to travel? By car, train, or bus? Don't you just love to travel? I do. I imagine that during the spring season, the country is beautiful. …

Walter, I truly need your prayers. My glee clubs, it seems to me, are singing poorly. I really have a time trying [to] *make tenors out of baritones. I usually have to lower the key to pitch the song so that the tenors can sing easily and unstrained. Raymund Goehring is doing quite well. Last Friday I practiced with him alone after school. Gordon Meyer has taken more interest in singing. Byron Dutoit just loves to sing. The mixed chorus hasn't practiced for a while, but this week I hope to spend much time on putting finishing touches on the song "Precious Wee One," which is one of their contest numbers. …*

I wonder when you will get here to Washburn. I hope that you will enjoy your stay. Maybe you won't like it here, but I do. Washburn isn't very large, but it is large enough for me. I'll show you the school, but I won't let you be in my classroom when I teach. I am not what I should be in teaching, so that's one of the main reasons for my prohibiting you from that place at that time. I wish that we could make more definite plans as to the future. I am so glad that I was rehired. I wonder what my pupils think about it. …

Well, Walter, I welcome you in Jesus's Name, and may God guide and protect you on your long journey. May His grace and peace be yours.

Yours in Christ,

Margaret

I wonder what made you so very happy in your last letter. … I just reread your letter, and I found out the reason for your joy. It was because I was seeking His kingdom & His righteousness. May I always give you that joy.

Apr. 3. 1938

Dear Margaret:

"Simon, Simon, behold Satan asked to have you, that he might sift you as wheat; but I made supplication for thee, that thy faith fail not; and do thou when once thou hast turned again establish thy brethren." Luke. 22: 31, 32.

It must have been a wonderful and strong comfort to Peter to know that Christ was helping him and Peter certainly made good upon the request of Jesus. For he did much to establish many of his brethren.

Margaret, I was a little blue when I came over to my place to write to you. But in sending in an order to the Augustana Book Concern and sending my congratulations and best wishes to Eagle Bend I have lost some of the color.

I really have nothing to complain about tho I lost some money in my farming & feeding others have lost much

April 3 [Postmarked April 3, 9:00 p.m.]

Dear Margaret:

"Simon, Simon, behold Satan asked to have you, that he might sift you as wheat; but I made supplication for thee, that thy faith fail not; and do thou when once thou hast turned again establish thy brethren." Luke 22:31,32

It must have been a wonderful and strong comfort to Peter to know that Christ was helping him, and Peter certainly made good upon the request of Jesus. For he did much to establish many of his brethren.

Margaret, I was a little blue when I came over to my place to write to you. But in sending in an order to the Augustana Book concern and sending my congratulations and best wishes to Eagle Bend, I have lost some of the color.

I really have nothing to complain about. Tho I lost some money in my farming & feeding, others have lost much more. Some sheep feeders lose 2 to 3 thousand dollars. So I have much to be thankful for.

Nevertheless, when I think of how I promised that I might be able to help buy a flute for you (by the way, it is an old instrument. Matt. 9) and painted other rosy pictures, it kind of makes me feel bad. But I have asked God to guide and lead me, and if it does not go in the way

I think it should, it is because I am not what I should be or it would not be for the best.

A disappointing bend in life's road can evoke complaints and plaguing thoughts over what might have been or what might lie ahead. Dad had a way of accepting the bend and heading off in the new direction. As noted in my February 5 reflection, with the four words "Somehow God would provide," Dad soon returned to his joy in his work. And I did too. It was more fun to join him than to sit alone and complain. In that sense, Dad modeled a way for me to negotiate a troubling bend in my path through life by accepting the past and the future in order to focus on the present even though I had yet to acquire his conscious faith in God's providence.

Ordinarily I should have had 5 to 6 hundred dollars left over. That with only fair crops and prices. As it is now, when I pay my bills, including Mother, I will not have much left. Of course I would not have to pay Mother, but she deserves it and has earned it. I would not feel right not to do so. Besides, I will have my horses and machinery with a little money to go on, in the clear.

Margaret, I have always said that I was going to wait and get married until I had plenty of money. But it seems that all things do not go as we plan.

I am going to set down some various possibilities and things we could do.

First we could go ahead into the summer … watching the prospects together. If we have no hail by the 20th of July we are generally safe, altho not always. By the 25th of July we are usually through threshing. If barley is a fair price, I can sell some. I am afraid when I talk about borrowing money that you are afraid of debt. Of course the bank only loans upon a part of your valuation. If by the 1st of July I could get by on $150, I know I could get enough to carry us through until fall. I borrowed $750 dollars last year, but I hope to get by on less this year. I know I can. Of course it might mean that you could not get a flute and we could not get a piano right away. Then farming works the opposite way from this year many times. If I got a good crop with fair prices, I could, or rather, we could, have from 1000 to 3000 dollars at the end of next March. My needs are not great. I like to work; in fact, it is my first joy. As for pleasure or diversion, I get that going to church. I shall not ever have much time to run around. I have always wanted to include in my plans some time for a vacation and a trip now and then. I cannot help believing that two young people *working in harmony and loving one another, with the love of Christ in them, have as much chance as our forefathers had. They often started with a debt to conquer. I know my folks did. I am not urging too strongly on you for wanting to be reasonably sure of the financial ends of starting a home. And I write these plain facts to help you make such decisions as you come to. My horses are young and except in the case of death will not have to be replaced. I need some more machinery, but as long as I am near home, there need be no rush for them. And from the beginning we shall plan and share together. To me it is as important to furnish the home as it is to keep up any other working equipment. A honeymoon trip we cannot miss, for coming to Colorado from Minn. merely means choosing a route which we would like best.*

If we did not want to take the chance, we would either have to wait for a whole year or, if my grain and beans turned out real[ly] *well in August and the other crops looked good, you would have to cancel your contract, and we could be married in Sept. or November. The grain and beans could bring in 5 to 800 dollars depending on the price.*

In connection with the above, the first suggestion, do you think a home can, by careful shopping, be furnished somewhat nicely and comfortably for $400?

Please ask any questions which you wish to, Margaret. Make any suggestions which you wish. Feel free to speak as you feel. I am not afraid at all to borrow even 750 dollars, for I could sell some potatoes and next year's crop and pay that. So if you would feel strong enough and would want to try to manage on a very little for a while, you need not fear to say so. For my part, I do. Just to have you near would help me more than you can know, and after all, we have to live by faith anyway.

Then again, if you feel it best that we wait either till fall or next year, feel free again to speak. I cannot come for Easter, for if we were to be married in the summer, it would be better to use the money required for the trip a little later. This may not sound as though I was doing this because I loved you but rather for a selfish reason. But I want to plan for as early a wedding as possible without using any influence or force urging in any way. This is hard to understand, but God will help you see it, and I shall pray that you do. I want you to be willing of your own free will and after careful thot to try it.

I am having my picture taken this coming Tues, and if all goes as I plan, I am sending it with a ring for Easter. I hate all these ifs, but it is that way with farming. If it doesn't hail; if the prices stay up, go up, or don't go down; if it rains or snows. But thru it all God sustains us, and I like it so much. Even today the birds sing, and the lawn and alfalfa fields are green with new life.

Now, although this letter is poor and may be hard to understand, it is written because I love you and would like to help you make your decision by telling you the truth & facts. I may not make myself clear, but ask any questions you wish to.

Then I want to leave one thing clear. That I love you. I pray for you always and about all the things which I have written, and come what may, I know that He leads us all the way; that you, too, are one of his children. I am not ashamed of my love or your love. It is not just desire or passion with me but a longing to have a companion in Christ to walk with and work with. …

This letter is not as I should like it to be but I want to send it tonight.

May God bless you and keep you,

Yours in Christ,

Walter.

Things also didn't go as planned for Dad the summer before I started college. My two older brothers found summer jobs to save up the money for their education. Dad said he would pay me if I stayed home and helped on the farm. I didn't really have a choice in the matter, but that was OK. Although farming was hard work, it wasn't boring, and I enjoyed working with Dad.

Summer rolled right along. My brothers received regular paychecks. I was looking forward to a single check at the end of the summer like my two Leaf cousins had received in earlier years after each had spent a summer working with us. In the middle of August, Dad apologetically told me that he wasn't going to be able to pay me until he had the money but that Clue Nelson would pay me a dollar an hour to drive an ensilage truck down the rows alongside his corn harvester.

Two weeks later I left for college with a little over a $100 in my pocket. Although I had a scholarship for tuition, I was charged $45 dollars for books and fees. I got an off-campus room and breakfast for $15 dollars a month and bought a used bike and oak desk for $5 apiece. I cleaned up a café in exchange for evening meals until my brother James introduced me to George W. Scott. He paid college students $1.25 an hour for up to forty hours a week to assemble souvenir rock collections. After receiving my first check, I opened a savings account.

April 4 [Postmarked April 7, 3:00 p.m.]

Dear Walter,

"Now unto him that is able to do exceedingly abundantly above all that we ask or think, according to the power that worketh in us, unto him be the glory in the church and in Christ Jesus unto all generations for ever and ever. Amen." Ephesians 3:20,21

Thanks for the letter that I received this morning. I am very sorry that you got less than you had planned to receive from your cattle. I know that it must be discouraging, but if you reread the above verse, one forgets discouragements. It must be hard for a person to lose as much as $25 per head of cattle. I am glad that yours was not any more than $6. I am beginning to wonder if you are overworking. I know you have much to do, but if my wanting to be married to be with you is causing you to overwork, I want you to let me know. I can easily teach another year or maybe more if I can have a teaching position. …

Wednesday evening

"For ye remember, brethren, our labor and travail: working night and day, that we might not burden any of you, we preached unto you the gospel of God" Rejoice always; pray without ceasing; in everything give thanks: for this is the will of God in Christ Jesus to you-ward."

These are some words which I believe mean much to you. I like to think how Paul labored with his hands. It puts me to shame. I pray that God may direct my work to His honor, but while in the midst of my toiling, I forget that that is my aim. …

My boys' glee club [is] *singing very poorly. I will just have to do something drastic or not allow them to enter the contest. I have not been as diligent in my practicing with them. I have not sought God's help often enough. I suppose that I can't make them enjoy singing. Walter, isn't that too bad?*

The girls' glee club [is] *doing quite well. They are very eager to get their dresses finished by the seventh. I hope that they all succeed. The girls' voices blend very well.*

I am not the only teacher having trouble. Each one of them is having obstacles to overcome. "Thru Christ we are more than conquerors," so I shall rejoice even when troubles rage.

Walter, I have a hundred dollars in the bank now. Last week I sent home forty dollars to pay on [the] *church building fund and for that which the folks need, and then also to buy a dress in the cities. I haven't bought a dress for spring. You recall the permanent that I was to have gotten in Bismarck. It was an end curl. Well, my hair grew so much that I had quite a time with it, altho it worked better than it usually ~~does~~ ~~had~~ did. Last Saturday I had that end curl cut off, my hair permanented, and now I don't know what you're going to think of my hair on me. It takes very little to work with it, however.*

You must feel pretty happy to pay your debt to the bank. I know it makes me feel joyful to pay that which I have borrowed. I hope you can get a good price for your potatoes. Our God will supply all our needs. Walter, could I eat my dinner out in the field with you? We could have a little devotional time, too, couldn't we? …

Walter, I met an old man on the street the other evening. He told me what his name was. He must be a Baptist because he was on his way to that church. He said he knew who I was because he had heard me sing several times. He asked me why I hadn't ever sung in the Baptist Church, [and] *then he said he liked to hear me sing. Wasn't that kind? Maybe that God touched him while I was singing.*

You made me very happy when you said you love me more and not less. I am the type of person that can be with a person a while but then I someway lose their love, but I believe that is because Christ does not shine through. My folks love me, altho I can't understand how they can at all times. … I am thankful that God has supplied me with what I have needed these past years, and I know that He will continue to do so. I am grateful for your prayers. I remember you to whom I know will bless you with every spiritual and temporal gift which He knows you can make use of.

Yours in Christian love,

Margaret

Figure 2. Margaret's family. Bottom row: John Peter Leaf, Margaret, Ebba, Bernard, Carl, Anna Leaf; back row: Evodia, Phillip, John, Ruth, Clara; desktop: Photo of Anna.

Washburn, North Dakota
April 6, 1938

My dear Walter,

"Let us therefore draw near with boldness unto the throne of grace, that we may receive mercy, and may find grace to help us in time of need" Hebrews 4:16.

I just finished reading from Hebrews. I think I can finish the Bible by Easter. It goes so fast but there are so many verses that I long to meditate upon. I will get that chance as soon as I finished the Book.

It is rather late but since I didn't send the letter I had ready to mail I shall write another. Walter, I appreciate your frankness. I am ashamed of myself. You see and weigh the problems of the future more than I which I admire but can not put into action. I am just not ready yet to be a married woman and so it is all working out fine.

Concerning the flute and your postponing other purchases and so on, don't even think about them. That would certainly be small of me to expect you to pay toward that flute. I think now I can buy one myself. I have wanted one for so many years so that if that wish can be realized I will be so very happy.

It surely is fine that you are going to be able to pay your debts. There are too many who do not ~~fulfil~~ fulfil their obligations. It seems when one gets behind it is almost impossible to catch up. If you are so loving toward your mother I do not fear that you will be different to me.

April 6 [Postmarked April 7, 3:00 p.m.]

My dear Walter,

"Let us therefore draw near with boldness unto the throne of grace, that we may receive mercy and may find grace to help us in time of need." Hebrews 4:16

I just finished reading from Hebrews. I think I can finish the Bible by Easter. It goes so fast, but there are so many verses that I long to meditate upon. I will get that chance as soon as I finish the Book.

It is rather late, but since I didn't send the letter I had ready to mail, I shall write another. Walter, I appreciate your frankness. I am ashamed of myself. You see and weigh the problems of the future more than I, which I admire but cannot put into action. I am just not ready yet to be a married woman, and so it is all working out fine.

Concerning the flute and your picturing other purchases and so on, don't even think about them. That would certainly be small of me to expect you to pay toward that flute. I think now I can buy one myself. I have wanted one for so many years, so if that wish can be realized, I will be so very happy.

It surely is fine that you are going to be able to pay your debts. There are too many who do not fulfill their obligations. It seems when one gets behind, it is almost impossible to catch up. If you are so loving toward your mother, I do not fear that you will be different to mine.

Walter, I know that it is discouraging to not do all that one plans. I truly do not want you to rush into matrimony without getting all arranged as you wish it. You have such high ideals that I can't understand how God thought of letting me be engaged to you. Your ideals are Christian through and through, and now you regret that you offered me that which you cannot fulfill. I am glad that you are telling me now and not waiting to let me find out that after we are married. I ~~wonder~~ believe if all men would do the same there would be less divorce. Well, we thru Christ shall be faithful to one another thru cloud and sunshine.

I will be so happy to get your picture and the ring. To think of it, here we were engaged on the great festive Christmas Eve, and now I am to get these gifts on the more wonderful Easter day. My prayer is that I may be worthy of you. May God grant me grace to follow in His footsteps throughout my lifetime. May we ever walk and talk with Him here on earth and be caught up in the sky to meet Him. That is the essential part of life. Our earthly home fades into oblivion when we think of the Home in heaven. If Christ should happen to come before we are united, we will not remember our disappointment in not having a home together. I am so happy that you love me with a pure love, so what care I if we have to wait? May I be ready when my bridegroom comes from Colorado for me.

Yours in Christ,

Margaret

I decided to send the letter which I mentioned. I don't plan to go to school this summer. I can study without being under an instructor. I plan to learn to cook and sew so that I, when the time comes, can be of more help to you. Walter, I love you dearly.

April 6 [Postmarked April 6, 4:30 p.m.]

Dear Margaret:

"Wherein ye greatly rejoice, though now for a little while, if need be, ye have been put to grief in manifold trials." I Peter 1:6

This is only a part of a joyful and strengthening passage. Please read it all. I suppose you are nearly up to it in your reading, or are you entirely thru?

This Chap contains not only wonderful promises, but much admonition, which if practiced will be much help and benefit to us.

But I like that part which says "If need be," "If we can take the Bible literally and that must be the only way to take it, or how else can the ordinary class of people who have no time to study the Heb. & Greek languages, ever understand it."

These words seem to indicate to me that it might be necessary for us to be put to grief in order that we might Glorify the Father and the Name of Jesus. What do you think? Please write your answer to me, and then perhaps we can make a better study of this together when God grants that privilege to us. ...

If possible and with God's will and help, I hope to work and save for a home of my own and enough to keep me and mine during the days when I can no longer do hard physical work, altho I never hope nor plan to quit working, but I do hope to have enough to be able to read and study more and perhaps be a better S. S. teacher and a leader and helper of young people. This is not just a dream but a plan, and it will be something for us to work toward, for I know from being with you what I have that you, too, are concerned with the many souls which are not anchored in the Solid Rock. We should, and I know you will include this in your prayers, Margaret.

Sometimes it hurts me so much when I think of the thousands who are not anchored in Christ that I cannot and do not do more. I would like to go out and tell them what they are missing, but to my mind comes the tasks of my work to be done; worries of my own overwhelm my thots of them, and I go plugging along in the same old way, and I say to God, within myself, Why? …

It is a human weakness to want to see results so that we may glory in them. This is truer of each of us than we want to confess or than we ever know.

I wanted the cattle and potatoes to bring me 5 or 6 hundred dollars. Then I would have thot that God surely means this so that Margaret and I can be married right away. This would be not so much my glorying as perhaps — yes, I must confess it — a keen desire to have you with me and near me. To hold you in my arms.

Last fall Dr. Miller talked about how hard it is to confess our sins, how our confessions are often excuses. He said in his case it was adultery, not the actual committing of the sin, but he said before he was right with God, he had to confess that he had the desire in his heart.

What I am getting at is this. We want to perhaps go out and tell many people of Christ and then know in our heart that we did this. That's putting it a little strong, perhaps, but it's true with me, altho it's hard to see. Oh. Yes, I want God's name to be glorified, but I would like to hear and know that people thot, "Yes, Walter Johnson has done so much."

So if we want to help others experience God's love, we must first come to Him, confess all our sins, which with me are many. Then take time and find time to pray for them, not just as Hallesby says in groups or [in] *general but individually. This is true even of mere acquaintances, neighbors, and those who we know are hardened sinners and perhaps to us hopeless cases.*

So again: Margaret, I ask you to pray for me. In my mind it is the work of the devil which makes us want to see results, makes us want to do great things, and then makes us discouraged when we do not see them.

I thank God today for carrying me thus far, and I hope that I will always remember that He knows what we do and will take care of others and us. All we need to do is come to Him, and that means often with our problems and with them on the wings of our prayers.

Now I have written much, but you will forgive me. These things I think of often. Please tell me your opinions. If it differs, please tell me that too.

It is 11.15^a.m. o'clock. I am inside because it is snowing and blowing outside. ...

This afternoon I go to town to have my picture taken. That will give me time to get it and the ring to you for Easter. I do wish I might see you. But I assure you that with that ring comes a deep and true love and, though I confess, a deep desire for you, it is God given, and I ask Him to control it, so that my love may be a true and lasting love of God for you. That it was and is I knew long ago. For such a fine Christian friend, I thank Him.

In Christ,

Walter

The phrase "taking the Bible literally" means different things to different people. Here Walter refers to the translational issues arising when trying to understand a passage originally written long ago in a foreign language and for an unfamiliar culture. Being bilingual, Walter is well aware of the beauty, style, and subtle meaning that are easily lost in translations.

"Taking the Bible literally" can also mean that one only accepts the most direct and factual interpretation of the text — a difficult and confining task. The Bible is rich and subtle in intent, form, content, and context. Mathematicians, scientists, accountants, and lawyers use explicitly defined terms residing in specialized dictionaries so that their communications can be taken literally, but ordinary adults don't speak that way.

When Peter says, "if need be, ye have been put to grief in manifold trials," Walter is well aware of the complexities of fully understanding what might have been meant. He knows that Peter spoke the crude language of a fisherman who earned his living casting nets into the lakes of Palestine roughly two thousand years ago. The trials alluded to in Peter's letter had much more to do with religious beliefs and choices than with financial loss arising out of a fall in market prices. Walter may have been aware that Peter likely spoke an ancient version of Aramaic and that his words were written down by someone fluent in ancient Greek. Walter is well aware that reading an English translation of Peter's letter is not to hear the intonations of Peter's Aramaic tongue. Still, Walter catches a sense in which

Peter is speaking directly to him because he is intent on understanding Peter's words even though he cannot directly ask Peter, "Now what exactly are you trying to say?"

April 9 [Postmarked April 9, 3:00 p.m.]

Dear Walter,

"Now unto him that is able to guard you from stumbling, and to set you before the presence of his glory without blemish in exceeding joy to the only God our Savior, through Jesus Christ our Lord, be glory, majesty, dominion and power, before all time, and now, and forever more. Amen." Jude 1:24,25

This is Saturday morning. I have received your letter mentioning that you are to have your picture taken. I presume before this letter reaches you [that] *you have received the proofs. I hope everything goes well for you. It will seem as though you are here when I have your picture. The ring will mean so much to me; you just can't realize how much. Will you send them, the picture and ring, to Underwood in care of Rev. Oscar Johnson. I plan to be at Johnson's home over Holy Thursday and Easter. I surely will appreciate having a vacation. …*

Walter, it isn't any rush, it seems, to get married, so I really don't have any questions to ask. I am so tired right now that what I am writing doesn't have much meaning. I am beginning to think that farming is very uncertain. I am just wondering if it is best to wait; it might turn out the same way next fall and next spring so that we couldn't get married then, either, if we wait because of money. Maybe, too, that waiting such a long time isn't good for me or for you either.

I believe that we could really live for a whole year on very little if we tried. I believe that God will supply what we lack. I have just been wondering if your folks are against your marrying this year. Well, be that as it may, I don't believe we should get married without your parents' willing consent, so I am willing to wait.

This afternoon we are to [have] *boys' glee club practice at four fifteen and mixed chorus at five o'clock. I wish that I had put in one more soprano in my chorus. We have our county contest on Wednesday the thirteenth. The state contest is to be held one week later at Bismarck. There is a lot to do. This evening I plan to write out six weeks' examination questions. Won't you come to help me write them?*

Walter, I can't understand why you worry about having too strong a desire for me. I am certain you don't. You say you love me, and I believe you, and that's all there is, so don't worry about it. If there is anything else we had better forget about one another, which will be impossible for me, but God can give me the needed strength for that too. There is a nook for me to fill, I am sure. I can't understand why I am writing this way because I really believe if money didn't stand in the way you would want to get married this summer. I believe that we could get married in the fall, but who am I to tell when we are to get married? I think if you wanted to, I could be ready by November. You said that the latter part of July you would know definitely if we could get married in November. I will make plans toward getting married then. Then, if it doesn't work out, I can return to Washburn to teach. It will all work out fine. …

I hope to finish the Bible either today or tomorrow. I am reading in Revelation now. You asked me about what I thought about a certain portion of I Peter. I agree with your thought. I like your plan of thinking how you can help win souls. That is my desire too. …

The girls are going for a walk, so I am going to send this letter with them. I hope you are feeling well as usual. I am well. I should do more work, but I just don't feel like working. I feel like going for a walk with you. I wish that I could see your chiffonier. So your house is all cleaned. That's fine.

Well, may God bless and keep you ever His and mine.

Yours in Christ,

Margaret

A Glimpse Back

March 30. Margaret, a high school teacher, doesn't think that she and Walter "should need so much money" to enjoy life together. Which of her understandings guide her thinking this way? What understandings determine how much money you feel is needed to enjoy living with someone? How do ways of acquiring the needed money enter in?

Margaret is "glad that the future is veiled." How do you reconcile that statement with her holding a salaried teaching position while contemplating life on a farm, subject to the caprices of the weather, infestations, and markets?

March 31. The thoughts in this letter were probably stirring in Walter's mind as he drove home from Denver after selling his cattle. He is thankful for being part of the people of God, sees a possible lesson in his loss, is thankful he didn't lose more, and finds hope in the law of averages. What thoughts would have been in your mind had you been in Walter's place?

April 3. In applying one of her selected verses, Margaret fears her epistle "this year has many blurred pages," yet she asks for mercy from "God who writes the words." In what ways might she feel that the issues, concerns, and understandings being placed on her heart are the doing of something outside of her control?

April 3. Three days after selling his cattle, Walter is still trying to wrap his loss in a positive narrative. How do you see the consequences of finding or not finding a positive narrative for a deep disappointment or a loss of a loved one? In what way might his selected Bible verse be relevant?

How do you see the comfort Walter finds in learning that "others have lost much more"?

April 4 and April 6. On Monday, April 4, Margaret writes a comforting letter to Walter but doesn't post it, possibly because of receiving and reading Walter's April 3 letter. In that letter, Margaret relates a comment from an "old man on the street" she had met. How would you characterize the effect of that comment on Margaret? On Walter? On you?

Margaret writes a follow-up letter that Wednesday, April 6, expressing her concerns with their engagement by saying she is "just not ready yet to be a married woman, and so it is all working out fine." Really? Factually? Literally? How would you characterize her use of words to convey and further what was going on in her relationship with Walter?

Margaret continues, "Our earthly home fades into oblivion when we think of the Home in heaven. ... So what care I if we have to wait?" Really? Factually? Literally? What do you feel Margaret was trying to get across to Walter? How apt were her expressions?

April 6. In getting his mind around his financial setback, Walter first writes, "It might be necessary for us to be put to grief in order that we might Glorify the Father." Later he writes, "It is the work of the devil which ... makes us want to do great things, and then makes us discouraged when we do not see them." How do you see each of these understandings figuring into Walter's search for a positive take on his financial disappointment? In what ways do you feel that major disappointments can lead to a more meaningful life?

April 9. When contemplating the possibility that things might not work out in her relationship with Walter, Margaret writes, "There is a nook for me to fill, I am sure." What understandings might give rise to such confidence when one's current relational and vocational hopes suddenly dim?

IF WE HAVE NOT ENOUGH FAITH

The tide comes in and the tide goes out while the waves advance and retreat along the shore. Palm Sunday begins the high celebration of the Christian Church, which is so much a part of Margaret and Walter's lives.

April 10 [Postmarked April 10, 6:30 a.m.]

Dearest Margaret:

Grace & Peace to you upon this beautiful Palm Sunday Morning.

It is truly beautiful Palm Sunday with a great deal of sunshine and warm weather again after a quite severe blizzard.

I wish you were here or I up there so that we could go to church together.

I am in quite a hurry, as you see. I suppose I always shall be and hope that you [will] *be able to overlook it. I am restless when doing nothing.*

Thank you for the letter. They mean so much to me, and that last one carried such a message of hope and confidence that it was a special help.

This afternoon I will answer it more completely, for there is much to write, as you may guess; this is Sunday Morn, about 7:45, and I have to be home for breakfast at 8 and leave for S. S. at 9:00.

I want this off to tell you a little about the ring. When you get this, you will have the ring. Should it be too large or too small, it can be sized by a competent jeweler for about 50¢. If there are no such jewelers near you, you can return it here. It will not cost me anything, but to insure and send it costs about 40¢ each time. Please write and tell me if you have to have it sized.

Though I cannot come up with it, I send my love with it and my wish and hope for God's richest blessing upon you for wearing it.

It hardly seems possible that you would. I hardly dared to ask you, but now I thank God for you and your love.

With much Christian love,

Walter

April 10 [Postmarked April 10, 10:00 p.m.]

Dear Margaret:

"Peace I leave with you; my peace I give unto you; Let not your heart be troubled, neither let it be fearful." John 14:27

Sometimes when I start a letter to you, I cannot immediately think of a verse which I would like to give to you. But I like to send one each time. So if I have difficulty in choosing one, I ask God's help even with that, and it seems I generally find one. …

This verse would indicate that Jesus meant us to have peace and confidence, but he does not say it is dependent upon any worldly things. It is a gift from God. At this time he was speaking especially to his disciples, which makes me believe that the peace spoken of is for those who believe in and are willing to work for our Lord and Savior.

Margaret, we have, each of us, I know spent much time thinking of the little problem which confronts us, "As to when we may be united in Holy Marriage." It is not wrong to plan and think for the future, but let us not let such thinking and planning go to the place where it robs us of the gift of Peace from Christ Jesus.

I doubt that it is necessary to make the detailed plans even for a wedding a great long while in advance. Each of us can and should use each coming day in preparation for that event and the days of life together afterwards. So again let us remember that we can, should, and I know we do have Peace in and thru our Lord and Savior. ...

Now to speak of other things, you mention an old man who liked your singing. I can imagine he did, for I certainly enjoyed your singing and most especially when you sang some of our common & beautiful hymns. I say this not to flatter you or make you feel good, except as it is true and may encourage you to know that you are helping in the kingdom. Margaret, I doubt that I ever flatter you, or anyone for that matter; I do not like it. But I shall try to be kind, truthful, and considerate to you, and I long for the day when we may work together, for after all, therein lies the joy in this life. ...

I want my Margaret to take an interest and know all my problems, and I want to share and know hers. Whatever we buy, if it be a plow or a rug, let us plan and discuss it together. It will help so much to keep things going smoothly, and besides, two heads are better than one.

Yes, you can have lunch with me in the field, and we will plan lunches and picnics together. I think that is a wonderful plan. I am so glad that you love nature and outdoor life. To be out a great deal will help you keep well also. ...

But I must close now, with the assurance that I love you very dearly and pray for you and yours always.

In Christ,

Walter

To be out hoeing beets or beans and see Mom walking up the field with homemade cinnamon rolls (or rusks with a biscotti's sweetness and texture) and a big thermos of coffee brightened even the cloudiest of days.

Washburn, North Dakota
April 10, 1938

My dear Walter,

"Behold, I come quickly; and my reward is with me, to render to each man according as his work is." Rev. 22:

"I will give unto him that is athirst of the fountain of the water of life freely." Rev. 21:6.

"He that overcometh shall inherit these things; and I will be his God, and he shall be my son." Rev. 21:7.

This morning is Palm Sunday. I just finished reading thru the Bible. I am so glad that I could read through such a wonderful book. It has and will mean much to me. It is much like a novel in that it has unity, plot, and setting as well as characters. One came from heaven to redeem us to God and returned to heaven to later bring us to Him. That truth is really great and marvelous. This holy week I hope to memorize the 13th. chapter of I Corinthians and relearn the 53rd " " Isaiah.

Last night when I returned from school I was so happy that I just wanted to shout. I was up at school to practice my solos and to write a six weeks examination. I got to thinking about what a Christian lover I have and that not to far in the future I will get to live with him until Christ comes to take us Home to Him. This so thrilled me that the girls wondered at my happiness.

Mother wrote that Ingeborg Peterson has returned to her work with John. She

April 10 [Postmarked April 12, 7:00 a.m.]

My dear Walter,

"Behold, I come quickly; and my reward is with me, to render to each man according as his works is." Rev. 22:12

"I will give unto him that is athirst of the fountain of the water of life freely." Rev. 21:6.

He that overcometh shall inherit these things; and I will be his God, and he shall be my son." Rev. 21:7.

This morning is Palm Sunday. I just finished reading thru the Bible. I am so glad that I could read through such a wonderful book. It has and will mean much to me. It is much like a novel in that it has unity, plot, and setting as well as characters. One came from heaven to redeem us to God and returned to heaven to later bring us to Him. That truth is really great and marvelous. This holy week I hope to memorize the 13th chapter of I Corinthians and relearn the 53rd chapter of Isaiah [a prophetic characterization of the nature and suffering of Jesus for Christians].

Last night when I returned from school, I was so happy that I just wanted to shout. I was up at school to practice my solos and to write a six weeks' examination. I got to thinking about what a Christian lover I have and that not too far in the future I will get to live with him until

Christ comes to take us Home to Him. This so thrilled me that the girls wondered at my happiness. …

Soon your picture and the ring will be here! I can hardly wait. There is so much happiness in my heart that I cannot know how to express myself. I do wish that you could put it on my finger. When I see you next, I'll take it off, and then you can put it on. Oh, God has truly been good to me, and if I would give myself more to Him, He would shower me with more gifts. I have given myself to you and see what I am receiving and am to receive more when the marriage rite has been performed. May God's will be done. Should it happen that something unforeseen happens so that we may not be married, may God always keep you and me in His mighty arms that we might not miss that Heavenly Home.

Yours in Christ,

Margaret

I just returned from our cantata rendition. It was fun to sing. There were a lot of people present. We stood during the singing of the cantata, which lasted almost an hour. …

So Frank Lunn is to help you this summer. You two must be wonderful friends. That will be grand for both of you, and I am sure that Evodia and Reuben will like to [have] *him help them in the church work. Does he ever mention concerning the trouble at Bethany of Uhe's resigning?* [In] *the last letter I received from Bernard he didn't mention anything, so maybe it has subsided.*

I am sorry that you have been feeling blue, and I am afraid that something I have written has made you feel that way. … That about your losing money on your cattle is disheartening, but I am glad that you still have your health and are able to pick up courage to continue your work. Money isn't everything. …

Now it is ten o'clock, so I guess I need to cease talking to you and go to sleep. I hope you will enjoy reading this letter as much as I have enjoyed writing it. I can hardly wait to get your picture and the ring. I hope they reach here in good condition. …

May God bless you and yours. May He hasten the time for us to be married. May He ever bless us as His children.

Yours in Christian love,

Margaret

April 11 [Postmarked April 12, 3:00 p.m.]

My dear Walter,

"I will lift up mine eyes unto the mountains:

From whence shall my help come?

My help cometh from Jehovah,

Who made heaven and earth."

Jehovah will keep thy going out and thy coming in

From this time forth and for evermore." Psalm 121:1,2,8

God is truly a wonderful God and to think that He has given me such a true Christian. This evening Helen and I didn't return from school until after six o'clock, so the post office was closed. There was a card in the box stating that some registered mail had come. Mr. Mann went down especially to get the mail for us, and it was the diamond. Walter, I truly am happy and grateful to you. Thank you and may God bless us both to ever be faithful to one another, and may He grant us to inherit eternal life in heaven. May God help us never to cause anyone to stumble but rather to help and bring them to Jesus Christ.

The ring is just beautiful. I am so happy that it is yellow gold. The diamonds sparkle so beautifully with many different colors. I regret that it is a little too large. I believe it must be about a size six or six and a half. This evening I tried on some of Ruth Loeppke's rings. She had one that was 4½ and that was too tight. She thought my size was

5½ or 5. I have wrapped tape around it so that I can wear it and not be worried about losing it. Walter, it is so beautiful. Oh, if you were only here! Mrs. Jefferis said she had had a very competent jeweler in Wilton to make her ring larger just a year ago or so. He has been a jeweler for a number of years. Should I have him make the ring (yours and mine) smaller, or shall I send it to you for you to bring it to the jeweler from whom you bought it, or should I wait until I see you this summer and we get it fixed in Minnesota, or do you have some other suggestion? I must have quite small fingers, but you don't care, do you?

The mixed chorus sang this evening, and they did exceptionally well. Now they are to try to learn to sing it acappella (spelling?). The contest is this coming Wednesday. The girls have not all finished their costumes, but there are but two who haven't finished. Tomorrow evening they are to sing as well as the boys. These groups are singing not as well as they should. Will you remember them in your prayers?

May God bless you, dear Walter, and may I be a true Christian helper to you as long as Christ wishes us to live together. "God is love his mercy brightens all the paths in which we move." "All the way (my/our) Savior leads (me/us) cheers each winding path (I/we) tread."

Yours in Christ,

Margaret

"In peace will I both lay me
down and sleep;
For thou, Jehovah, alone mak
est me dwell in safety."
Ps. 4:8

April 12 1938
8:20 P. M.

Dear Margaret;

"Now the day is over,
Night is drawing nigh"
Another beautiful day is over, but before I seek sleep and rest I want to write to my Margaret.

First, I want to say that I am sorry to have caused you some worry and uneasiness and then I ask to be forgiven. I do not remember what my ob-ject was in writing as I did. I must have been in too big a hurry and did not make myself plain. But this day has not been very pleasant, knowing that something I wrote, caused you even to think of forgetting each other. Please forgive me.

Now to answer a question in your mind. My folks would not care if I would be married tomorrow, in fact they would like it, and joy with us. They have no objections whatsoever. They are entirely in favor of you, and Irene, asked me the other day when she

Altho, I have been staying and eating at home for the last 2 years, because it adds to convenient, I am working on my own and financing myself [illegible] even. But the home upon the mortgage of I have to borrow money

April 12 [Postmarked April 13, 8:30 a.m.]

Dear Margaret:

"Now the day is over,

Night is drawing nigh"

Another beautiful day is over, but before I seek sleep and rest, I want to write to my Margaret.

First, I want to say that I am sorry to have caused you some worry and uneasiness, and then I ask to be forgiven. I do not remember what my object was in writing as I did. I must have been in too big a hurry and did not make myself plain. But this day has not been very pleasant, knowing that something I wrote caused you even to think of forgetting each other. Please forgive me.

Now to answer a question in your mind. My folks would not care if I would be married tomorrow; in fact, they would like it and joy with us. They have no objections whatsoever. They are entirely in favor of you, and Irene asked me the other day when she could see Margaret. I think a lot of my father and mother and brother and sisters. But I have often wished that we would have had and did have family devotions. It seems to me that the Bible is so much a foundation in any life that a study of it and a time of communion with God adds so very much to each life. That is one of the reasons why I should like a home of my own as soon as possible. …

Figure 3. Dad's family. Bottom row: Mabel, Claus Johnson, Bernice, Hilda Johnson, Irene; top row: Walter, Bruce.

Farming can be a tiring, sweaty, muddy, and greasy business. Yet Dad always washed his face and hands and combed his hair before sitting down to eat a meal Mom had prepared. Every meal began and ended with our saying, and sometimes singing, grace together and, except for noontime lunch, was followed by devotions. In the morning, we used a devotional book and read the selected verses from the Bible. In the evening, we used *Egermeier's Bible Story Book.*

We took turns reading. One of us would pray. I most enjoyed hearing Dad pray. His prayers updated us on what needed prayer and what deserved our thanks. After saying the Lord's Prayer together, we would go to the piano and sing a hymn. Mother usually played, but each of us had the opportunity once we could play the melody. Those who could, sang parts. Once my voice changed, I especially enjoyed singing the melodic bass of the hymn Walter's introductory quote just brought to Margaret's attention.

Those family devotions became a living cultural heritage that would later color my understandings of life's many issues and choices. Their influence is inextricably woven into my reflections on their letters.

Margaret, as I rode the cultivator today, preparing the ground for grain and wishing I might spend Easter with you, I thot we could set a time Saturday night, say about 9:00 for you and 8 for me, in which we could come to our Heavenly Father in prayer and ask his help, direction, and guidance in all things. Could we do that? As I may not get an answer by then, I will promise now to do that. …

Speaking of going for a walk, I would like to be outside walking with you now. Just before I came in, I fed the horses and put the grain in the boxes for them for morning. It was so comfortable and warm, with a big moon in the sky and hundreds of stars blinking already. Over half of the heavens were hung with rippling white clouds, which reflected the moonlight. A fresh breeze brot air to you, which you could not get 1/2 enough of.

Working in the field now is a joy, and the new upturned earth has a fresh and fragrant smell. As I drove along, I turned up hundreds of earthworms and other insect life. When coming home from the field last night, a hen pheasant flew up. She must have gone near to a meadowlark's nest or prospective nest because Mrs. Meadowlark took right in after her. I didn't know the lark was so aggressive, but she flew right up to the pheasant, lit on its back, and pestered it until it had to land in order to drive off the pursuer. …

In addition to the southwest quarter of the square mile on which we lived, Dad farmed fifteen acres owned by Claude Stone, a retired ditch-rider who shared Dad's interest in water rights. Cottontail rabbits scurried under Mr. Stone's sheds whenever we arrived in a tractor or pickup. We were often reminded to leave them alone. After the pickup was turned off and the silence of the yard returned, the cottontails would soon stick out their quizzical noses before again hopping about.

A small pasture separated Mr. Stone's land from a rise that defined the horizon of the sparsely populated dry lands to the east that evoked thoughts of coyotes and rattlesnakes. Hawks, buzzards, and an occasional eagle lazily circled overhead. An intermittent creek lined with cattails wound through the pasture. Its larger pools teemed with minnows and frogs. When I lay in the nearby grass with the hot Colorado sun warming my eyelids, the songs of the nesting red-and yellow-winged blackbirds occasionally lulled me to sleep.

One hot afternoon, while I was cultivating sugar beets, a baby cottontail jumped up and scurried down one of the rows. I stopped the tractor and gave chase. The bunny darted about for a while before I caught it. At first it quivered in my hands, but it soon settled down as I gently petted its soft, furry body. When I put it back down, it scurried before becoming a camouflaged bump on the ground alongside a nearby beet row.

A large hawk, perched on a fence post about a hundred yards away, caught my attention as I mounted the tractor. Seconds later, it lifted off the post and glided silently a few feet off the ground toward the baby rabbit. There was a swoop, an extending of talons, a short squeal, and then a flying off to a nest in the distance — a life-and-death interaction comprising crisscrossing moral threads I could not unravel.

Margaret, I love to get your letters so much, but when you are too tired or sleepy, I will forgive you if you seek rest instead of writing to me. Especially now toward the end of school, I know that you work hard and worry quite a good deal. I never taught, but remembering my school days makes me think that teaching is the hardest the last 2 months. Is that right? When you get home, perhaps you can write more often because I miss them a great deal. You have written regularly and often as well as read a great deal lately, so I know you must be busy.

Have you taken a walk along the Mo. river lately? It will soon be teeming with new plant and animal life along its banks, will it not? …

I must soon retire, but speaking of money and our getting married, if we have not enough faith, not enough hope, and our love is not strong enough to face the future together, come what may, then it is hopeless even with a million dollars. God has always provided plenty for me. I've had the blues, but everything always turned out many times better than I expected.

Let's quit talking about If, When, and How (I guess I did the most of that) and go right ahead and plan to be married as soon as possible.

If some catastrophe should happen, that will be time enough to talk of waiting for another year. I have a good supply of clothes, and my personal expenditure has never had to be large.

After all, it would be fun to work together toward a goal. We appreciate what we have only to the extent of what we put into it. Is that not true? The old saying easy come — easy go is pretty true after all.

I know that you love me and that you have had to work for all you ever got. I love you, and I like to work. God has not promised to help those who are not willing to help themselves. It was not money that led our forefathers out across the plains to settle and build up this great nation. It was Faith, Hope, and Love. …

In Christ,

Walter.

"In peace will I both lay me down and sleep; For thou, Jehovah, alone makest me dwell in safety." Ps. 4:8

Altho I have been staying and eating at home for the last 2 years because it was so convenient, I am working on my own and financing myself. Dad does not even put his name upon the mortgage if I have to borrow money.

Who cannot hear what resonates with Walter's joy? It's not the money; it is God having "always provided plenty." It's not the achievement; it is working "together toward a goal." It's not a Pollyannaish hope; it is heading forth "to settle and build."

April 16 [Postmarked April 16, 4:30 p.m.]

Dear Margaret:

"He is not here; for he is risen, even as he said" Matthew 28:6

This morning as I write, I can hear robins and many other varieties of birds singing, and their joy is catching, and perhaps they have caught some of mine.

They may have. Our feathered and furry friends easily distinguish between a merry whistle, an angry shout, a jaunty step, an aggressive stride, an ignoring shuffle, or an inquisitive halt as we pass their way.

I am glad that you are well and happy; able to carry on your work each day.

I received your last two letters the same day. The ring must of arrived safely, but I, too, am sorry that it is too large, but that is easy to fix, and if there is a competent jeweler at Wilton, I believe it best to fix it there, altho I guess the danger of loss by registered mail is not great.

You worry about little hands and feet, and my sisters worry about big ones, so I guess its human nature to be a little dissatisfied. But I know you do not mean it that way, and I also know those little hands can do much work.

I wish you were here, Margaret, to behold the beautiful sunrise, the drifting clouds, green lawn, and alfalfa fields. I have not been in the mts. yet this year. When you are here, we shall go as often as possible, for drives and picnics.

We had a very good rain Thurs. nite, so I could not be in the field at all the rest of this week. Maybe I can a little Sat afternoon.

How did the glee clubs work in the contest? I suppose you are worrying about the state contest now. It is not wrong to be concerned in anything we do and also to strive to do it well, but if we trust in God, He will carry the worries better than we can.

I just thot, as I started writing, what a joy it must have been to the two Marys to hear the message of the Angel, altho they might have been a little concerned at first.

They were promised that they might see him in Galilee. May we so live and do as to see Him and be with Him when He comes for us. …

In Christ,

Walter

So much hinges on the words Walter quotes regarding the open tomb, "He is not here; for he is risen even as he said." For some, their basic outlook on life rests on the physical resurrection of his crucified body — an extraordinary event that can be believed but not evidentially documented outside of biblical testimony. But suppose you identified with the vision and the way of Jesus. How might a change in the tangibility of that event affect your way of life? That is the issue in the next chapter.

A Glimpse Back

April 10. In his second letter on the tenth, Walter claims that "peace and confidence … is a gift from God." What do you feel supports that personal claim other than his belief in his opening quote? On what understandings and experiences do your peace and confidence reside?

Walter longs for the day when he and Margaret may work together, for "therein lies the joy in this life." What steps do you see him taking to assure that joy?

April 10. On hearing about the ring in her April 9 letter, Margaret confides, "The ring will mean so much to me." In her letter the next day, she "just wanted to shout." What do you feel may have elicited her new elation?

April 12. Walter feels that a study of the Bible and communion with God, especially through daily devotions, "adds so very much to each life." How would you summarize the benefits to Walter of that study and communion? What daily rituals add significant meaning to your life?

April 16. Walter writes that he "can hear robins … and their joy is catching" and that he feels they have caught some of his joy. In what ways do you feel that being in touch with nature ties into one's sense of self?

Seeing Jesus: Same World, New Eyes

Like all Christians, my faith is centered on the transformative experiences that took place among the disciples of Jesus before, during, and after the resurrection. Before he died, Jesus left his followers with a vision of a new kingdom on earth and of eternal life. In the account of Matthew 28, both Mary Magdalene and Mary the mother of James were probably attracted to that vision before his death. If so, that vision may have faded, possibly dramatically, right after his crucifixion. We don't know. We do know that the reality of that vision began its dramatic dispersion when both Marys miraculously experienced the presence of Jesus two days after his death, a day now commemorated by millions as the first Easter. The "open tomb"[53] gave new meaning to the words Jesus said in John 12:24 shortly before his death, "Unless a grain of wheat falls into the earth and dies, it remains alone; but if it dies, it bears much fruit."

We cannot know what happened to the disciples, physically or mentally, that made these experiences transformative. We can only believe and try to infer what went on based on the memories of his followers. The treasured anecdotes and narratives circulated and continued to evolve until those concerned stabilized their veracity by writing them down. It would be nice to have the original manuscripts. We have only the results of copied and recopied parchments, easily torn and lost.

The earliest historically definitive manuscript, extant only as a copy, is a letter. According to Edgar Krentz in *The Harper Collins Study Bible,*[54] that letter, I Thessalonians, was either penned or dictated by the Apostle Paul around 50 CE, roughly two decades after Jesus was crucified. In a subsequent letter, I Corinthians 15:3 – 8, Paul documents a number of different instances when Jesus first appeared to some of the followers and, roughly three to five years later, appeared to him. The letter is written in Greek. I have added in brackets the relevant Greek word Paul used for "appeared":

> For I delivered to you as of first importance what I had also receive, that Christ died for our sins in accordance with the scriptures, that he was buried, that he was raised on the third day in accordance with the scriptures, and that he appeared [*horao*] to Cephas, then to the twelve.
>
> Then he appeared [*horao*] to more than five hundred brethren at one time, most of whom are still alive, though some have fallen asleep. Then he appeared [*horao*] to James, then to all the apostles.
>
> Last of all, as to one untimely born, he appeared [*horao*] also to me. For I am least of the apostles, unfit to be called an apostle, because I persecuted the church of God.

The inspired authors of our scriptures, although human, were skilled in communicating the central truths that had changed their lives and were changing the lives of their fellow believers. Paul notes his singular unworthiness in receiving the experience that transformed his life from the worthiness of Jesus's disciples, Cephas, and James. Due to our "modern" interest in "getting the facts straight," it is surprising that Paul did not differentiate the nature of his "seeing" experience from that of Cephas and James, for Paul was still persecuting the early Christians after Jesus had ascended to heaven.

I, like Walter, have no time to study the centuries-old Hebrew and Greek dialects in which our earliest copies of the New Testament manuscripts were written. However, I can use *The NIV Exhaustive Concordance*[55] to illustrate two critical semantic distinctions that the Greek manuscripts make that are easily lost in English translations of what it meant to "see" Jesus. The issues are present in the flexible ways we can use the verbs "to look" and "to see" to change the expression and meaning of the sentence: He saw her and he looked at her, and as he looked at her, he saw into her.

The critical distinction between seeing something through one's physical eye and experiencing a revelation through one's "mental eye" is evident in Paul's defense of his actions before a riled-up crowd of fellow Jews in Jerusalem that occurred roughly two and a half decades after his vision of Jesus. Luke and his colleagues gathered and wove into a gripping and unifying narrative the stories and recollections of Paul's defense some years after Paul had traveled to Rome. It comes to us in Acts 22:3 – 4, 6 – 14.

> I am a Jew, born at Tarsus in Cilicia, but brought up in this city at the feet of Gamali-el, educated according to the strict manner of the law of our fathers, being zealous for God as you all are this day. I persecuted this Way to the death, binding and delivering to prison both men and women.
>
> As I made my journey and drew near to Damascus, about noon a great light from heaven suddenly shone about me. And I fell to the ground and heard a voice saying to me, "Saul, Saul, why do you persecute me?" And I answered, "Who are you Lord?" And he said to me, "I am Jesus of Nazareth whom you are persecuting." … And when I could not see because of the brightness of the light, I was led by the hand by those who were with me, and came into Damascus.
>
> And one Ananias … came to me, and standing by me said to me, "Brother Saul, receive your sight." And in the very hour I received my sight and saw [*anablepo*] him. And he said, "The God of our fathers appointed

> you to know his will, to see [*horao*] the Just One and to hear a voice from his mouth.

Jesus anticipated issues his followers would raise on seeing him after the crucifixion. What was new that they hadn't seen or realized before? What was critical for those who saw Jesus after his crucifixion and for those who didn't? How is it some could see Jesus after his body no longer walked this earth? His words are given to us through the memories of his followers as they were trying to comprehend and share the different post-crucifixion experiences of Jesus that were transforming their worlds. These memories are mainly recorded in the Gospel of John, written fifty or sixty years after the crucifixion.

That those who had walked with him would come to a new sense of the presence of Jesus after the crucifixion is suggested in the writer's careful juxtaposition of two Greek verbs in John 16:16:

> A little while, and you will see [*theoreo*] me no more; again a little while, and you will see [*horao*] me.

The difference between seeing the significance of Jesus through the mental eye as opposed to the physical eye comes across in the juxtaposition of these two Greek verbs in John 20:11 – 16.

> Mary stood weeping outside the tomb, and as she wept she stooped to look into the tomb; and she saw [*theoreo*] two angels in white, sitting where the body of Jesus had lain, one at the head and one at the feet. They said, "Woman, why are you weeping?" She said to them, "Because they have taken away my Lord, and I don't know where they have laid him." Saying this, she turned around and saw [*theoreo*] Jesus standing, but she did not know that it was Jesus. … Jesus said to her, "Mary." She turned and said to him in Hebrew, "Rabboni!" [which means "Teacher"]. Jesus said to her, "Do not hold me, for I have not ascended to the Father; but go to my brethren and say to them, I am ascending to my Father and your Father, to my God and your God." Mary Magdalene went and said to the disciples, "I have seen [*horao*] the Lord."

It was implicit in the words and actions of Jesus while he walked this earth that his physical presence was not a prerequisite for experiencing his love; you had only to believe in the power of that love. Moreover, his followers had heard the understandings in John 14:21: "He who has my commandments and keeps them, he it is who loves me; and he who loves me will be loved by my Father, and I will love him and manifest myself in him," expressed in many different ways. But after his crucifixion, there would be some who would not be able to say with Paul, "he appeared [*horao*] also to me." What about them?

Paul dedicated an answer to this question in a letter written for him by Tertius. Paul said in Romans 1:16 – 18, "For I am not ashamed of the gospel: it is the power of God for salvation to every one who has faith … For in it the righteousness of God is revealed through faith for faith; as it is written, 'He who through faith is righteous shall live'" — the latter quote being a possible rendering by Paul of Habakkuk 2:4. Some years later, the writer of Hebrews would describe in chapter eleven the critical role faith played in the lives of the founding fathers of the Abrahamic religions. The chapter opens with the central theme, "Now faith is confidence in what we hope for and assurance about what we do not see."

Two, maybe three, decades later, the writer of John 20:26 – 29 recalls the words of Jesus — specifically the importance of seeing through the eyes of faith.

> Eight days later, his disciples were again in the house, and Thomas was with them. The doors were shut, but Jesus came and stood among them, and said, "Peace be with you." Then he said to Thomas, "Put your finger here, and see my hands; and put out your hand, and place it in my side; do not be faithless, but believing." Thomas answered him, "My Lord and my God!" Jesus said to him, "Have you believed because you have seen [*horao*] me? Blessed are those who have not seen [*horao*] and yet believe."

* * *

The accounts of the life of Jesus come to us from those who walked with him. Much of our Christian theology comes to us through the teachings and writings of Paul. The early followers of Jesus were amazed at the teachings of Jesus, "for He was teaching them as one having authority, and not as the scribes" (Mark 1:22). The source of that authority troubled the religious leaders of his time when they asked him in Mark 11:29: "By what authority are You doing these things?"

It is a question that all of our spiritual pathfinders end up having to eventually address in one form or another. Paul does in Galatians 1:11 – 23:

> I would have you know, brethren, that the gospel which was preached to me is not man's gospel. For I did not receive it from man, nor was I taught it, but it came through a revelation of Jesus Christ. For you have heard of my former life in Judaism, how I persecuted the church of God violently and tried to destroy it; and I advanced in Judaism beyond many of my own age among my people, so extremely zealous was I for the traditions of my fathers. But when he who had set me apart before I was born, and had called me through his grace, was pleased to reveal his Son to me, in order that I might preach him among the Gentiles, I did not confer with flesh and blood, nor did I go up to Jerusalem to those who were apostles before me, but I went away into Arabia; and again I returned to Damascus.

> Then after three years, I went up to Jerusalem to visit Cephas [Peter], and remained with him fifteen days. ... I was still not known by sight to the churches of Christ in Judea; they only heard it said, "He who once persecuted us is now preaching the faith he once tried to destroy."

Paul points out that the backdrop of his seeing (*horao*) Jesus differed in a fundamental way from that of the earlier followers of Jesus. These early followers who saw (*horao*) Jesus after his crucifixion came to see his actions and teachings in a new light, but they had already loved and pondered his words while he walked with them on earth. Not so with Paul. The Christians he was pursuing when Jesus questioned his actions were not, in his mind, revering the Judaic law and traditions he zealously studied. More fundamentally, in the traditions of his fathers, there was no man who walked this earth whose voice could be experienced as the Voice of God — yet, that was the experience with which Paul had to come to grips. The Voice of God came to him through the words of Jesus.

When struggling with a relational problem among many interrelated pieces, it occasionally happens that all the pieces start coming together once a critical piece falls into place. The relief experienced at that moment is well conveyed in a verse of a popular song by Johnny Nash: "I can see clearly now, the rain is gone,/I can see all obstacles in my way/Gone are the dark clouds that had me blind/It's gonna be a bright (bright), bright (bright)/Sun-shiny day." In the song, the obstacles don't suddenly disappear; indeed, many may still need to be resolved. But they no longer block the road ahead.

For Paul, who "persecuted the church of God and tried to destroy it," the "rain" must have been a downpour before the clouds broke and that first critical piece fell in place by means of a simple question: "Saul, Saul, why are you persecuting me?" The release he felt occurs throughout his teachings: "But by the grace of God I am what I am" (I Cor. 15:10); "For the law of the Spirit of Life in Christ Jesus has set me free from the law of sin and death" (Romans 8:2); "He [God the Father] has delivered us from the dominion of darkness and transferred us to the kingdom of his beloved Son" (Col. 1:13).

Paul was just another human with unique gifts and talents by which he became a leader of those arresting the early Christians. Yet there was within him, as in us, a vast knowledge with which he had only occasional conscious contact. He may have never questioned — most of us don't — how in his mother's womb, starting out as a fertilized egg, virtually invisible, he somehow had within himself the needed biological knowledge to grow a body by which to effectively move about and to fashion a brain by which to recognize and enjoy parents, siblings, and friends. However, like each of us, he was quite aware of his world and respectfully remembered Gamaliel, at whose feet he learned the teachings and traditions of his fathers through which he saw his world. In that world, there were the fortunate few, the Jews, chosen by and covenanted with the one true God, and the less fortunate, the Gentiles, attracted to foreign gods.

Paul's sense of things totally changed when the clouds broke — same world, but a whole new kingdom and a new set of eyes through which it could be seen. Time would be needed to contemplate this new view of life and to gather into words, phrases, and thoughts the vast difference between the old and the new. He put his sword away and set off for Arabia.

After one or two years, he came back using words like "his Son in me" and "God, who set me apart from birth" to explain his conversion and new identity, words very much in line with how the followers of Jesus came to understand his words in

John 14:20: "In that day you will know that I am in my Father, and you in me, and I in you." He came back talking of an all-inclusive sense of self that bridges the many different religious, national, cultural, social, and genetic differences that often underlie intimidation, exploitation, and aggression. But that is to use thoughts and expressions of my time and place. While recognizing our individuality through "gifts that differ according to the grace given us" (Romans 12:6), Paul pictures a new kingdom using words of his time and place: "There is neither Jew nor Greek, there is neither slave nor free, there is neither male nor female; for you are all one in Christ Jesus" (Galatians 4:28).

Paul was soon recognized as a new and different leader of the emerging Christian Church. He was not authorized as one who had walked with Jesus or as a student of the first apostles but as someone authorized by the voice that gave him new eyes through which he could see the kingdom he was called to proclaim.

* * *

Hundreds of years later, we are still trying to understand the depth of the transformative experiences of the early followers of Jesus. Our efforts necessarily operate within the limitations imposed by the current understandings and methodologies for ascertaining truth in its various forms. Philosophers can't help us. They have been unable to deduce either the existence or nonexistence of God via any universally accepted set of assumptions on the nature of God and, consequently, how a human can be experienced as God. Artists, on the other hand, have the creative freedom to produce any number of scripts in which a human is experienced and worshiped as God. But who could have faith in such a mind-boggling event when it is sourced in a writer's imagination? Science cannot help us, even with its rigorous methodologies and theories for how things come about. Its specialized dictionaries lack the needed terms, such as *miracles* and *God*. As we have just seen, the revelatory experiences of our spiritual leaders, in stark contrast, are central to their testimonies of miracles and lived metaphors. We may or may not ever comprehend the material means by which their experiences came about, but we have the reports of those experiences in our scriptures and the teachings and understandings that flow from them.

In his introductory chapter "The Problem of Pain,"[56] C. S. Lewis illustrates some assumptions to which a skeptical scholar can be driven in trying to understand the central truth of those who have experienced Jesus as God. He recognizes that "numinous awe is as old as humanity itself" and either "is a mere twist in the human mind … serving no biological function … or else it is a direct experience of the really supernatural, to which the name Revelation might be properly given." He goes on, "The second element in religion is the consciousness not merely of a moral law, but of a moral law at once approved and disobeyed. This consciousness is neither a logical, nor an illogical, inference from the facts of experience; if we did not bring it to our experience we could not find it there. It is either an inexplicable illusion, or else revelation." He continues, "The third stage in religious development arises when the Numinous Power to which we feel awe is made the guardian of the morality to which we feel obligation. … It may be madness — a madness congenital to man and oddly fortunate in its results — or it may be revelation." He ends with a fourth assertion, "There was a man … who claimed to be, or to be the son of, or to be 'one with,' the Something which is at once the awful haunter of nature and the giver of the moral law.

The claim is shocking … and … only two views of this man are possible. Either he was a raving lunatic … or else He was, and is, precisely what he said. There is no middle way."

I sympathize with the significance of the distinction but differ with regard to the nature of the distinction that Jesus claimed. It is true that Jesus claimed God as his father, but he claimed the same for all desiring that relationship. He did claim to be the prophesied Messiah, the Christ who, through his teachings, life, death, and resurrection, would inaugurate the coming of the kingdom of God on earth. For me — and, I believe, for those wanting peace and freedom to reign on earth — the radical choice is between a "raving lunatic" and the Messiah.

That, for me, is the choice, made both consciously and unconsciously, each day: Do I truly want to be a part of the coming kingdom of God on earth that he proclaimed? It is similar to the choice of joining in a game in which everyone is welcome to play. You don't have to join, and you can always leave if you don't care for the game. But if you really want to be a part of what is going on, you must learn the rules and strive to play your part even though your playing may be far from perfect.

That we do not have to have an unexpected, sudden, and life-changing experience to join and play is profoundly assuring. Conversely, for the early Christians who did, the presence of Jesus following that experience became more real than his death. Faith in that presence quickly became the grounding understanding of all of his followers. The question arises whether such experiences still happen today.

William James, an eminent psychologist and philosopher of the late nineteenth and early twentieth centuries, thought it might. In his chapter on mysticism in *The Varieties of Religious Experiences,*[57] he proffers some marks of "mystical" experiences. Because many of his interviewees gave the impression that the experience defied expression, he suggests that what they described "must be directly experienced" and "cannot be imparted or transferred to others." His studies led him to believe that these mystical experiences often give rise to "insights into depths of truth unplumbed by the discursive intellect." He goes on to say, "The mystic feels as if his own will were in abeyance, and indeed sometimes as if he were grasped and held by a superior force."

Roughly seven decades later, Abraham Maslow focused on these unusual experiences in his monograph *Religions, Values, and Peak-Experiences.* He writes, "It is quite characteristic in peak-experiences that the whole universe is perceived as an integrated and unified whole,"[58] and he adds, "The peak-experience is felt as a self-validating, self-justifying moment which carries its own intrinsic value with it."[59]

William James suggests there are no sure ways of having a peak experience. Yet something elicits them. Here are two recently shared occurrences that followed profoundly emotional searches.

The first, a contemporary version of the miracle of the five loaves and two fish found in all the gospels, illustrates the breadth of identity that can be experienced. In this case, a young mother shared her experience over the radio in a Ted Talk. Her child had perished in her womb. At her doctor's request, she agreed to donate the organs in its body to medical research. (I like to think a spirit of love for others and the value of even the small life that she lost somehow spoke to her in her grief.) Her stillborn child somehow lived on in her mind. A couple of years later, through a series of odd occurrences, she ended up visiting a research facility that had received, I believe, the eyes of her infant. The researchers explained to this young mother how the cells from her deceased infant's eyes had been used to bring sight to others. She wanted to learn more. At her request, the researchers helped her locate other recipient facilities. Each time in talking with the doctors at those facilities, she was tearfully struck by the many ways various individuals had been helped through her gift. While trying to get her mind around all the good that had flowed from the little gift whose emotional separation had torn her in so many ways, everything came together in a totally new way. I recall her saying, in effect, "I was no longer a boat tossed about on the ocean. I was the ocean."

The second, a testimony of a leading scientist, illustrates the profound mystery of interconnectedness that can be experienced. In discussing his spiritual walk in the "Truth Seekers" chapter of his book *The Language of God: A Scientist Presents Evidence for Belief*, Francis Collins notes that he became first an agnostic, then an atheist, then a believer in God, and finally a Christian. His answer to the vexing problem of the existence of God came in a metaphorical experience when, in 1989, he traveled to a small mission hospital in Nigeria as a result of his and his daughter's "harboring a desire to contribute something to the developing world." (I feel that they, like the young mother, were urged on by a spirit of love for others.) In

Nigeria, he realized that "the majority of diseases I was called upon to treat represented a devastating failure of the public health system." At the hospital, he encountered a patient who changed his life. He writes:

> The only chance to save him was to carry out a highly risky procedure of drawing off the pericardial fluid with a large bore needle placed in his chest. … Nearly a quart of fluid was drawn off. The young man's response was dramatic. … For a few hours after this experience I felt a great sense of relief, even elation. But by the next morning, the same familiar gloom began to settle over me. … Even if he survived the disease, … the chances for long life in a Nigerian farmer are poor.[60]
>
> With those discouraging thoughts in my head, I approached his bedside the next morning, finding him reading his Bible. He looked at me quizzically, and asked whether I had worked at the hospital for a long time. I admitted that I was new, feeling somewhat irritated and embarrassed that it had been so easy for him to figure that out. But then this young Nigerian farmer, just about as different from me in culture,

> experience, and ancestry as any two humans could be, spoke the words that will be forever emblazoned in my mind: "I get the sense you are wondering why you came here," he said. "I have an answer for you. You came for one reason. You came here for me."
>
> I was stunned. Stunned that he could see so clearly into my heart, but even more stunned at the words he was speaking. I had plunged a needle close to his heart; he had impaled mine. …
>
> The tears of relief that blurred my vision as I digested his words stemmed from indescribable reassurance — reassurance that there in that strange place for just one moment, I was in harmony with God's will, bonded together with this young man in a most unlikely but marvelous way.

As a research scientist, Francis Collins naturally sought an explanation:

> Nothing I had learned from science could explain that experience. Nothing about the evolutionary

> explanations for human behavior could account for why it seemed so right for this privileged white man to be standing at the bedside of this young African farmer, each of them receiving something exceptional. This is what C. S. Lewis calls agape. It is love that seeks no recompense. It is an affront to materialism and naturalism. And it is the sweetest joy that one can experience.[61]

At that point in his life, Francis Collins must have loved Jesus in some deep sense. For Jesus said in John 14:21 that "he who keeps my commandments loves me" — and one of his commandments is to love one's neighbor as oneself. Yet, Francis Collins writes:[62]

> Lewis was right. I had to make a choice. A full year had passed since I decided to believe in some sort of god, and now I was being called to account. On a beautiful fall day, as I was hiking in the Cascade Mountains during my first trip west of the Mississippi, the majesty and beauty of God's creation overwhelmed my resistance. As I rounded a corner and saw a beautiful

> and unexpected frozen waterfall, hundreds of feet high, I knew the search was over. The next morning, I knelt in the dewy grass as the sun rose and surrendered to Jesus Christ.

Following this experience, Francis Collins became a leader and spokesman for many who believe in Jesus even though he did not describe his experience as seeing (*horao*) Jesus in the sense of Paul.

These life-changing experiences may be rare, but they have been happening for a long time. After writing *Brave New World,* Aldous Huxley began studying the understandings that have flowed from the more noteworthy ones. He organized these understandings in his book *The Perennial Philosophy,* which the *New York Times* called "The Masterpiece of All Anthologies." In the introduction, Aldous Huxley writes:[63]

> *The Perennial Philosophy* is primarily concerned with the one, divine Reality substantial to the manifold world of things and lives of minds. But the nature of this one Reality is such that it cannot be directly and immediately apprehended except by those who have

chosen to fulfil certain conditions, making themselves loving, pure in heart, and poor in spirit.

These conditions seemingly flow from the beatitudes and teachings of Jesus that permeated the emotional hearts of his followers as he hung on the cross. After his crucifixion, his followers would be asking, "What now? We left everything to follow him." At the same time, his words "Seek and you will find" and "After I am raised up, I will go before you to Galilee" may have been stirring in their minds.

Whatever the reasons, news that many of the followers of Jesus saw (*horao*) him after his crucifixion spread like fire. But to appreciate the speed and extent, we must mentally toss out our cell phones and computers, turn off our TVs, and burn the presses that print our books, magazines, newspapers, and promotional brochures. Back then the only news that came your way came from the lips of the speaker who arrived on foot, by donkey, or by boat.

Should you have asked a follower of Jesus, "How do you know it's true someone has seen Jesus?" he or she might have replied, "Well, that's what my friend said."

"But how do you know what your friend said is true?"

"Well, my friend said that Mary, who had walked with Jesus, said she SAW him after he was crucified. My friend goes to the synagogue all the time, and she said that Jesus was the prophesied Messiah. ... Why don't you come to the next meeting at my friend's house? She said a new follower of Jesus, a rabbi, will be there and will read from a scroll containing what the prophet Joel said would happen when the Messiah comes. Others will be telling stories they have heard about Jesus, what he said and what he did back when he was with his disciples."

According to many Christian scholars, conversations along these lines probably started a half century or more before concerned proclaimers of the acts and teachings of Jesus and his disciples got together with the author of Luke as he began penning his gospel with the words:

> Inasmuch as many have undertaken to compile a narrative of the things which have been accomplished among us, just as they were delivered to us by those who from the beginning were eyewitnesses and ministers of the word, it seemed good to me also, having followed all things closely for some time past, to write an orderly account.

That the news of Jesus's resurrection quickly spread by word of mouth is dramatically conveyed in the second chapter of Acts:

> When the day of Pentecost had come, they were all together in one place. ... Parthians and Medes and Elamites and residents of Mesopotamia, Judea and Cappadocia, Pontus and Asia, Phrygia and Pamphylia, Egypt and the parts of Libya belonging to Cyrene, and visitors from Rome, both Jews and proselytes, Cretans and Arabians, we hear them telling in our own tongues the mighty works of God. And all were amazed and perplexed, saying to one another, "What does this mean?" But others mockingly said, "They are filled with new wine."
>
> But Peter ... addressed them ... "This is what was spoken by the prophet Joel: 'And in the last days it shall be, God declares, that I will pour out my Spirit upon all flesh, and your sons and your daughters shall prophesy, and your young men shall see visions, and your old men shall dream dreams; yea, and on your

men servants and my maidservants in those days I will pour out my spirit; and they shall prophesy.'"

So where does that leave us? As Yuval Harari notes, quoted earlier, "Since we might soon be able to engineer our desires too, the real question facing us is not 'What do we want to become?' but 'What do we want to want?' Those who are not spooked by this question probably haven't given it enough thought." I believe that should we ever start wanting to want to bring about a greater spirit of universal self-worth, more of us will start seeing (*horao*) an embodiment of the spirit bringing about the kingdom of God on earth. Should that time come, even more of our daughters and sons will prophesy, even more of our young men and women will see visions, and even more of our elders will dream dreams.

SO FILLED WITH QUESTIONS

*A*s the seasons come and go, many of life's doors open and close as well. Spring brought for Walter a welcome return to fieldwork but also the forced sale of his cattle. It brought for Margaret the success of her vocal groups but also a continual reminder of the teaching contract waiting for her signature.

April 17 [Postmarked April 18, 8:30 a.m.]

My Dear Margaret:

"Pilate said unto them, Ye have a guard; go, make it as sure as you can." Matt. 27:65

My Dear; I would greet you and ask you how you feel. Have you had a pleasant vacation and rest? I am sure you will go back to Washburn with renewed strength. Since I cannot come up there, I want to greet you and tell you that I love you.

Did you have nice Easter weather, and did you hear an inspiring message of both word and song? Perhaps you were asked to sing while you visited at Rev Johnson's. It has been a beautiful day in this part of Colorado. Our church at Greeley was filled to capacity, and we enjoyed a fine message, as we heard again of a new day, for all who are in Christ. A new day; made possible thru Christ's death and resurrection. Tonight the choir renders its cantata, directed by Gilbert Sattoff.

The thot never occurred to me before, but there were those in that day who actually feared that Christ might rise again, Matt 27:63. At the same time, the ones who had been near him during his ministry were fearing that he would not rise again, even though he had told them that he would. The opposition and doubters here present a testimony which is wonderful. Tho they believed not his teaching because it convicted them of their sin, yet they were afraid that he might rise again and made physical preparation against such an event. Even Pilate's answer carries a doubt in it, as to their ability to prevent his rising. I think Pilate came very near to becoming a follower of Christ on the day of the trial, but fear of the mob and love of the power which he had kept him from eternal life. Do you think this to be right? And I wonder how often this is true today.

How careful we should be of all our thots and decisions. Pilate thot for a moment, and his decision was to crucify the Savior. As I think back, I see this same guilt in my decisions. A second to speak a word and a lifetime of eternal separation from the only true source of life. A few brief years of power and then even that taken away from him. …

Although Dad always spoke lovingly of Jesus, he saw Jesus as something of a radical when he walked this earth. Jesus often associated with "sinners" and outcasts. He was at odds with much of established religious practice and assailed many of its leaders. To revitalize the spirit of the law, he was willing to break the letter of the law. Not only that, Jesus claimed to be the Messiah foretold in the scriptures. More than once, Dad wondered aloud to me if he would believe and follow a man doing such things today.

Tomorrow I begin planting barley, if the weather permits. This is the first planting I will do. About the 5 of May I will plant corn, and beans about the 20th of May. We plant potatoes round the first to the 25th of June. I will plant around the 20th of June. We plant beets between the 1st of April & 1st of May.

I wish you were here to bring me a cup of coffee and a sandwich, also one yourself to share with me. Then to share a moment together with God and the day would go much better.

Now as things begin to green up, they look much brighter. We also have the best prospects for water that we have had in several years. It is very encouraging to know this.

I have not sold my potatoes yet. I probably will sell the remainder this week.

Frank Lunn has not mentioned anything concerning the affairs at Bethany except as he started, he said that things were not as they should be.

Has Bernard said anything more about oil around Lindsborg? …

Is the grass greening yet, up there? Is the wheat up, and are the prospects for a crop pretty good this year?

It must be discouraging to have failures year after year. Nevertheless, I believe there are many more true Christians in those sections than in the prosperous ones. Don't you think so?

Now I must go to bed, and I pray that God may direct all your ways and keep you ever in Christ.

Yours in Christ,

Walter

April 18 [Postmarked April 19]

My dear Walter,

"Jehovah is nigh unto all them that call upon him,

To all that call upon him in truth.

He will fulfil the desire of them that fear him;

He also will hear their cry, and will save them." Ps. 145:18, 19

This is early Monday morning. I have longed so to write to you before, but truly, Walter, I haven't had the chance. I really do love to write to you. When I tell all that has happened, you'll understand.

First of all, this diamond has called for a lot of explanation. So many have wanted to see it and have asked about you. The teachers were so filled with questions that I almost wished you could have been here to answer some of them. Mr. Fahrer said he is afraid you're not good enough. Isn't that something? Well, it didn't take me long to put him in the true light of all your merits. The pupils have said that they have seen us together on two occasions recently. I can't understand that because I haven't been with any man except you since last August, and you already know about that affair. I explained it to you. Walter, this diamond draws me nearer to you because every time I see it, I know it is an expression of true Christian love. Last Saturday I had it made smaller, so now it fits very well. It is size five. …

The contest is over, and am I glad and thankful! We tied for first place with Turtle Lake. I had the privilege of going up to get the plaque. The pupils sang very well. The mixed chorus sang acapella with no difficulty. The tenors just soared up there. The judge said that my mixed chorus had just leaped ahead this year from last. (He judged last year's contest.) The outcome, I am certain, was just an answer to prayer. God truly loves us children. May we ever delight in His guidance. I'll tell you more about the contest when I get the chance to speak with you. …

The time that I spent at Underwood was so joyous except for this: I didn't get a chance to write to you. The children seemed so happy to have me with them. Walter, [the] *Johnsons have six children, and they didn't get married until they were thirty-three years of age. We can wait until later to be married. I would just as soon teach another year anyway. I believe that if I would room with Helen one more year I would be a more efficient wife, but now I am thru with ifs. …*

I lost my music stand in Turtle Lake at the contest. The case which contained the stand had my name on it. Would you remember this loss to God? I need it quite badly.

In Christian love,

Margaret

Prayer has always been a part of my life. It takes many forms. Meditative prayer consciously sets aside time to simply be with God, occasionally sharing a concern and sometimes receiving an urging or a direction. Public prayer voices concerns in the minds of the participants. Reactive prayer instinctively wells up with an unexpected need or appreciation. Yearning prayer has an undercurrent of persistent desires that are incorporated into, and sometimes conflict with, our other prayers.

Walter's praying in his December 5 letter, "for the day to come, soon when my first thot shall be for the Kingdom of God," is a meditative prayer based on a scriptural understanding that eventually anchored his joy in life. Walter and Margaret's interests in public prayer are clearly expressed in his April 12 letter when Walter suggests they set aside an agreed-upon time to pray for "help, direction, and guidance in all things." Margaret closed her letter by asking Walter to join her in asking for God's help in finding her music stand, thus making public what must have been at first a reactive call to God for help when first realizing it was gone.

I remember an occasion when I received a dramatic answer to a reactive prayer for something lost. My son, Joel, was showing me his new stunt — riding his bicycle off the end of a ramp on the dead-end road by our house. Something twisted or gave way, and he went flying over the front of his bicycle. With one arm obviously broken and blood dripping out of his mouth, he looked up and pleaded, "Dad?"

Martha and I rushed him to the emergency room. We learned that one of his two adult front teeth was pushed into his upper gum and would in all likelihood descend and reseat itself. The other was missing. We were told that if the missing tooth could be found and quickly reinserted into the cavity, it, too, might reseat itself.

I raced home to scour the pavement where he fell. The road was a collage of tooth-sized bits of white and light gray rocks embedded in an old asphalt mix. I was quickly losing hope of finding the camouflaged tooth when I stopped and asked God for help. The help came during my plea: *Lie flat on the ground with one eye flush with the pavement.*

I flattened my ear against the pavement. The tooth stood out like a pimple! I grabbed it, put it in my mouth, and raced back to the emergency room.

Would the idea have come to me had I not prayed but simply stopped to think up another way to look for the tooth? I don't know, but during my prayer, I somehow broke loose from what was quickly becoming an unpromising effort. The answer came wrapped in a thankfulness that I had been taught to pray.

April 19 [Postmarked April 20, 7:00 a.m.]

Dear Walter,

"He will not suffer thy foot to be moved: He that keepeth thee will not slumber." Psalm 121:3

I just love this verse. I am sure that it means much to you also. O, Walter, I am sure that you love to meditate on Scriptural passages. The precious gems which God gives to us in a certain way are like receiving diamonds from Him.

Last Saturday night I prayed at the same time as you did. It was just as though you were praying by my side. May God always grant that our knees will be ready to bend to Him. Isn't it fun to come to such a loving Father for guidance, help, and strength for the future? How did you happen to think about setting a certain time for prayer? I wish we could continue to do so.

Now I have your picture before me, and it seems just as though I were talking to you. Have you had a hard time in the field today? Won't you come to eat supper? We're to have fried potatoes, juicy beef steak, fruit salad (ready all but mixing it together, which I want you to do), sauce, and cake. The bread is ready because I just finished taking it out of the oven. I am sorry, but it got a little burnt. I hope the coffee isn't too strong; just as I [was] *putting in the coffee, the telephone rang, so I missed my count. Oh, it's a grand feeling to have you so hungry and the food ready for you. But you look a little tired — what have I done to make you look that way? I know — I forgot to meet you at the door with a great big kiss. Here it is! Now let's eat. Isn't God grand to us to give us so many blessings? This was imaginative, but it's been fun.*

Although Walter announced his time of arrival over the past Christmas vacation by telegram, no telephone calls are mentioned in these letters. Back then, each phone was connected by wire to the town switchboard. To place a local call, you dialed the number. The alerted telephone operator created a continuous connection by inserting both ends of a connecting wire into the two switchboard slots corresponding slots for your number and the dialed number. Because multiple phones were often joined to the same telephone wire, people with phones on the same "party" line could listen in on each other's conversations. Doing so was severely frowned upon, but privacy could not be guaranteed.

Still, privacy would not have been Walter and Margaret's main reason for not calling each other. Long-distance telephone calls were complex and expensive endeavors. Switchboards of small towns were connected by continuous telephone lines to central switchboards. Placing a call through even one central switchboard required the joint effort and conversation between three operators, a nontrivial matter. Routing a call from Washburn to Greeley probably entailed at least one central switchboard in North Dakota, another in Wyoming or Nebraska, and another in Colorado. One can imagine how much they would have liked to hear each other's voices. The fact that no calls are mentioned in the letters suggests that the needed long-distance call was either not possible or prohibitively expensive.

A long time ago you asked me how much it would cost to furnish a home. The home economics class has been busy estimating such costs. I asked Helen to have one of the pupils plan a home such as our home. She has done so, but the reports have not been handed in. The girl who used a house like ours had one that was larger than ours and furnished the house completely with new furniture and much that was not necessary to have for at least a five-year period for $600. I wish you were nearer so that we could talk about it. I believe that we could get along with much less, don't you? Helen said this girl really bought much not necessary to have and paid more for articles which she could have gotten for less. …

This evening I got the Reader's Digest. *I plan to read several articles this evening. I enjoy reading this magazine. Thank you so much for sending that to me. …*

I finished the Bible on Palm Sunday, I believe was the day, and now I have tried to memorize two chapters, so I haven't any definite plan. Schoolwork seems drab without some special Bible reading before and after. Should I read the gospels, or the epistles, or psalms or reread the Revelations?

Has Mr. Brown ceased from drinking liquor? I am glad that he has stopped asking you. [It] *may be that God sent you to this place to be an instrument in God's hand to draw him to Christ.*

This ring that you gave me is so very pretty. I just wish that you could see it. It fits me so nicely. I wear it all the time. When it gets dirty, I can clean it with some very soft, thin paper.

I am enclosing the picture we took last Christmas. How is your back now? I hope it is as strong as it was before you fell. Walter, how tall are you? So many have asked me to describe you, and one of the first questions seems to be, How tall is he? I am proud that you are Swedish. You know, I believe we have a lot in common.

Tomorrow evening the squad that I am in is to meet at the parsonage. …

The juniors are busy working on their class play. They are busy planning the junior-senior banquet. This evening Mr. Thorson handed out slips which asked the parents to say yes or no in regard to having the class sponsor a prom. He said that no outsiders were to be allowed to be at the prom. Will you remember this in your prayers? I have neglected to pray about it, but since this request was made after four o'clock, I was reminded of my negligence. …

Yours in Christ,

Margaret

We have just been invited to come down to eat some ice cream. It is Mrs. Jefferis's birthday. Come go along.

Margaret's quest for and discovery of gems in the Bible brought to mind the time she helped me find some blue barite crystals near Stoneham, Colorado. I had talked my brother James into driving the ninety miles east with me to look for the crystals. On hearing about our plans, Mom turned the trip into a family outing.

Stoneham, a small general store with a gas pump, was situated on a crossroads in the middle of the dry lands. Fortunately, the store was open. We walked in and asked the attendant if he knew anything about some barite crystals in the vicinity. He pointed to a couple of parallel tire paths and said, "Take this road a couple of miles north, and you will see some excavations where people look for them."

We took off and after a mile or two came across a small gulley with exposed dirt. The clumps of grass and dirt slopes didn't look hopeful, but we got out and started looking. After about fifteen minutes, our suspicions were confirmed — dirt and grass.

We drove on until we found another equally unpromising cutaway. We stopped and scoured around more earnestly, thinking these had to be the desired excavations. The floor and sides of this pit, like the first one, were largely dirt with crumbly clods and clumps of grass. Our enthusiasm quickly waned in the hot afternoon sun as we dug around. We were about to head home when Mom brought a fist-sized clod and asked me, "Why is this so heavy?

A light went on. Barite had roughly twice the specific weight of the weathered rocks from which the soil was derived. As I hurriedly scratched away at the outside of the clod with my pocket knife, a pale blue cluster of crystals emerged. Soon we were all crawling around the cutaway searching for unusually heavy chunks of dirt. A couple of hours later, we headed back with a small bag of barite crystals and crystal clusters thanks to Mom's seeing the unusual in a place where the rest of us saw only dirt.

April 19 [Postmarked April 20, 8:30 a.m.]

Dear Margaret:

"Grace and Peace to you, in Christ Jesus."

This evening I can imagine you, working at lesson plans for the morrow and perhaps grading the work done today. Did the vacation make the work more pleasant and lighter? Have you completed the six weeks' examination papers which you spoke of.

Perhaps you are reading the last Companion. ... Pastor John P. Milton has an interesting article in this issue, which contrasts two viewpoints in our church. The name of it is (Lutheranism or Revivalism). It would take a lot of time to discuss this article on paper, and maybe you do not care to, for I know you are very busy now. Nevertheless, I shall put down a viewpoint and observation and ask your opinion of it.

We all know that there is a difference of opinion on all things and among all men. Within our church and without. That in itself is not wrong, I believe (for Paul & Peter differed upon some things at times) Gal. 2:11 [Now when Peter had come to Antioch, I withstood him to his face because he was to be blamed; for before certain men came from James, he would eat with the Gentiles; but when they came, he withdrew and separated himself, fearing those who were of the circumcision.] *It would perhaps even be possible to criticize in a careful and constructive way with love as the guiding factor. I believe even though Paul & Peter did differ somewhat at times that they prayed for each other out of a common love of Christ. Don't you?*

I have wondered and thot often about whether or not any fault in another, which we readily see and often criticize, is so much an overabundance of that fault in them, or is it a lack of love on our part which leaves us unable to see anything but the fault in them? God created each and every one of us, and I doubt that he failed to keep the proper balance of all things when he did so. But as men fell into sin, they fell away from God, who we are told, and read also, is Love. So if there is a lack in us, it is Love. Certainly most of us have to confess *that (Love or God) does not dwell in us as was intended before the fall of man and is now made possible through the redemption, bought for us by Christ.*

I doubt that we would criticize so much, even 1/10 as much, if we in love would come to God in prayer, for the one with whom we differed and for ourselves. Am I right on this?

Oh, that I might learn always to do this. …

I worked in the dugout today sacking some potatoes I have to sell, about 150 sacks. I shall try to sell them this week. I can't keep them much longer as they will rot. …

I also helped Father and Bruce butcher a hog today. Come down and you can have some fresh spareribs and sauerkraut. …

I am yours in Christ.

Walter.

April 20 [Postmarked April 21, 3:00 p.m.]

My dear Walter,

"Be ye also ready: for an hour that ye think not the Son of Man cometh." Luke 12:40

This is Wednesday night, nearly eleven o'clock, but I want to speak a little to you before falling asleep. I found the above verse which always seems so searching for me whenever I read it. How wonderful God is to give us this warning. He truly wants us to be with Him. May He ever be with us!

I received your letter this evening which mentioned about your family reunion at Eastertide. We haven't had one for a long time. It seems the only times we gather is at the saying farewell to some member of our family. Death has been reaping in our midst. Since the Savior has seen fit to call them Home, I can't help but rejoice that they were ready in the hour when He called.

This evening I was over to a committee meeting for a Luther League social. We have it all planned. I am to play a flute solo. It seems I never play on my flute; now I shall start. Flute music carries quite well, so maybe, speaking in the hyperbole, if you strain your ears and stretch your imagination, you will be able to hear me play on May the fifteenth.

Mr. Thorson had a little confidential talk with me this evening before I went to Rev. Berg's for the committee meeting. He wanted to know if I planned to teach next year. I told him that nothing definite had been planned but that we had planned to get married this fall, but then you had not made that which you had estimated in the stock. I presume I should have said that you had really lost but I didn't think of that. Mr. Thorson is going to school in the East, to Columbia, so he would like to get it all straightened out before he leaves. He said that it would be all right to wait with knowing. I told him that I could maybe tell him definitely just before school is out. I like to teach here, but it is an awful long distance from my folks and you. …

Walter, I would have enjoyed having been with you on Easter Sunday. Just think, then I could have met your folks. I can hardly wait to talk with your father because I long so to have one since my father has left me. I do wish that you could have known my father.

I am glad to hear that the cantata was performed so well. Who accompanied the choruses? I can't recall the organist's name; perhaps she did the playing. I hope Robert Johnson's voice will not be impaired for a very long period of time because of his tonsillectomy. Now I guess I have talked long enough, and I do need some sleep, so I want to say Good Night and may God bless us while we are absent one from another.

Margaret

A large, oval photograph of Morfar, Mother's father, hung on the wall of an unused room in the bunkhouse where my brothers and I slept when we were teenagers. His eyes seemed to focus on something deep inside me with a kind but objective stare. His picture now hangs lovingly on my wall, and his well-used *Funk & Wagnall's Dictionary* rests on one of my bookshelves. My oldest brother has his brass microscope.

I learned from Dad that Farfar, Father's father, came from Sweden as an indentured servant and that he paid back every cent of his fare through seven years of hard work on a farm. Dad often remarked on how hard his father had worked and had expected Dad to work as a young boy. More than once Dad mentioned that his father was a founding member of the Swedish church we attended, that he had served on the school board of Dad's grade school, and that he had been well liked and respected in the Greeley community. I learned from Mom that my paternal grandfather once became so drunk that he drove his car into a ditch.

John Carlson, an older Swede in our church, was the only living grandfather-like figure in my early life. He had thick white hair and held an eminent position in my mind by virtue of Dad's respect for his judgment and character. It helped that when he was younger, he had gone trout fishing with Dad. We didn't talk much, but I enjoyed sitting with Mr. Carlson in church. He enjoyed my wanting to see his Red Ibis trout fly in his tie clasp and always offered me a peppermint or two.

I don't recall when he passed away. Maybe he never did. His image still signifies for me the calming presence an older person can bestow on a young child once he or she gains that child's respect.

April 21 [Postmarked April 21, 8:30 p.m.]

My Dear Margaret:

"For ye know the grace of our Lord Jesus Christ, that, though he was rich, yet for your sakes he became poor, that ye thru his poverty might become rich." 2 Cor. 8:9

We (you and I), also others, are indeed rich in Christ, and I am so thankful for his guidance and leading and most especially in his leading us together. There was an article on marriage and choosing a life companion in the L. Comp. [Lutheran Companion] *for Apr. 21. Did you see it? I am certainly glad that I did ask God's help in this matter and then to think that he would make it possible for me to meet such a fine Christian girl.*

Mr. Fahrer is right. I am not worthy of you, but with God's help I shall try to do and become more so.

I am so sorry to hear that you are not feeling so well. I know that you work very hard and with these contests to work upon, I am afraid you worried quite a bit. Do not worry too much; but it is not lack of faith which causes it. It is a human weakness found in nearly all men, especially those who work and accomplish anything. Nevertheless, past the point of diligent concern for your work, let your burdens rest upon Christ. I pray for you, Margaret, tho I am afraid I am weak and do not give myself to Him in prayer as I should. I am glad that you finished so high in the contest. It is gratifying to know that one's work has been of some avail and also to know that God has been and is with you. ...

It is not easy to know when to stop worrying. I sometimes liken my interactions with life to a person hitting tennis balls served up by a tennis coach. You concentrate on the ball coming at you and hit it as best you can. Once you have hit the ball, it momentarily lies outside of your ability to affect its course. You might as well attend to a more immediate responsibility — which may be to relax and enjoy the moment.

It's not quite that simple when Life comes at you from many angles. But I like to think of the ball you just hit as falling into God's hands or, to use Walter's phrasing, letting your burden "rest upon Christ," or, to use a less spiritual phrasing, just "letting go."

The fields are greening rapidly now. It is beautiful to be out in them. [The] *Browns have been planting flowers and cleaning up the yard. It really looks very nice. When it gets some greener, I shall take a picture and send to you. I finished planting barley today. Tomorrow I will plow irrigation ditches in the grain and hay, and after that I will start plowing for potatoes and beans. You probably will understand this better a few years from now, for I want you to know and will help you all I can.*

I got my soil conservation check from the govt. yesterday, and it was much better than I had planned for. I thot I would get about $40 but I got $82.15. It paid for some bean seed and hay that I had to have for the horses. They are fat and stand the work very well. I like to be around them and work with them. They seem and are so understanding and loyal. One especially just loves humans and will come to them whenever possible.

Tomorrow night is League, and I was to church last nite, so I had better get to bed.

Goodnight. Pray for me and rest in His peace.

In Christ,

Walter

Although Dad's workhorses had been replaced by tractors by the time I came along, their harnesses hung in the barn. He often remarked on how the horses liked to work, but when evening came, they let him know it was time to quit. He said they looked forward to being fed and receiving a good rubdown after their harnesses were removed.

April 23 [Postmarked April 26, 3:00 p.m.]

Dear Walter,

"Ask, and it shall be given you; seek, and ye shall find; knock, and it shall be opened unto you; for everyone that asketh receiveth; and he that seeketh findeth; and to him that knocketh it shall be opened." Matthew 7:7,8

This is Saturday. I have experienced an answer to our prayer concerning my music stand. It has been found. It was in the car in which several searched but didn't seem able to find it. Mr. Holton found it. Doesn't prayer change things, tho? I have had a feeling all along as I prayed that the stand would be returned to me. The stand was given to me from my mother and father, and the case John gave me. I do treasure them a great deal, and God wanted me to have them returned. Walter, that's the way God will always take care of us. …

So you have about 150 sacks of potatoes to sell! Well, I hope that you receive a good price for the potatoes. I am beginning to realize that there is much speculation in farming. One needs to have power from above to be able to know when to sell or buy.

Bernard did mention about drilling for oil, but I don't happen to remember what it was, but I know this much: that he said it was very encouraging. My father bought some land near Marquette, which is not very far from Lindsborg. We still own the land. Wouldn't it be marvelous if the land would go up in value? Then we could get rid of some of our debts. …

I've no recollection of Mom or Dad mentioning any land or money when Mormor (Mother's mother) died. The farm on which Dad grew up went to his younger brother Bruce, who was farming the land. I vaguely recall Dad being disappointed in the share of the inheritance he received, but he did receive some. It was about that time we acquired a piano.

It seems our prayers about not having a Junior Senior prom have been answered too. I have heard it said, but not from Mr. Thorson, that we are not to have one. I hope the report is authentic.

Walter, I wish that I possessed more love for my fellowmen. I believe, too, if each one of us possessed more love we would criticize less severely. "Love covereth a multitude of sins." I know one thing: that when I am helping a pupil, if I pray that God will give me more love for him, the pupil seems to grasp the information much more easily, and I feel more satisfied.

It is time for me to be asleep, so again I wish God to watch over us his children who long to [be] *united in Christian matrimony when He sees fit.*

Yours in Christ,

Margaret

Sunday morning.

"I was glad when they said unto me, come let us go unto the house of the Lord."

I can't recall the exact quotation, neither can I remember where in the Psalms it is found, but I do love the verse. Let us go to church together in spirit, Walter. This is such a beautiful morning. Last night it rained, so everything in nature seems in joyful tune with me that this is the Sabbath day. Of all the days of the week, this one I love the most.

This noon we start on our choir trip. It has been said by some that the ferry is not safe. I plan to say no about going if the report is not better because, you see, I have you and my dear ones for whom I do not want to needlessly endanger my life because I do so want to live with you. I can't help if I do. [I do] *have some solos to sing,* [but] *the choir can easily get along without my singing them.*

Thanks for the invitation to eat spareribs and sauerkraut. I do like that kind of dinner. …

Monday evening

"And him that cometh unto me I will in no wise cast out." St. John 6:37b.

How time flies. I am glad that it does because then I will sooner be in Clarissa and it will not take too very long before we will be together again. Thanks for the letters I received from you. I truly enjoy getting them.

I have finally found out why the report is out that I am engaged to a minister. I had a picture of Philip on the dresser, and I guess some folks had seen it and so had just made up the story. I have told them about the mistake. Last night we stopped in at a beautiful ranch home. When this lady, Mrs. Tindall, learned that you are a farmer, she just clapped her hands, and her husband's face just beamed when he said, "So she's not going to be a "prest-fru" but instead a farmer's wife." Mrs. Tindall said, "Oh, but you'll enjoy living on a farm. I never have regretted living on a ranch." Tindalls have four children, and they surely are happy. …

Walter, I have read the article in the Lutheran Companion *"Keeping Fit for Marriage." I agree with the author. I am sorry that I do not always get enough sleep in, but I'll try to do better because, really, I do so want to keep fit. I am liking to teach more and more but, oh, that urge to be with you for the rest of my life counteracts it. …*

Yesterday it went easy to sing in the afternoon but not so easily in the evening. I think it was because I was tired out. Walter, don't think I am all worn-out because I am not. I weigh 127½ lbs. and I have so much happiness, so if I feel tired sometimes I can't help it. I long to see you, but if you can't come until the wedding, it will work out. I'll not leave you. God has blessed us richly thus far.

Yours in Christ,

Margaret

We rode on the ferry and worked fine. When I see you I will tell you about the interesting trip.

This letter and the following one were mailed in the same envelope.

Dear Walter,

"Rejoice in the Lord always; again I say, rejoice."

We are having such cloudy, damp weather, but it is ideal for vegetation. Last night it thundered & lightninged, but I didn't hear it, so I slept very soundly. This noon I hurried down so that I could write a little to you. …

I learned that the prom is to be held. I surely am sorry, but I am sure that I haven't prayed and should have. I am not going to go. I have been told that I am not an educated person because I disapprove of sponsored dances. May God help me to be an epistle that the others can read and long to be Christian.

With Christian love,

Margaret

A Glimpse Back

April 17. Walter believes that "fear of the mob and love of the power" resulted in a decision Pilate later regretted. What unwise choices have you made or seen others make that resulted from fear of others or the draw of power?

April 18. Margaret wanted Walter to pray to God about her lost music stand. To where do you turn when you've looked for but can't find something you want?

April 19. How do you see Margaret's search for spiritual "gems" interlinked with her joy? What gems have encapsulated your understandings and where do you find them?

April 19. In saying, "a difference of opinion on all things and among all men … in itself is not wrong," Walter expresses support for freedom of expression. He then wonders if it is "a lack of love on our part which leaves us unable to see anything but the fault in them." Recalling how, in his February 5 letter, he "read *Main Street* quite thoroughly," a book containing viewpoints authored by a "rank atheist," how do you see his love of others expressed in his understanding, his reading, and his criticism?

April 20. In his courtship letter of December 8, Walter speaks of "the shadow of that mysterious will" when writing about the accidental death of a young mother. When writing about death in her family, Margaret sees death "reaping in our midst" and the Savior "[calling] them Home." What words and metaphors help you wrap the death of a loved one in a freeing narrative?

April 21. Walter feels Margaret's worrying "is a human weakness found in … especially those who work and accomplish anything. Nevertheless, past the point of diligent concern" for her work, she should let her "burdens rest upon Christ." What revisions in his expression would make it speak to you?

April 23. Margaret feels that when trying to help a pupil, if she prays that God will give her more love, her pupil always seems "to grasp the information much more easily." Assuming she is faithfully reporting her experience, why do you feel those particular prayers are consistently answered?

Why do you feel Margaret wants her life to be "an epistle that the others can read and long to be Christian"? How do you see the consequences of her epistle? How do these letters play a part in her "epistle"? Why should one be concerned about the consequences of one's "epistle"?

WE ARE SO HESITANT

*T*he seasons regularly open and close so many doors, but not all of them. Readers of the *Greeley Tribune* learned on April 26 that plane sales to England were worrying Washington and on May 1 that the Senate approved a billion for naval expansion. Those same readers also learned on May 6 that the French and British decided to warn Hitler and on May 7 that the federal relief for the year might soar to three billion.

April 24 [Postmarked April 24, 4:30 p.m.]

Dear Margaret:

"For I am ready not to be bound only, but also to die at Jerusalem for the name of the Lord Jesus." Acts 21:13

How is my darling this morning? This beautiful morning. Are you rested some and feeling better now?

Thank you so much for the verses you have been sending to me; I am glad that you do that and especially glad that we do have so much in common, for I do believe we do. It will be a great help to us in the days to come when God grants to us the privilege of living, working, and planning together.

This verse from Acts is found in our Sunday School lesson for today. (My class's lesson.) Paul's assurance is certainly a challenge even today, and I can almost see him as he makes this statement. To someday meet Paul is one of my keenest desires. Wouldn't you like to meet him and shake hands with him?

Margaret, you are up against a hard question, and I want to help you. I believe I can help you from here just as much as I could if I were there, for I shall pray God to guide you and direct your decisions. I refer to the question Mr. Thorson asked you, whether or not you would teach another year.

It is easy to look ahead until Nov. and say, "Maybe it won't turn out so well with the crops, and I had better teach until we have enough money to be sure of our needs."

Now God says not to be anxious of the morrow. Now in these uncertain times, it is impossible to know anything about anything in Nov. except that it will come if God lets us have that much grace of time.

Even those who have not Christ, have to and do launch out on faith. They call it forth in our country and people, but we have a faithful, ever-loving father in whom we can and must trust. Of course I could be entirely wiped out as far as money goes. It could happen. But if things just go in the ordinary way, I feel I have a pretty good start in my occupation.

Weigh these carefully, Margaret, but remember that God will help us and [that] *we must live by faith and in hope. I think you fear that I would feel that you were a burden unless I had as much money as I wished to have and have sometimes planned to have. Of course I would like to give you many things and fulfill some of the rosy pictures I fear that I painted for you, but it is because I love you that I wish them for you. Now I am leaving this matter in your hands with the assurance that I want you and your help even tho I have nothing. I do not believe we make much being apart. It costs you more to live and me also. I either have to board at home or hire a man and batch. You could just as well have those wages, could you not?*

But if you would rather wait and be more certain, I do not blame you at all. I love you and pray for you. I know you will be guided by him.

I think you will be required to make a decision pretty soon, and I will be with you in prayer and in Christ.

We can set a date later on, can we not?

There is more to write, but I must go to breakfast. Maybe I can write some more tonight. …

May God bless you and keep you for Christ and for me.

I love you dearly.

Yours in Christ,

Walter

In commenting on his Sunday School class, Walter writes that he would like to meet and shake hands with Paul the Apostle. Walter may not see it this way, but that part of Paul's identity that ultimately concerned Paul will also be in Walter's class. If Paul were not somehow present in his teachings and were not somehow associated with the consequences of his teachings, what interest could Paul possibly have had in sharing them and in their going out to the ends of the world? Somehow a particularly important bit of Paul, not a relic or some other memento, but a living part of his identity must be in his expressions if we are to appreciate the concern embodied in his statement, "If I speak in the tongues of men and of angels, but have not love, I am a noisy gong or a clanging cymbal."

Walter is among those who have ingested Paul's words through scripture, writings, and the sharing of teachings of writings. And yet, it goes much deeper. Walter is among those who have digested those words. Walter has not only met Paul, but he and Paul are joined at the heart through their love for Jesus. Walter says he wants to shake Paul's hand. I like to think they are already wrapped in each other's arms.

April 26 [Postmarked April 27, 8:30 a.m.]

My Dear Margaret:

"Serve Jehovah with gladness: Come before his presence with singing." Psalm 100:2

It is quite late, but I have a deep longing to talk to you today. I would like to know whether or not you are well. Are you happy in your work, and do you feel at peace within yourself?

I wish that I might write something that would make the load of work lighter and easier.

Wed Morn.

God indeed is good far beyond measure [of] *my own worth.*

I started this letter last nite but was so tired I could not make it sound sensible, so I put it up and went to bed. The wind was blowing hard, the sky was heavily clouded over, and it was raining a little at the time.

Now the ground is covered with little pools of water, and the air is so fresh. You know the feeling of a fresh rain, though, don't you? Do you have much rain up there? We have had between 1/4 and 1 inch of rain each week now for 3 weeks, and the fields are certainly beautiful.

I didn't answer your last letter very well, altho I wrote one since I received it. You do write such nice letters; it is almost like talking to you. I, too, imagine or live in my imagination at times, but I do not allow myself to do so often, for I would be so lonesome if I did.

Last Friday we had League. I am sending one of our quarterly programs, and you will see the program which we enjoyed. The talk by the Indian girl was unusually interesting. She is a quarter-blood Sioux Indian. Her father is Norwegian. She came here (to the college) from the reservation in S. D., I believe the Rosebud Reservation. Is there such a name for one there? …

Are you able to take time enough for a walk in the fresh spring air now and then?

It would be fun to walk along the little creek around Eagle Bend now, wouldn't it? It must be beautiful in spring.

I have not been up to the mts. yet. I wish you could go with me soon. The anemones will be up now. Was it not Browning who wrote an ode to an anemone? I am not sure if it was he, but I thot so. They are beautiful.

But I must go now to milk the cow and then home to breakfast.

I wish this letter might make it easier for my little lady to smile and let her light shine forth from her eyes.

Would 8 o'clock Sun. morn. be a good mutual prayer hour for you? That would be 7 for me.

I John 1 "Walk in the light as he is in the light and ye have fellowship one with another." So thru Him we have fellowship, and I ask Him to keep you for His and mine always.

In Christ,

Walter.

Margaret is in Walter's mind as surely as she is in her letters and in the styling and scripting of her sentences. The paragraphs in the preceding letter are short, much like they are in the give and take of a conversation. He sits down and dashes off a Bible verse about singing. Margaret may have spurred his interest in singing, but she is 500 miles away. On his own, the conversation lags. He's tired and goes to bed.

The next morning, he returns to his letter with every intention of updating Margaret about what's going on in his life in Colorado. The wind is blowing; the ground is wet; the air is fresh.

Margaret interrupts. It's almost like talking to her. But when he imagines being physically near her, instead of warmth comes loneliness. He returns to his physical world by telling her what is going on: The league met. Margaret wasn't physically there, so he writes about the interesting Indian girl at the meeting.

Margaret interrupts by bringing to mind her joy in nature. Walter suggests a walk along a creek or in the mountains where the anemones are displaying their beauty. The disappointment of Margaret being in North Dakota probably sweeps through Walter even before scribbling the suggestion on the piece of paper that lies before him. It's not a useless invitation. Margaret will like the thought when she reads the letter.

His mind turns to his chores and breakfast.

Margaret interrupts. The thought of her smile prompts him to write something that will keep the twinkle in her eye. Walter would like less evanescent ways of being together. Spiritual togetherness, like the fellowship they share in Christ, seems a more real possibility given the distance. Their mutual prayer hour comes to mind.

Was Margaret with Walter in Colorado when he wrote this letter? It depends on how you see her identity — all the ways she can be present and of the varied manifestations of those different ways.

April 28 [Postmarked April 29, 7:00 a.m.]

Dear Walter,

"For Thou has been my help,

And in the shadow of Thy wings will I rejoice" Ps. 63:7

It seems such a long time since I have written to you. My fountain pen is out of commission, so I have not had the facility that I have needed. The pen that I am using is Dorothy's. I broke the point of my pen because I screwed the cover on too tightly. I have sent it in. Since the pen has a lifetime guarantee, I don't believe it will cost much to have it fixed. …

Walter, you surely can read me like a book. I can't understand it. I am glad that you have that book-reading gift in regard to human nature. You guessed right when you said I felt that [I] *was afraid that I would be hindering you from experiencing the completion of your plan in regard to having a good financial standing before getting married. I am glad that you think that maybe with frugal living we could get along all right, but maybe it wouldn't be best.*

I wish that you could hear this wonderful flute concert that I am listening to over the radio. It is just marvelous. …

You should hear the lessons that I am taught about farming at the noon table. One day it was all about animals; another day, dairying; a third day, gardening. Helen said, "It's lots of fun to farm, but oh, it's hard work with little or no let up. The janitor constantly says, "You aren't responsible for your actions from now on." It is not all like they say, but I know one thing, I do so long to see you sometimes that I wish that you weren't so far away. ...

I hope soon to return the books which you have let me read. Someday I hope to reread them in our home. I can hardly wait to see the interior of it. How is Mr. Brown in keeping sober? I can't understand how Mrs. Brown can tolerate it. Oh, I am so glad that you do not have that terrible home-breaking drinking habit.

This letter seems so short, but I just haven't time to write more. I must finish the novel The Vicar of Wakefield in reading. I don't even recall how the story ends, and tomorrow the seniors are to complete it.

The lawns are so pretty in their green color. I saw another flock of cranes; they are making a squeaking sound, it sounded like.

May He guide you all your journey thru life with or without me as He chooses.

Margaret

I presume you are quite busy working or building your irrigation ditches. It reminds [me] *of Holland. Shall we someday go to Europe? I don't believe we would get very seasick. It would be enjoyable. John and Phillip want to go to Sweden. They haven't had that longing for a goodly number of years.*

April 28 [Postmarked April 29, 8:30 a.m.]

My Dear Margaret:

"And lo, he speaketh openly, and they say nothing unto him. Can it be that the rulers indeed know that this is the Christ." John 7:26

I marvel at the number of times which the opponents of Jesus admitted his deity. Pilate did; the Pharisees did several times, of course somewhat indirectly. It was interesting to see that they requested an armed guard to keep a dead man in a tomb, but they did.

How are you today? I was glad when I read your letter today to see that you are not losing any weight. Soon you will be in Clarissa, and you can rest some then.

Thank you for the interesting letters. I cannot write in such [an] *interesting style as you do. Reading your letters is almost like talking to you*

I reread some of your last letters & find I did not answer some of the questions.

For one thing, I am 5 ft. & 11 in tall. 6 ft. in my shoes. …

In your last letter you ask God's help to be a living epistle in order to lead others to him. I have dreamed and hoped and prayed that our home might have such an influence on people. …

Even those who do not have a conscious sense of making the world a better place to live in cannot avoid impacting the world with all they say and do. If we had an influence Geiger counter, it would be going off the scale in our workplaces and homes. Our influences — for better and for worse — spread like waves that can pass through seemingly impenetrable walls and end up resonating in the lives of others in ways we can never know.

You asked me what book you should read now that you have finished the Bible. This is merely a suggestion, but why not make a definite outline study of Paul? For instance, you might outline his conversion, his travels; record the number of churches he started, the number of letters he wrote. For me, this would be an interesting study and would be valuable in S. S. teaching or leading a Bible study on the life of Paul.

I do hope that the land which you have in Kansas will go up in value. I have heard quite a bit about the oil work there. Mr. Brown has relatives near there also.

We should remember Mr. Brown to God. I would like to show him the Way everlasting. I don't pray about this as I should. It is not easy to remember those who are not so near & dear to us. Is it?

Frank writes that they are having quite a time at Bethany. I guess it is quite a rotten mess. But he says not to say anything about it, at large because he said it is pretty hard on even those with a strong faith. He says Dorf is trying to straighten it up.

It is hard to say now how things will go, but I don't think I can wait until fall to see you if we have to wait until then to get married.

The work slacks up in Aug., and I shall try to see you then, and we could talk things over much better than we can write them.

God has indeed been good to us, and He will lead and provide in the days to come. …

I must get to bed. I hope this imaginary hand clasp and embrace will let you know that I would like to share my confidence with you. …

In Christian love.

Walter

April 30 [Postmarked April 30, 3:00 p.m.]

Dear Walter,

"Blessed be Jehovah,

Because he had heard the voice of my supplications.

Jehovah is my strength and my shield;

My heart hath trusted in him, and I am helped,

Therefore my heart greatly rejoiced;

And with song will I praise him." Psalm 28: 6 – 8

This is Saturday afternoon. This morning I had my dental work completed. It cost me thirteen dollars. … I returned home to get my knitting. It was so still except for a soft breeze, so I decided to go to the river. It wasn't long before I reached the riverbank and had found a nice rock to sit on, and after I had prayed, I commenced knitting. It was very pleasant. …

Yesterday Mr. Thorson gave us our contracts with the board signatures on them. We haven't talked anything more about next year. I am so happy because now I have $130 in the bank. I just wonder what I should do with the money when I leave after school closes. I have it in [a] *savings account which gets 4% interest. I think with my last month's check I can almost get along until August. Of course I could put it in savings in Clarissa. I have twelve dollars in cash for this month. I plan to send five dollars home. … I think I can get along on* *six dollars if I have to. I have paid my room rent for May. Mrs. Jefferis asked me if I didn't want to start paying some for next year so that she would be sure that I would be coming back.*

You mentioned about a talk on Indian life. There are quite a number of Indians near here. At our music contest there is one Indian school that is always represented. Last year the pupils seemed so very shy, but this year they seemed to have overcome much of their bashfulness. …

The time 8 o'clock a.m. suits me just fine because I usually get up a little before that every Sunday morning. I think that that mutual prayer hour will be a solid foundation on which to build our home. Prayer does much, and to think God urges us to pray; He loves to answer too. May His will always be done.

Yours in His Son,

Margaret

A century and a half before Margaret went to pray and knit on the bank of the Missouri River, Lewis and Clark wintered among the Mandan Indians a few miles west of where she sat. I expect many a Mandan Indian meditated on the source and creative spirit of their lives when sitting on the banks of that great river.

Unexpected lengths in time and idiosyncratic places come into play in puzzling ways when trying to connect all the events that are incorporated into one's spirit. Roughly three-quarters of a century after Margaret sat on that riverbank south of Washburn, I also sat there watching the Missouri River silently and dutifully carry truckloads of dirt downstream as it has done over the centuries — spans of time that are to Mother Earth what seconds are to me, all part of something vast and eternal.

May 1 [Postmarked May 3, 7:00 a.m.]

Dear Walter,

"When Jesus therefore had received the vinegar, he said, 'It is finished:' and he bowed His head, and gave up His spirit." St. John 19:30

This is the verse for our Sunday School lesson next Sunday. I marvel that the words "It is finished" were said by our Master. He embodied truth, so I know all was completed for our salvation. To think that thru His grace and merit we may someday be in heaven with Him. Our traveling days here on earth may be very few, but may He ever be our guide, always drawing us nearer to Him. …

Walter, I surely thank you again for this beautiful diamond ring. It is so very precious to me. I can hardly wait until you can put it on my finger. I wish my fingers could and would be more swift to do acts of kindness for Christ's sake.

This evening I get the chance to sing in a mixed quartet. The music text is that of Sibelius's "Finlandia." It is so much fun to sing. I am sure you know the selection "Finlandia." …

During that mutual prayer hour, I didn't spend the whole time in prayer because I just felt like singing, so I sang some hymns that voiced my prayer for our lives. … It just thrilled me. …

I haven't been to many conference meetings, but I have attended at least three synodical meetings. I hope that you and I can attend some synod conventions together. I do enjoy them very much. Perhaps you have attended some, and so you know how inspirational and educational in church doctrine and how practical they are. … Wouldn't it be fun to go this year? John is planning to go. …

This is the day of May baskets. One little neighbor boy said, "If Virginia gives me a basket, I am going to catch her and give her a real smacker." I just wonder how it turned out. Many baskets have been brought to Dorothy and Ruth from their pupils. …

To think that your horses are doing such fine work. What is the name of that one who is so friendly toward people? That's the one I hope to ride on. …

There are but twenty more days of school, and then home I go. I will have such an enjoyable summer, sewing, cooking, and planning for our future home. Walter, it is so much fun; I believe you're enjoying your work of preparing the home as much as I. Don't you enjoy it, though? …

Now may He continue to make our bond of love deeper until we are married, and may it burn more fervently afterwards. …

Yours in Him,

Margaret

May 3 [Postmarked May 3, 4:30 p.m.]

My Dear Margaret:

"Who would have all men to be saved, and come to the knowledge of truth." I Timothy 2:4

You mention that God loves to answer our prayers. That is true, and this verse certainly supports that idea, altho the 1st verse does even more so. I am glad He wants us, for I am so imperfect that only the perfect love of God could be strong enough to blot out my sins.

How is my darling this morning, for it is morning, about 10 after five? Margaret, I long so to see you and talk with you. I try not to let it take up too much of my time, but I cannot help wishing once in a while that I could see you. I do love you so much. …

Margaret, if God grants us soon to be together, and if we can soon get a piano, I want you to sing a Swedish song for me. … Evodia & Reuben … sang it beautifully, and many of the old Swedes wept as they listened. Even tho they were singing, you could have heard a pin drop. …

Last Sunday afternoon I had such an intense longing to see you, so I went to see a young couple named Arthur Carlsons, married last June. He is a member of our church; she is a Methodist. He does not go often, but I think they alternate between them. They get along fine and are very nice. We drove into the mts. for a while up the Buckhorn, where we came down when we saw the beaver. It was wet and snowy but beautiful. Quite a few flowers are out already. How I do long for the day when we can go together not only to the mts. but everywhere. To that end I shall work and will not spend much money that does not work to that end. I am pretty lucky to be fixed as I am, the banker says, considering that I only started two years ago and this was a bad year. I can easily borrow all I need. …

I must close.

I love you, Margaret. May these words convey my love and longing to you. I miss your smile and comforting personality. This is very true. May God bless you.

In Christ,

Walter.

I know now I shall see you this summer. I just have to. God will provide a way.

I would come to know the Carlson family through their daughter, Janet, who was in my confirmation class. The drive they took was one of Dad's favorites. The Buckhorn was a little mountain stream we occasionally fished when I was little. I don't know that it flows anymore except after a heavy rain.

May 4 [Postmarked May 5, 10:00 a.m.]

My Dear Margaret:

Honor thy father and thy mother, that thy days may be long upon the earth, which the Lord thy God giveth thee!

Soon after you receive this it will be Mother's Day. I am often ashamed when I remember the impatient answers and unkindnesses, which I am often guilty of, toward my parents and loved ones. Mother's Day should be every day, and so should Father's Day. …

I thot often of you today, my dear little lady. I am sorry to hear … that the pupils are not all doing as they should. I think you worry needlessly there. But I am glad that you are so honestly conscientious that you do worry about your work and your pupils.

I am glad that you have so much knitting done and that you like to knit. Yes, I do enjoy working toward the preparation of our home. Never has the work been so easy, light, and enjoyable. As I work I often dream of the day when I will come in from my work to meet you and eat supper with you, then help you with the dishes, so that you may sit beside me or in my lap as you knit. But you are not always going to knit or work, for sometimes you're just going to sit in my lap and rest. …

Sometime and somehow, I shall manage to come to see you this summer. I want to place that ring upon your finger and talk with you and walk with you, and together we may talk and walk with Him who has led us this far and who ever cares for us.

I know that you love me and long to see me more often because my longing to see you and talk to you becomes almost unbearable at times. I felt that I would like to drop everything and start for N. D. But God will give us strength to be patient. I am going to spend money enough for one trip to Minn. this summer. But I must try to get along with one for it is far and costly, and every cent I spend before we are married will lessen our chances of being married soon.

Could you speak privately to Mr. Thorson, asking him if it would be all right for you to accept or reject your contract by the 5th of Aug?

I want to be married at the very latest this fall in Nov. If possible sooner.

Could we shop carefully for some used furniture and fixtures and get along until we had more money? I would rather buy used furniture for cash than new furniture on time, wouldn't you? My car is good and would do for 2 or 3 years. (I got 20 miles to the gallon of gas taking Reuben to Denver.)

I have now borrowed 2 hundred dollars, paid all my debts, got all my seed and feed, and have over 30 dollars to go on for a while. I can get at least 500 dollars If I need it for my summer expenses (200+300 more). If I need more I could get it because the banker asked me if I was *sure that that was all I needed. Last year I borrowed 750 dollars, but I had a man at 60 per month for 8 months, bot some high-priced seed potatoes ($135 worth), and was not too careful about expenditures. Though last year was a poor year as a whole, this farm paid me over $2500; of course I had to pay for all the seed, work, and cost of operation out of that. Last year I planted 600 dollars' worth of potatoes. This year they are worth about 150 dollars.*

With a fair year and fair prices, I should do very well, for I can and will cut expenses down a great deal.

If these figures are hard to understand and are confusing, just forget them until we see each other. I just put them down to give you an idea of the situation. I do not believe economic conditions will get better, so we had better plan to be married before the next election; for though I may be wrong, I think we shall yet experience a harder depression than the one of 31, 32 & 33.

In hard times a farm is the best place in the world to be. You at least have enough to eat, clothes enough for comfort, and a little money for fuel.

I believe that once you and I could get enough to furnish this little house and pay for it ^the furniture that we could get along very well with a few chickens and cows. It would cost us very little to live.

I love the farm and country, and I know you will too.

In all our decisions let us always come to Him and be found in Him.

Yours in Christian love,

Walter

This letter was mailed on May 5. Two days later, Margaret responds, starting off on a positive note.

May 7 [Postmarked May 7, 3:00 p.m.]

Dear Walter,

"All the paths of Jehovah are loving-kindness and truth unto such as keep his covenant and testimonies." Ps. 25:10

It surely feels fine to get a chance to write to you again. I haven't received my fountain pen since I had the druggist send it in to the factory to have it repaired. My eversharp is also being fixed. During this past week, I have misplaced two ordinary pencils, so all in all, I have been in dire need of writing instruments. Now I am using Ruth's pen. The druggist said that he thought the pen would come sometime next week.

Thank you for the letters that I have received. Walter, you mention that you were lonesome last Sunday afternoon. I surely would have enjoyed spending the afternoon with you. I would like to ride with you in your car. We could go to see our home to be, couldn't we? Would you take me to your folks' home so that I could meet your mother and sisters? …

Walter, your letters sound as if you were soon coming to see me. I can hardly believe it possible that you want to see me, but you have said that that was the only reason that you came last Christmas. Whenever you can come, I shall be glad to receive you. I know that the folks will welcome you also. I don't know just which Swedish song you had in mind when you asked about my singing it for you, but whichever it is, I will enjoy singing it for my dear Walter. I know quite a number, but I will have to have the notes before me because I cannot play without them except to chord. I enjoy Swedish and I am grateful to God that you love Christian hymns and have not a dislike for the Swedish language. …

I should be up studying, but when Saturday comes, I don't feel like doing schoolwork. … I plan to make out one final examination today. Then I plan to do some more work up there. I want to be thru with my work on Thursday morning so that I can complete packing on Thursday. Friday home I go as fast as the bus can take me. …

I haven't spoken to Mr. Thorson about next year. I just don't know what to do. It seems that you are encouraged about the crops and your banking account. I feel just like coming back next year, but I would like to teach nearer home, but then again I get lonesome to be with you, and I feel that maybe if we wait, we don't know what might happen; if something would happen to break our engagement, I don't believe I could stand it, but God, of course, can supply all my needs in His own way and own time. … Walter, you mean more to me than any career that could be given to me, however rosy it might be. Then I begin to think maybe God has something that He wants me to do and that is the reason we are so hesitant about setting any definite time for a wedding. I know one thing: that I am not the cook, seamstress, housekeeper that I should be, but you said that others have gotten married who weren't any more prepared than I. This summer I plan to learn to do better work. I really like to work in the house and in a garden, but I can't do the work in any artistic manner. Evodia would help me, I know. Well, Walter, I just don't know how you feel about it. I do know that you would be able to supply all that we would need, and anyway, money isn't everything. I would be afraid to marry anyone who wasn't a Christian, but I know that if all wouldn't go so smoothly in regard to helping you, you would forgive me, and then we could take it to God in prayer, and He would help me. If we wouldn't plan to get married (sometime this next school year), then I believe that I had better say that I am coming back because I really need money to get along and to help pay off some debts. I love you so much that I don't know how to express myself, but I don't want to tell Mr. Thorson that I won't be coming back if we don't plan to get married until a year or two. I maybe could get piano pupils in some town during the school year, but it wouldn't pay me as much as teaching school. I really believe that our love is mutual, but maybe the time has not reached the time for the wedding. What do you think?

Now may God direct you in your planning. I am looking forward to prayer hour together tomorrow morning.

In Christian love and fellowship,

Margaret

Margaret closes her letter after placing things in "God's hand." Morning brings another day and a chance to write a short note before posting the letter.

This noon I just finished eating my dinner of wieners and sauerkraut. After dinner I knitted about ½ an inch.

There is so much to think about that rather inspires me. The thought that someday I will get to be with you, so I guess that is what helps me along. …

Now I must leave off writing.

Margaret

A Glimpse Back

April 24. Walter recognizes that Margaret is "up against a hard question" in deciding if she should teach another year. In trying to help out, he addresses the question from a number of different angles. Which of his comments do you feel most attracted Margaret?

April 28. At night, Margaret is likely to be contemplating her future alone on the farm with Walter. During lunch, her colleagues are teaching her about life on the farm. What might she enjoy and not enjoy about those "lessons"? How do you feel Walter would answer that question?

April 28. Walter "dreamed and hoped and prayed" that his home might lead others to Christ. What messages about you does your home send to others?

May 4. Walter was in his early twenties during the Great Depression. In the year of this letter, he lost money because of the current economic downturn. He notes that he thinks the downturn will be "a harder depression than the one of 31, 32 & 33." What understandings do you see as keys to his joy with Margaret when he writes, "We could get along very well"?

May 7. Margaret sees a disconcerting possibility in teaching another year when she writes, "If something would happen to break our engagement, I don't believe I could stand it." Some possibilities have crossed her mind. If you were a novelist, how would you finish out their letters knowing that they will eventually meet at the altar?

EPILOGUE

In their early courtship letters, Walter and Margaret enthusiastically explored the joy they found in each other. Four months later when Walter hitched a ride on a stock train to celebrate Christmas with Margaret at her home in Clarissa, Minnesota, they agreed to get married.

As we saw in this second phase of their courtship letters, financial concerns delayed by three and a half months the symbol Margaret needed to slip on her finger before she could publicly share that marital commitment. The letters ended with Walter anticipating "a harder depression than the one of 31" and Margaret wondering why they "are so hesitant about setting any definite time for a wedding."

In the coming third and final phase of their letters, Margaret's colleagues will teach her about life on the farm before sending her on her way. Later events will take charge of the wedding date, the ceremony, and their future home as they anticipate their first night together. In all this, they will see God's mysterious and loving hand.

A comment by Margaret will bring back the time Mom had to find a salaried job a few years before Dad was asked to leave the farm. A comment by Walter will resurrect the unlikely occurrences that ended my search for a lifetime partner. And an answered prayer of Margaret's will bring back a silent plea that miraculously ended an unrelenting argument from which I saw no escape.

More significantly, a religious conversion that puzzled Walter will motivate an extended take on a spiritual experience that changed my life. That experience will be seen to underlie my interest in these letters, to color the twists and turns giving rise to this trilogy, and to govern my takes on the three pivotal issues just addressed.

That said, the book you hold would never have been published had Walter's and Margaret's interest in sharing their Christian faith with others not permeated their courtship. In struggling with how best to share their thoughts, I found it necessary — and clarifying — to share essential aspects of my faith.

If you found this combination of letters and reflections helpful and engaging, your telling others why in a review on Amazon, Goodreads, Facebook, or any other suitable venue would be greatly appreciated by others.

ACKNOWLEDGMENTS

I greatly appreciate but cannot acknowledge all who, through interest and conversation, are a part of this book. My brothers and sisters provided helpful recollections of our childhood experiences. Helene Leaf and Paul Johnson straightened out my vague recollections on my grandparents. The *Washburn Leader* staff graciously let me browse their archived newspapers. Lois Barliant spurred my interest in the letters by having them scanned into an accessible PDF file. Pastor David Pierce clarified a number of the translational complexities of Greek expressions surrounding what it meant "to see" the resurrected Jesus. Topics and thoughts encountered in the spirited book discussions of the Palms Presbyterian Sack Lunch Theology group have inevitably colored my philosophical and theological digressions. The time line of world events and the self-exploratory questions were suggestions by Claire Barliant and Diane Shepard, respectively. Both contributed portions of the preliminary edit. Kirsten Balayti, developmental editor, meticulously edited the grammar and the spelling of this final document. Lois and Ron Barliant and Anna Johnson pointed out a number of needed clarifications. Martha, my loving life companion, carefully critiqued the many drafts and significantly influenced the focus while lovingly supporting the drawn-out effort from beginning to end. My thanks to all and especially to her.

ABOUT THE AUTHOR

Mark Johnson has enjoyed a career as a scientist in computer-aided drug discovery for a major pharmaceutical company. He has enjoyed living with Martha in North Carolina, Michigan, and now Florida. Along the way he has served as both an elder and a deacon, coached youth soccer and baseball, and enjoyed golfing, cycling, and riding his Honda Helix. Since moving to Florida, he has taken up again his interest in singing and playing the trumpet.

Mark was embarking on an effort to share his enthusiasm for life in a book on our fundamental sources of truth (science, art, religion, and philosophy) when he was handed copies of the courtship letters of his parents. Upon finally bothering to browse the letters, he found carefully scripted answers to a question he had, as a teenager, put to his dad: "Why are you a Christian?" He eventually saw in the letters an inspiring resource for his trilogy *A Lettered Courtship* on how our most basic sources of truth enrich our daily lives and shape our views of God. You can follow his encounter with these letters at https://www.facebook.com/FindYTK/ or share your reactions to his thoughts at mkfytk@mindspring.com.

---

[1] D. O. Lamoureux, *Evolution: Scripture and Nature Say YES!* (Grand Rapids: Zondervan, 2016).

[2] Ibid., 17.

[3] In one of life's many ironies, Duane and I are among the coauthors of the paper: W. J. Wechter, M. A. Johnson, C. M. Hall, D. T. Warner, A. E. Berger, A. H. Wenzel, D. T. Gish, and G. Neil, "Aracytidine Acylates; Use of Drug Design Predictors in SAR Correlation," *Journal of Medicinal Chemistry*, 18, 339-344.

[4] S. J. Gould, *Rocks of Ages: Science and Religion in the Fullness of Life* (New York: Ballantine Books, 1999).

[5] Ibid., 4 – 5.

[6] Ibid., 56, 62.

[7] I. E. Edman, ed., "Euthyphro," in *The Works of Plato* (New York: Random House, 1928), 41.

[8] R. M. Hutchins, ed., "On Interpretation," in *Great Books of the Western World*, vol. 8 (Chicago: Encyclopedia Britannica, 1952), 25.

[9] R. M. Hutchins, ed., "Discourse on the Method of Rightly Conducting the Reason and Seeking for Truth in the Sciences," in *Great Books of the Western World*, vol. 31 (Chicago:

Encyclopedia Britannica, 1952), 51.

[10] R. M. Hutchins, ed., "Of the Proficience and Advancement in Learning: Divine and Humane," in *Great Books of the Western World*, vol. 30 (Chicago: Encyclopedia Britannica, 1952), 14.

[11] R. M. Hutchins, ed., "Novum Organum: Aphorisms Concerning the Interpretation of Nature and the Kingdom of Man," in *Great Books of the Western World*, vol. 30 (Chicago: Encyclopedia Britannica, 1952), 180.

[12] J. Bartlett, *Bartlett's Familiar Quotations*, 16th ed. (Boston: Little Brown & Co.), 303.

[13] J. Hutton, *Theory of the Earth* (Sioux Falls: NuVision Publications, 2007 [1788]), 14, 16, 17, 53, 73 – 75.

[14] "Hutton, James," in *The New Encyclopedia Britannica*, 15th ed., 32 vols. (Chicago: Encyclopedia Britannica, 2010, final print version, continued online, as *Encyclopedia Britannica*, at https://www.britannica.com/).

[15] P. Toghill, *The Geology of Britain: An Introduction* (Marlborough, UK: Crowood Press, 2000), 14.

[16] D. J. Bronstein, Y. H. Krikorian, and P. P. Wiener, *Basic Problems in Philosophy: Selected Readings with Introductions* (Englewood Cliffs, NJ: Prentice Hall, 1955), 52.

[17] T. S. Kuhn, *The Structure of Scientific Revolutions* (Chicago:

University of Chicago Press, 1970).

[18] M. F. Bear, B. W. Connors, and M. A. Paradiso, *Neuroscience: Exploring the Brain*, 4th ed. (Philadelphia: Wolters Kluwer, 2016), 24, 44, 85, 101.

[19] J. H. Woodger, *Biological Principles: A Critical Study* (London: Routledge & Kegan Paul, 1929), 58.

[20] Bear, Connors, and Paradiso, *Neuroscience: Exploring the Brain*, 653.

[21] M. Meyer, *The Bedford Introduction to Literature* (Boston: Bedford Books of St. Martin's Press, 1990), 313.

[22] Ibid., 356, 357.

[23] Ibid., 462, 463.

[24] P. W. Russell, B. W. Clayton, and B. Freeman, *Dixieland* (New York City: Coronet Records, CX-163, n.d., 33 1/3 rpm).

[25] J. Legge, *Confucius: Confucian Analects, the Great Learning, and the Doctrine of the Mean* (New York: Dover Publications, 1971). This is the source of all of my quotations of Confucius.

[26] B. Nanamoli and B. Bodhi. *The Middle Length Discourses of the Buddha* (Boston: Wisdom Publications, 1995), 339 – 340.

[27] Ibid., 106.

[28] *The Holy Qur'ān*, trans. Maulana Muhammad Ali, 7th ed. (Columbus: Ahmadiyyah Anjuman Isha'at Islam Lahore,

1991). This is the source of my quotations from the Quran.

[29] A. Berlin and M. Z. Brettler, eds., *The Jewish Study Bible* (New York: Oxford University Press, 2004), 111.

[30] L. Yutang, *The Wisdom of China and India* (New York: Random House, 1942), 583 – 624. This is the source of my quotations from the *Tao Te Ching*.

[31] R. Hammer, *The Classic Midrash: Tannaitic Commentaries on the Bible* (New York: Paulist Press, 1995), 85.

[32] D. Howard, ed., *A Buddhist Bible* (Boston: Beacon Press, 1970), 498.

[33] S. Radhakrishnan and C. A. Moore, eds., *A Sourcebook in Indian Philosophy* (Princeton: Princeton University Press, 1989), 292 – 325. This is the source of my quotations from the *Dhammapada*.

[34] B. S. Miller, trans., *Yoga: Discipline of Freedom, The Yoga Sutra Attributed to Patanjali* (New York: Bantam Books, 1995), 29.

[35] National Aeronautics and Space Administration, "The Relentless Rise of Carbon Dioxide," last updated July 26, 2018, https://climate.nasa.gov/climate_resources/24/.

[36] N. H. Harari, *Sapiens: A Brief History of Humankind* (Israel: Kinneret, Zmora-Bitan, Dvir; author translation, London: Vintage Books, 2011), 463 – 464.

[37] Ibid., 28.

[38] Ibid., 42.

[39] Ibid., 234.

[40] Ibid., 74, 82.

[41] N. Davies, *Europe: A History* (New York: Oxford University Press, 1996), 759.

[42] Ibid., 763.

[43] Ibid., 874 – 875.

[44] S. Pinker, *The Better Angels of Our Nature: Why Violence Has Declined* (New York: Penguin Books, 2011), 475.

[45] "Joseph Roux," Brainy Quote, last updated 2018, https://www.brainyquote.com/search_results.html?q=joseph+roux.

[46] In a forward to the book, Michael Meyer writes about the author, "Dorothy Thompson, his second wife, had interviewed Hitler as a foreign correspondent in Berlin and had written a series of articles between 1932 and 1935 warning Americans about the Nazi propaganda machine that masked the vicious persecution of Jews and the growing number of concentration camps designed to annihilate them."

[47] H. Lindsey and C. C. Carlson, *The Late Great Planet Earth* (Grand Rapids: Zondervan, 1970; reprint, New York: Bantam

Books, 1980), 43.

[48] Bulletin of the Atomic Scientists, "The Doomsday Clock: A Timeline of Conflict, Culture, and Change," last updated 2018, http://thebulletin.org/timeline.

[49] J. D. Crossan, *The Greatest Prayer: Rediscovering the Revolutionary Message of the Lord's Prayer* (New York: HarperCollins, 2010).

[50] A. Lavrov and I. A. Kosevich, "Sponge Cell Reaggregation: Mechanisms and Dynamics of the Process," *Russian Journal of Developmental Biology* 45, no. 4 (2014): 205 – 223.

[51] Yutang, *The Wisdom of China and India*, 587.

[52] F. S. Collins, *The Language of God: A Scientist Presents Evidence for Belief* (New York: Free Press, 2006), 125.

[53] Many have struggled with what we can know about what took place when "the stone was rolled away." Objectively, very little, according to Bart Ehrman, the James A. Gray Distinguished Professor of Religious Studies at the University of North Carolina and author of *How Jesus Became God: The Exaltation of a Jewish Preacher from Galilee* (New York, HarperCollins, 2014). He notes that Jesus and his disciples were not particularly noteworthy; otherwise, their lives would be documented somewhere in the many writings and

historical artifacts of that time. Moreover, Ehrman claims there is no evidence that a crucified person, especially a non-Roman, would have been allowed a dignified burial. He also notes that Paul never mentions a tomb in his epistles about Jesus written roughly two decades after the crucifixion. The open tomb first occurs in our gospels written roughly one or two decades after Paul's exhortations. There the stone that sealed the tomb of the dead and buried Jesus is rolled away. What, then, should we make of the New Testament narratives? It may help to bear in mind the earlier quote by Tim O'Brien. Reflecting on his example of a "true war story that never happened," he says, "In the end, of course, a true war story is never about war." In the end, the narratives of the open tomb are about events and experiences that changed the course of world history by changing and resurrecting one individual life after another.

[54] E. Krentz, "1 Thessalonians: Introduction," in *The HarperCollins Study Bible,* W. Weeks, gen. ed. (New York: HarperCollins, 1993), 2218.

[55] E. W. Goodrick and J. R. Kohlenberger, III, *The NIV Exhaustive Concordance* (Grand Rapids: Zondervan Publishing House, 1990).

---

[56] C. S. Lewis, "The Problem of Pain," in *The Complete C. S. Lewis Signature Classics* (New York: HarperCollins, 1940).

[57] W. James, *The Varieties of Religious Experience* (New York: The Modern Library, 1929 [1902]).

[58] A. H. Maslow, *Religions, Values, and Peak Experiences* (New York: Penguin Books, 1983 [1970]), 59.

[59] Ibid., 62.

[60] Collins, *The Language of God,* 215.

[61] Ibid., 217.

[62] Ibid., 225.

[63] A. Huxley, *The Perennial Philosophy* (New York: Harper & Row, 1990 [1944]), viii.

www.ingramcontent.com/pod-product-compliance
Lightning Source LLC
Chambersburg PA
CBHW071402090426
42737CB00011B/1315

* 9 7 8 1 9 4 5 9 7 6 0 5 6 *